Sybil,

This book wouldn't exist, except for your encouragement and support. Thank you.

Jeff

The Soul of Cyberspace

Transformations: Awakening to the Sacred in Ourselves
(with Tracy Cochran)

THE
SOUL
OF
CYBERSPACE

HOW NEW TECHNOLOGY IS CHANGING OUR SPIRITUAL LIVES

Jeff Zaleski

Harper*Edge*
An Imprint of HarperSanFrancisco

HarperCollins®, ♨®, HarperSanFrancisco™, and HarperEdge™ are trademarks of HarperCollins Publishers Inc.
Harper*Edge* Web Site: http://www.harpercollins.com/harperedge

FIRST EDITION

Library of Congress Cataloging-in-Publication Data
Zaleski, Jeffrey P.
The soul of cyberspace : how new technology is changing our spiritual lives / Jeff Zaleski.
p.   cm.
Includes bibliographical references and index.
ISBN 0–06–251451-2 (cloth)
ISBN 0–06–251452-0 (pbk.)
1. Religion—Computer network resources. 2. Internet (Computer network)—Religious aspects. 3. Cyberspace—Religious aspects.
I. Title.
BL37.Z35   1997
200'.285'46—dc21   97-12611

97 98 99 00 01 ❖ RRDH 10 9 8 7 6 5 4 3 2 1

For Tracy

Contents

Acknowledgments

Many people contributed to the writing of this book. I'm grateful to them all. To my colleagues at *Publishers Weekly,* particularly Sybil Steinberg, for her generous encouragement and support; Daisy Maryles, for accompanying me into the world of Hasidism; and Jon Bing and Mike Scharf, for numerous favors. To Leslie Miller, who showed me how to look at cyberspace in new ways; Mitch Kapor, whose analysis of the original outline of this book prompted a better one; and the late Lex Hixon, who urged me to write this book. To Aly Sujo, for giving me a laser printer when I most needed one. I also owe thanks to those who gave of their time and energy to be interviewed for this book, and to those who facilitated the interviews.

A big thank you goes out to Lisa Bach, my editor at Harper*Edge,* for her enthusiasm and her literary skills. Thanks, too, to my agent, Wendy Schmalz.

I'm especially grateful to my family—my brother, Phil; my sister-in-law, Carol; my sister, Susan; and my mother, Jean—for helping in myriad ways. Above all, I'm grateful to my wife, Tracy, who inspired me to write this book, and to my daughter, Alexandra. Their love makes it all worthwhile.

Partenia

Partenia is a place of freedom.
— BISHOP JACQUES GAILLOT

Before the World Wide Web, before Windows and *Wired,* there was Winky Dink.

Winky was a cartoon elf who couldn't stay out of trouble. By 1958, when his TV show went off the air, his big heart and sense of adventure had endeared him to young kids across the country, including me. But what kept us rushing back to our sets every weekday morning was what lay behind the title of Winky's show. The show was called *Winky Dink and You.* What counted was the *"and You."* In one episode, a giant chased Winky to the edge of a cliff. Across a yawning chasm, too wide for little Winky to jump, stood another cliff. How would Winky reach it to escape being eaten by the giant? Only one way—by each of us placing a special *Winky Dink and You* sheet of transparent plastic (available at toy stores everywhere) on the screen and using a crayon to draw a bridge for Winky to scamper across.

I don't know if Bill Gates or Steve Jobs or John Perry Barlow or any of the other pioneers of cyberspace ever watched *Winky Dink and You.* They might have. I do know that my own involvement with interactive media, and by extension with cyberspace, began the first time I changed Winky's world, and thus my own, by drawing on that sheet of plastic. Back then, I couldn't have asked what the spiritual implications of that involvement might be. Recently, I learned of a latter-day Winky who brings this question to the fore.

With his small body, happy smile, and pointy ears, Bishop Jacques Gaillot looks amazingly like Winky, but it's his big, adventurous heart that seals the comparison. As the Roman Catholic bishop of the diocese of Evreux, in Normandy, Gaillot had throughout the early 1990s spoken his conscience on controversial issues including priestly celibacy, homosexuality, and the ordination of women. In each instance, what he said veered from the Church's teachings as proclaimed by the Vatican.

By January 1995, the Vatican had heard enough from Gaillot. Calling him to Rome, Cardinal Gantin, prefect of the Congregation for Bishops, informed the wayward cleric that in twenty-four hours he would no longer be the bishop of Evreux. Instead, he was to shepherd the faithful in the diocese of Partenia. But where was Partenia?

Partenia is what is referred to in Church parlance as a *titular see*. It is in fact nowhere, or as close to nowhere as possible. Fifteen hundred years ago, it bustled with nomads and perhaps a settlement or two. But Partenia lies in Algeria, on the slopes of the Atlas Mountains, and over the centuries the Sahara has spread implacably over its dominion. Now it hosts only the scorpions, lizards, and flies that crawl over its sands, plus some Muslims who couldn't care less about what Gaillot might say. There, the Vatican must have reasoned, Gaillot could preach as much as he liked to a congregation of one: himself.

Nine days after his appointment to Partenia, Gaillot delivered a farewell homily at Evreux Cathedral. Tens of thousands came to listen. "As far as I am concerned," he announced to the throng, "in communion with the Church, I will pursue my way, bringing the Good News to the poor. The Gospel is a message of freedom and love. To proclaim God, today, is to fight for people's freedom."

Gaillot moved to Paris, where in a ritzy neighborhood he turned a large building into a squat for 150 homeless and took up residence with them. Seven months later, he wrote to Pope John Paul II, asking to meet the pontiff and offering to bring to the meeting not rebellion but "a listening and open mind, ready to humbly receive your advice on what you wish to notify me."

The Pope granted Gaillot's wish. Four days before Christmas, the two met in Rome. Photographs depict the clerics standing side by side. The Pope looks down, his left hand resting lightly on Gaillot's wrist. Gaillot, dressed in black, looks smaller still next to the taller, sturdier, white-clad pontiff. Gaillot is smiling broadly, looking positively Winky-like. Why?

A press release issued by the Holy See gives a hint. After noting that John Paul II has urged Gaillot to "commit himself more and more to the service of the ecclesial fellowship," the release reiterates the Vatican Council II statement that "the care to announce the Gospel on all the earth has been entrusted to Pastors as a body."

"On all the earth. . . ." Has the Pope spoken these words to Gaillot? Have they sparked an unexpected fire in the mind of the bishop of Partenia? Returning to Paris, Gaillot gets in touch with his friend Leo Scheer, media philosopher, author of the book *Virtual Democracy*, and, most crucially for Gaillot, the man with the plastic sheet and the crayon. If the Vatican has exiled Gaillot to a diocese that is, in effect, a virtual diocese . . . very well, then, Gaillot will embrace that virtuality, in order to announce the Gospel *on all the earth*. On January 13, 1996, exactly one year after his appointment to his new diocese, Gaillot, with the help of Scheer's computer, leaps the chasm from the real world to the virtual world by moving Partenia into cyberspace, onto the World Wide Web.

Partenia is one religious site on the Web. No one knows how many more there are. The Web is too big, too fluid, for an accurate count. Old sites disappear every day even as the total number doubles every six months. Jews, Christians, Muslims, Hindus, and Buddhists have established beachheads on the Internet. So have Druids, Pagans, Taoists, Zoroastrians, Gnostics, Sikhs, Mormons, Jains, New Agers, Twelve-Steppers, and Satanists. The digital crusades are here, and this time the prize isn't Constantinople but the entire earth.

To visit the Virtual Diocese of Partenia (at *http://www.partenia .fr*) is to witness one small foray in these crusades. Yet the questions that Partenia inspires are large ones, and they apply to every religion and spiritual movement in cyberspace. (The fluidity of cyberspace manifests in the mutability of its sites. As this book was about to go to press, the Partenia homepage located at *http://www.partenia.fr* was superseded by a more colorful Partenia homepage at *http://www.partenia.org*. The original Partenia pages remain at their original addresses, however, and the questions raised by them and by the new Partenia pages remain intact. No doubt other sites discussed in this book also will change in the near future, or perhaps even disappear.)

Partenia is a fully empowered Catholic diocese. Through its Web site, the Church is extending its reach to thousands, potentially millions, of people previously barred from its teachings by law or force of circumstance. Anywhere and anytime, anyone with Net access can now learn something about Catholicism, or about any other religion. How will this ease of access to the universal store of sacred knowledge reshape the spiritual life of our species? Will religions keep their belief systems and their body of believers intact in a virtual world where it takes only a click of a mouse to jump from one temple, one mosque, one church to the next?

Although Partenia is a Catholic diocese, its Web pages reflect the particular understanding of Jacques Gaillot. The site presents not papal encyclicals but letters and bulletins in which Gaillot continues to lobby for causes he deems important. Even as the Web carries organized religions into cyberspace, it allows a worldwide hearing of every voice within these religions. And online, not only can every voice be heard, but all voices are equal. Online, the words of the Dalai Lama look no different than those of an everyday Buddhist practitioner. How will this potential eroding of hierarchy change the way we worship?

The information highway is a two-lane road. On one page of Partenia, an icon invites visitors to send an instant message to Gaillot. This immediate give-and-take isn't religion from the top down but from the bottom up, from the grass roots. The highway is a Möbius strip, moreover—a road that circles back on itself. The Web is organized laterally rather than vertically. It lacks a center, and any site may be linked to any other site. In what ways will this decentralizing of communication alter organized religion?

Further questions arise. The first image that unscrolls on Partenia's homepage is of a map of central North Africa that marks the location of Partenia in physical reality. To the left of that map is displayed an image of a computer screen with Gaillot's face at its center. The legend on that image reads "Virtual Diocese." Where, in fact, does the Virtual Diocese of Partenia exist? In central North Africa? Where does any Buddhist, Muslim, Hindu, Jewish site exist? In the computer that hosts the site? In the computers that log on to its pages? In the minds of those who read the pages?

Partenia, and the rest of the Net, bends the contours of reality—physical, psychological, and spiritual. Partenia links to many other sites. At what point in the linkage does Partenia begin or end? A visitor to Partenia, or to any other Net site, can take on any identity he or she pleases. Who am I when I visit Partenia? Where do I myself begin and end when, sitting at a computer, I inhabit real and virtual space at the same time?

The photograph of Gaillot posted within the Virtual Diocese of Partenia is a simulated Gaillot, a virtual Gaillot. Like the map of Partenia, this Gaillot exists in two dimensions only. He does not breathe, and no living presence shines from his eyes. On his upturned face, no sunshine plays. Nature—the "dearest freshness deep down things," in Gerard Manley Hopkins's words—withers to memory in cyberspace. The online world is a world of mind alone. How will the human spirit fare in such a realm, sundered from the mystery of the flesh? And what of the artificial intelligences—bodiless minds—that are beginning to populate cyberspace? Do artificial life-forms have artificial souls?

What effect does surfing the Web have on mind, on consciousness, and, most importantly, on attention—the basic tool of spiritual realization? Partenia houses no cathedral, no cross, no explicit reminder of the sacred. Most noticeably lacking are the sacraments. Does sacred ritual have a place in cyberspace? Is cyberspace sacred space?

These questions are new because cyberspace is new. The first electronic computer, EINIAC, made its initial computation—for the U.S. Army—only half a century ago. The first linking of computers took place only in 1969, when researchers connected computers between four campuses in the American West. Tim Berners-Lee invented the World Wide Web only in 1991.

This book aims to explore these questions rather than to answer them. Like all books, it has tangled roots. They entwine with the magic of *Winky Dink and You* and of the text adventure games I played on my first computer (and later wrote for an outfit called Angelsoft). They coil through hours, weeks, years spent exploring the Net—in newsgroups, in virtual communities, and on the Web. The roots twist as well through my Catholic upbringing and with the religions and spiritual movements I've participated in as an adult, and with *Transformations*, a book I wrote with my wife, Tracy Cochran. Some of the research for that book consisted of collecting accounts of transforming moments in people's lives. On Tracy's suggestion, I went online to do this. Many people I met in cyberspace spoke of moments of grace, but to my astonishment not a single person mentioned experiencing a transforming moment while online. Does cyberspace, I wondered, present a particular challenge to spiritual work?

To find out, I decided to go to the source: to basic spiritual truths, to cyberspace, and, above all, to the spiritual teachers who are colonizing cyberspace and the scientists who are making this colonization possible. Sometimes these teachers and scientists are one and the same. This book presents their views as well as my own, for, ultimately, cyberspace is the voice of all humanity.

As far as I am concerned, to go onto the Internet is first of all like a dream. It is the dream of a child who walks along a sand beach and looks at the ocean. He feels lonely and weak in front of the vastness of the ocean. And suddenly the wish to start a dialogue with all the people of the world who live on other shores grows on him.

To go onto the Internet is also a venture. It is a magnificent venture which offers itself to me. I take the risk to let myself be welcomed by all women and men, whose face I do not know.

Partenia calls to mind faraway lands, yet unknown.

Partenia is a place of freedom.

—BISHOP JACQUES GAILLOT

CHAPTER 1

Judaism

Is TCP/ IP another name for God?
— RABBI YOSEF Y. KAZEN

The buildings in this part of Brooklyn are rundown, scarred by graffiti. Iron grates cover nearly every window. Aside from a few cars, nothing moves beneath the hot summer sun. No wonder my cab driver has his pedal to the floor.

In the distance, a billboard appears high on a wall. An old man with a white beard looks out from it. He is the late Rabbi Menachem Schneerson, the seventh Alter Rebbe of the Chabad-Lubavitch sect of Orthodox Judaism. The taxi passes the billboard, and everything changes.

This new block sparkles. It teems with dozens of men in dark trousers, some wearing dark jackets despite the heat, all topped with yarmulkes and sometimes black fedoras, milling, talking, laughing, gesticulating. A handful of women and children pick their way through the crowd. The action seems to swirl around a rosy brick Italianate mansion with a multipeaked facade. This is 770 Eastern Parkway, in Crown Heights, a building known around the world to Orthodox Jews simply as "770." It is the global headquarters of the Lubavitchers and the home of their late Rebbe, who died in 1994 at the age of ninety-two.

I've come to 770 to meet Rabbi Yosef Y. Kazen, director of activities of the Chabad-Lubavitch Web site, to talk with him about his outreach program in cyberspace and about some of the questions I have regarding spiritual work online. I know what Kazen looks like because I've seen a picture of him on the Web. (Nearly all of the research for this book was conducted on the Net.) Still, when I spot him it is a shock to match this exuberant man who greets me like a friend to the tiny black-and-white photo digitized in cyberspace.

Rabbi Kazen is middle-aged, tall, and husky, casually dressed in a white shirt and dark trousers. He wears glasses, and his carrot-colored beard is streaked with gray. The men he's talking with glance at me curiously, for I am the only person on the block in light-colored clothes and with an uncovered head. Kazen offers me a cigarette—like many of the religious digerati, he smokes incessantly—and we stand and puff and chat for a few minutes about the weather, the air, the neighborhood. We are waiting for my colleague Daisy Maryles, the executive editor of *Publishers Weekly*. A modern Orthodox Jew, Daisy, who coordinates the religious-book coverage at *PW*, has offered to join me here, out of professional and personal interest but also to act as my guide in this unfamiliar corner of Brooklyn.

After Daisy arrives, Kazen leads us down some steps into the modern building that hunkers next to 770. Inside, the secular twentieth century seems to give way to another time, another spirit. Women clad in head scarves and long-sleeved dresses bow, murmuring prayers in Hebrew. We walk down a narrow corridor. At a bend, a tiny window opens to an impossibly large room filled with Orthodox standing and talking, reading. It was in this room that Rabbi Schneerson enthralled his followers with his talks on God, Judaism, and the Torah. I want to linger, to marvel at the sight, but Kazen draws us away, through a side door and up four flights of battered stairs.

We enter a tiny room crowded with chairs and desks, modems and computers, a watercooler, bookcases, and workbenches. Cables snake everywhere. Cheap wood paneling covers the walls, and scratched linoleum adorns the floor in a checkerboard pattern. Most everything is scuffed and stained, a bit grimy, except for the glass over the picture of the Rebbe that hangs on one wall.

We each find a seat. The room is hot, the air close. I eye the watercooler. Its level will drop precipitously before we finish talking.

"The room you have here is ten by fifteen," Kazen tells us, the words spilling out of him in a high, happy rush. "But it's divided into three segments. One deals with people on the Internet, for mailings that go out weekly to individual questions and discussions. There is the computer development area. And then we've got the office end."

"How many people work here at one time?" asks Daisy.

"We can have up to five."

"I hope you like each other," she jokes.

The five are Kazen; Eli Winsbacher, the director of systems for the site; two programmers; and the site's webmaster, or chief programmer, Kazen's son David—who is all of fourteen. That's young for a webmaster, but not very young. Cyberspace is a romper room of sorts. Bill Gates was nineteen when he founded Microsoft.

"My son used to watch me sitting at the computer, and he always wanted to know what was going on." Kazen smiles at the memory. "So at about eleven and a half he created a little program, just for the sake of it. Basically, he created our homepages."

The room that the five elbow into is typical of other religious Internet launching pads. It doesn't take much to put up a Web site. A personal computer, a modem, and a table to put them on will do. With few exceptions, spiritual sites on the Net are financed on a shoestring. What money there is goes into hardware and operating costs. There's no need for a fancy office. The thousands of people who log on to the Chabad-Lubavitch site each week won't see this room, for cyberspace conceals as much as it reveals.

The Web site that Kazen directs is sleek and colorful, however. Its main page is topped by a picture of the Rebbe, along with the legends "Chabad-Lubavitch in Cyberspace" and "Judaism on the Internet at the speed of light." The page is festooned with icons of red, blue, green, yellow, purple, and gold. There's not a stain, scratch, or scuff in sight. Chabad-Lubavitch in Cyberspace is a bright, upbeat place, reflecting the good cheer that is characteristic of the followers of this branch of Hasidic Judaism.

Hasidism, or the Way of the Pious Ones, arose under the guidance of the great Jewish mystic known as the Baal Shem Tov in Eastern Europe in the mid-eighteenth century. (The style of clothing worn by Lubavitchers is a legacy of that time and place.) Hasidism emphasizes the individual's relationship to God and devotion toward others. Chabad-Lubavitch was founded in turn by the first Lubavitcher Alter Rebbe, Shneur Zalman, toward the end of the eighteenth century. Rabbi Zalman stressed the importance of the intellect in Jewish mystical practice, as well as the central role of the zaddik, or enlightened saint, in the religious life of the community. The succession of Lubavitcher rebbes is dynastic, generally from father to son, although Rabbi Schneerson was the son-in-law of the previous rebbe.

It is difficult to overestimate the influence of the rebbes, and of Rabbi Schneerson in particular, to Chabad-Lubavitch. So powerful was Rabbi Schneerson's presence that toward the end of his life many Lubavitchers declared that he was Mashiach, the long-awaited Messiah. When he died, hundreds danced in the streets, certain that the era of Mashiach was at hand. Throughout his leadership, which began in 1950, the Rebbe promoted an energetic outreach program to non-Orthodox Jews that made inspired use of high-tech equipment: radio, television, telephones, beepers, and, finally, computers. By Rabbi Kazen's estimate, approximately fifteen thousand Lubavitchers live in the Brooklyn community in Crown Heights, while another five hundred thousand are scattered worldwide. The numbers were significantly smaller before Rabbi Schneerson ascended to the leadership of the movement, and most of his followers take their outreach very seriously

Chabad-Lubavitch in Cyberspace has venerable roots by online standards. In the 1980s, electronic networks like Fidonet connected the digerati, who participated in electronic bulletin boards like Keshernet, a Jewish BBS, or bulletin board system, that Kazen joined late in the decade. In 1989, through Keshernet, Kazen received e-mail from a Reform Jew in Texas who told him about a Jewish woman who had expressed alarm at the flood of e-mail she'd received from Christian missionaries. The woman was eager to read Judaic writings, but there was a problem: she was allergic to ink.

"I said to myself," Kazen tells us, the wonder of it glowing in his eyes, "'One second! Here's a niche that hasn't been filled!'"

The rabbi e-mailed the woman some Jewish material on prayer. "I then turned around and started asking publishers within the organization to provide materials for me. The basic text of the Chabad philosophy, called the Tanya, is a five-volume book that has daily lessons. I got this book from the typesetter, had to remove the Hebrew, had to play around with the italics and whatnot. So it was quite a bit of work."

Kazen made the Tanya and other key Judaic texts available to whoever online wanted them. Along with other members of Keshernet, he then went where all in the community would go for the final word: to Rabbi Schneerson. "I asked the Rebbe if it would be worthwhile to look into going onto the Internet. Because in 1990 the Internet was starting to make a few waves, but we were apprehensive because it was a Wild West. And the Rebbe said to go ahead with it—absolutely to pursue it."

"A friend of mine, Eli Winsbacher," explains Kazen, "is a computer whiz. I spoke to him about it and I said, 'We've got to develop an electronic Chabad house.' An electronic Jewish center. And he said, 'You're nuts.'"

Kazen laughs. "You know, a lot of people tell me that. But I finally convinced him."

Barreling forward, the two went to Long Island City to meet with officials of the Dorsai Embassy, a not-for-profit corporation that provides computer services to other nonprofit groups. "They looked at us and they said, 'You know, rabbi, it's going to take away time from being home, and time to study this stuff and learn it. Are you ready for it?' And we said, 'Yeah, we're ready for it.'"

Kazen shakes his head. "Two and a half years—every night, night in, night out—we spent time there. They gave us our first computer, and they taught us how to put stuff on a gopher [a menu-based program that displays Internet resources such as text files]. So I took everything off the 40-megabyte hard disk I had, and put it on the gopher site.

"We asked the Rebbe if we could go with the name Chabad. [*Chabad* is an acronym for Hebrew words that mean "wisdom," "understanding," and "knowledge."] He said yes. At the end of '93 we came online as chabad.org. We eventually moved our computers from the basement of my house into this building, and moved the servers [computers that serve data or processing power to another, usually smaller, computer] over from Dorsai to here, got the T1 [an advanced phone-line connection to the Internet], and we're running."

That running costs substantial coin, but Chabad-Lubavitch in Cyberspace receives minimal outside funding. Most of the expenses are paid out of Kazen's and Winsbacher's own pockets. "Between the two of us," Kazen reckons, "we actually sank our savings. The return here is spiritual. There's no financial return here." Like most religious Web sites, Chabad-Lubavitch carries few advertisements from outside parties. The site does market a scattering of items, including a menorah-building kit, membership in a tape-of-the-month club, and a cooking video, *A Taste of Shabbos* ("Cholent? Babaganoosh? Kugel? Are these code words that Unlock the Mysteries of an Ancient Civilization?"). In early 1997, it presented advertisements from several "sponsors," including a commodities broker based in Florida.

"The idea," Kazen declares with a wave of his hand, "is that Judaism has to be free!"

Kazen's site functions primarily as an educational outreach. This is true of most religious outposts in cyberspace. But when Daisy asks him how many "Chabadniks" are linked to the server, his answer comes as a surprise.

"Of our own people, a small percentage—a very small percentage."

"Really," Daisy remarks. "So this is not for your own."

"Our setup was never for our own group. On the contrary, this was set up strictly to deal with the outside world. I don't know if your average Chabad person is going to want his kid running around on the Net. It's like putting him in the middle of a newspaper store with all the magazines there. So we've never come out within the community to try and push it. My perspective here is of getting out to the world. Getting a message of Judaism to the Jew who doesn't know much, to the Gentile who is interested in finding out what Judaism has to offer."

The Chabad and other Orthodox aren't the only Jews promoting Judaism online. Scores of Conservative, Reform, Reconstructionist, and Humanistic Jewish groups have established sites on the Web. Pages aimed at Jewish students flourish, particularly on sites connected with Hillel, the global Jewish campus organization. Several thousand Jewish sites probably exist on the Web all told. Chabad-Lubavitch in Cyberspace alone reaches a lot of people—over 2 million in 1995, according to the rabbi. Its pages now average, he reports, "twenty to thirty-five thousand hits a week. And that's just our site." (A Web page receives a hit each time anyone downloads any file—text, visual, audio—from that page. One person may visit a Web page once, therefore, and account for many hits.)

And there are numerous other Chabad-Lubavitch sites online, Kazen points out. This seems natural for a movement that has physical centers in scores of cities in the United States, Canada, and Europe, as well as in eight cities in Morocco, and one center each in Peru, Kazakhstan, Singapore, Hong Kong, and Zaire, among other locales.

"Are the sites connected in any way?" asks Daisy.

"They're all linked," Kazen says, leaning forward with excitement. "The material is all based on the Rebbe's teachings or on general Judaica, but there's a lot of local flavor. For instance, the Baltimore-Washington area is starting to zero in on women in Judaism. There's a guy in Marin County who is zeroing in on games and Judaism, dealing with questions such as, What does polo have to with Judaism? How can you learn a lesson from it? We've got another guy in California who's presenting kosher recipes from different places around the world."

The online visitors who make Kazen shout for joy are the wandering Jews who respond to the electronic call and return to the fold. He tells us of a police dispatcher in Philadelphia who not only came back to Judaism because of Chabad activities online but now spends the holidays at Kazen's house.

"I had a student in New Mexico," Kazen remembers, "who's very interesting. He wrote to me because he wanted to know if it was permissible to smoke marijuana on Saturday morning in preparation for prayer, so that he could be more astute." The rabbi chuckles at the thought.

"I wrote him back that, within Judaism, the concept is that the prayer itself gives you the high. Also, that you don't smoke on Saturdays. He ended up spending his summer here, at a yeshiva, and he's planning to pursue additional studies next year. I met him earlier this year, and he said that because I'd answered him in a positive way and didn't throw off his question, I had a profound effect on his life."

This student contacted Kazen through "Ask a Question," a Web page on the site that offers a field where the curious can type in a question and then, by clicking on an icon, e-mail it to the rabbi. Kazen reports that he spends an average of six hours a day dealing with this interactive tool. "Yesterday," he recalls, "I got a question from a woman who had bought an Egyptian pitcher with two handles and wanted to know if she could use it to wash her hands—the ritual hand-washing before eating bread. Very interesting. A student at Brandeis University who had cut her finger with a knife while she was peeling an apple wanted to know what to do with the knife—whether it was kosher or not, because of the blood.

"These questions come in at eleven at night, twelve at night, and they want to know it now. They don't want to have to wait until who knows when."

Kazen doesn't answer all the questions himself. Sometimes he farms them out. "I will usually try to find out where the questioners are located, who they are, whether they have a contact with a local rabbi or Chabad representative, and send them out there," he says. "I think the good part about the Net is that it allows for people to sit on their own, read, study, question, ask, ask, and ask, until they're comfortable enough so that they don't care whether they're associated with a specific stereotype. And that's what I have found to be the power of this thing."

"In other words," Daisy says, "it's an anonymous power when you first ask these questions."

"A totally anonymous power."

"It makes you comfortable asking anything."

"Anything. I've had people who are coming from all walks of life, who ask questions about homosexuality, transsexuality, bisexuality. I've had a psychiatrist from Australia who asked me how he was to cope with patients who are being tested for genetic diseases and who are going to die a horrible death young. The guy isn't American, he doesn't know what I look like, he doesn't even know whether I'm real or not."

Most of the material available on Chabad-Lubavitch in Cyberspace—grouped into areas like "The Jewish Woman" and "Jewish Mysticism," interactive Torah lessons in Hebrew and English—is text-based (although there are graphics and downloadable audio clips, including clips of Chabad songs like "Oh Rebbe"). This seems appropriate for the People of the Word. It's the bells and whistles of cyberspace, however—the interactive visuals, especially in 3-D—that can attract visitors to Web sites just as nectar attracts bees. Kazen knows this.

"Over the years, we've always had an event called *Hanukkah Live* on cable TV," he says, "with satellite hookup links all over the world. We figured that this year, we're going to take this to another level." What Kazen is referring to is the "Festival of Light!" (*http://www.festival.chabad.org*), an ambitious online program for the 1996 Hanukkah season that would, as a press release puts it, "utilize the power and reach of the Internet to raise the moral and ethical barometer of our planet."

The primary utilization is through "The Global Interactive Database of Good Deeds," intended as a permanent site where, Kazen tells us, "people will be able to participate in lighting their own menorah, by typing in an act of goodness or kindness or a positive thing that they did. And by having a map of the entire world, as every person types in something good that they did, another part of the world will be lit up." This database, he explains, adheres to "our perspective that the Internet is a fulfillment of Isaiah's prophecy of swords into ploughshares."

Kazen's plans for cyberspace are ambitious, but he is cautious about what he puts online. Among the many documents connected to his site, one set is notably absent: the very foundation of Judaism, the first five books of the Bible. When I ask him why, he grows somber and explains that although he makes numerous biblical commentaries available, "the actual Bible is not on there. To market it on the Net, to say that 'here is an authentic version of the Bible as provided by the movement'—that's a very, very big responsibility. Anybody can walk into a store and buy a King James Bible. They don't need me for that. I'd much rather go with a synopsis and get the person to go to the synagogue and participate."

"What about the possibility of putting a synagogue on the Web?" I ask. "Can a synagogue be duplicated online?" This seems a crucial question. For religions to move fully into cyberspace, they will have to bring their rituals and sense of community along with them.

"It can be duplicated," Kazen answers, "but only to a certain extent. There are limitations. For example, in Jewish life, the man who is above the age of thirteen has to put on tefillin [leather pouches containing scrolls of Torah passages] every weekday. It's an actual physical act. You're taking a leather box, and you're putting it on your arm, and you're wrapping it on your arm and you're putting it on your head and you're saying a specific prayer. Yes, the prayer itself can be read off the Net. But the actual act needs to be done by a physical person. The concept of Judaism in general is using the material—the animal cowhide, the hair of the lamb created into wool—so that there's actual participation in all the different four levels: the inanimate, the flora, the fauna, and the human being—all into one aspect.

"Can I have a virtual meal?" he continues. "How long is it going to hold me for? I can read a recipe, but I still have to go out there and buy the eggs, buy the sugar."

I ask Kazen whether there are other aspects of Judaism that may not be transferable to cyberspace.

"Well, you can't have a minyan online. You cannot have a quorum of ten people."

I don't understand this. I fail to see why ten Jewish men can't meet in a real-time chat room online and thus constitute a minyan—the minimum number, according to Jewish tradition, necessary to pray and worship communally.

"That's very interesting. Why not?"

"Because the quorum of ten people requires ten physical bodies. Each individual person has a spark of godliness within them, which is the soul. It requires the quorum of ten people, which reflect the ten different levels of godliness. So therefore you can have nine people who might not be religious at all, and one person who is religious. Their religious commitment doesn't matter, as long as they're Jews."

"And male," Daisy gets in.

"And male, over the age of thirteen. But the concept is that if you have those ten people, you're bringing down a higher level of godliness that will allow you to say the Kaddish prayer."

"But why," I ask, "can't that take place in a virtual chat room with ten males?"

"Because there's no physical presence. We don't necessarily see the spiritual reality of what is happening at that time, but certain things have to be done with physical people, just as food has to be eaten by physical people."

"So you couldn't have a bar mitzvah," Daisy points out.

"Right. And then don't forget, the clock stops at the end of six days. There is a concept in Judaism called Shabbos, or Sabbath. That day in the week is when we turn off the world and get out and walk into a whole different island in time. That is an aspect that cannot be handled on the Net."

Even so, Kazen and other Chabad have extraordinarily high hopes for the Internet. "Modern Technology and Judaism," an essay posted on the site and based on talks that Rabbi Schneerson gave in the late 1960s and the early 1980s, makes this bold claim:

> The advance of scientific understanding is increasingly revealing the *inherent unity in the universe*, as expressed in the forces of nature.
>
> Being aware of this can serve as a preparation and prologue to the Era of Mashiach, for at that time the Creator's simple, uncompounded Unity will become evident.

The Rebbe is speaking here specifically of radio and television, yet no doubt he would have extended these thoughts to computer-mediated communication.

Kazen confirms this. "This concept of inherent unity in the world," he says, "is very, very strongly shown through the Net, perhaps even more than through radio and television. Because if there's an effect between myself and a person who's in Beijing, or myself and a person in Antarctica, and it's an instant communication, what is the lesson showing us?"

"Is computer-networked technology then a holy technology," I ask, "in that it's serving a holy end?"

Kazen's face lights up as if I've said the magic word. "Yes. Humanity in the years past was glorified for war. All the monuments that you see are glorified about war. And Isaiah's prophecy is that there shall be no more war, that there shall be swords into ploughshares. So, how does the world come to that?

"My question is, in a humorous fashion, Is TCP/IP [the dominant Internet communications protocol] another name for God? Because in essence, this is a way that you're finding a unity between people. Sure, there are haves and have-nots. But ultimately everyone's going to have a piece of the action. So yes, in my opinion this is a means toward the era of Mashiach."

Kazen draws a deep breath, then rushes on. "Let's learn from the lesson we had fifty years ago. The most advanced technological country in the world, by not putting godliness within itself, created a nation that annihilated millions of people. Hopefully the Net, which is our latest technology, will bring humanity together for a better purpose, and will not be abused. There's a concept of good and light in the world, and this is a technology that can be the means toward that end."

On that inspiring note, we conclude our formal talk and leave the room, picking our way back down those four dismal flights of stairs. Outside, Kazen lights a cigarette and inhales like a man smoking his last smoke. He directs us down the block, into the main entrance of 770 and along a short corridor. To our right, through interior windows, we see a room filled with rows of young males bent over books. At the end of the hallway, we slip into a room lined with banks of telephones and a huge switchboard. This is the ancestor of Kazen's Web room, the media command center from where Lubavitchers around the world were relayed the Rebbe's speeches via telephone linkups. I recall how, as the Rebbe aged into his nineties, beepers were distributed to all of his male followers in order to alert them whenever he came out of his private quarters to pray.

These are, I think, very wired people.

Finally, Kazen leads us upstairs to Rabbi Schneerson's library. The room whispers of sacred history. In glass cases, mementos of rebbes past—photographs, documents, letters, Bibles—are preserved with great care. In one case I find a passport worn with use and age, evidence of the legacy of the Diaspora, the global scattering of the Jews. It occurs to me, looking at it through the glass, that in a virtual way the Internet has, by making possible a convergence in cyberspace of Jews around the world, spurred the reversal of the Diaspora as surely as has the establishment of Israel.

I run my hand along the polished side of an old grandfather clock that marks the moon according to the Hebrew calendar. The wood presses back warm against my fingers—so different, I think, so much more generous to my senses than the Windows clock that ticks off the minutes on my computer screen. A bit later, I press my hand in Kazen's hand, saying good-bye. His hand is warmer still than the wood of the grandfather clock. Touching his hand, I know that I am touching one spark of the living reality behind cyberspace.

The homepage of Chabad-Lubavitch in Cyberspace is located at *http://www.chabad.org.*

KEY SITES

The following ten Internet sites, like all the sites discussed in this book, provide keys to understanding the workings of the human spirit online. Most of these sites represent the best of the Net, but some illustrate its downside. Each site listed offers free access and is open to all.

Shamash (*http://shamash.org/trb/judaism.html*)

There's no better place to begin exploring the Jewish Internet than Shamash, a bonanza of Judaic resources cataloged and maintained in pristine order by Andrew Tannenbaum, a computer-systems architect in Burlington, Massachusetts. A table of contents divides the hundreds of listings on Shamash into fourteen categories such as "Jewish Communities," "Yiddish," "Museums and Exhibitions," "Books," and "Jewish Studies." Though Tannenbaum's presentation covers every available type of Jewish resource on the Net, including Usenet groups, mailing lists, and chat rooms, it emphasizes quality over quantity. Rather than simply listing resources by name, as so many Internet indexes do, Tannenbaum includes a brief description of each of his selections. This intelligent, informative page is a model of what an Internet index should be.

Havienu L'Shalom (*http://www.havienu.org*)

One of the most exciting developments in cyberspace is the advent of the virtual congregation, a religious grouping that has no real-world counterpart but exists solely on the Net. Havienu L'Shalom is one such congregation, apparently Orthodox—a "merger," as its Web site proclaims, "of advanced technology, the Internet, and traditional chaplaincy, to increase access to Jewish services, education, and guidance." Havienu L'Shalom claims a membership of several hundred, ranging from computer programmers in Melbourne and Jerusalem to a "rocket scientist" in Boston and a social worker in Atlanta. Anyone interested in joining can do so by e-mail. Its beautiful homepage displays an image of the Cabala's tree of life; otherwise, it is a text-only site. Among the services offered are a discussion forum, an electronic newsletter, and messages from the congregation's rabbi, Meilech Leib Dubrow. The site boasts great ambitions, including the building in cyberspace of the Third Beis HaMikdash, or Third Temple, but as of now it's more a fascinating experiment that is well worth observing.

The Virtual Shtetl (*http://sunsite.unc.edu/yiddish/shtetl.html*)

The patch of rough stone wall that greets visitors to the Virtual Shtetl reminds them that in the real world, shtetls, the small Jewish towns once found in Eastern Europe, were never as sleek as this excellent site. Set up like a small village, the Virtual Shtetl contains a "library" of Yiddish-oriented documents, a "school" with links to Yiddish teaching and learning centers, a "memorial" dedicated to Holocaust pages, a "post office" that provides Yiddish mailing lists, a "station" with links to documents concerning various historic shtetls around the world, an "art center," a "synagogue," and a "kitchen" complete with recipes and a database of kosher restaurants. That the Internet belongs to everyone is indicated by the identity of the man who maintains and designs this site. He's neither a computer professional nor a religious leader, but a research assistant professor in the School of Pharmacy at the University of North Carolina, Chapel Hill. His name is Iosif Vaisman.

Congregation Emanu-El of the City of New York (*http://www.emanuelnyc.org*)

Unlike Havienu L'Shalom, this Web site is rooted in a real-world congregation. Congregation Emanu-El of the City of New York is the largest Reform Jewish congregation in the United States, with more than ten thousand members, and is housed in the largest synagogue in the world, located in Manhattan at Fifth Avenue and Sixty-fifth Street. Congregation Emanu-El's site is typical of many well-run Web sites that are geared toward promoting the message and activities of one particular congregation. The site contains a message from the congregation's senior rabbi, Ronald B. Sobel; news of upcoming events; and a "Virtual Tour of the Temple" that consists of a series of color photographs that display the power as well as limitations of a two-dimensional simulation of three-dimensional space. What distinguishes this site, though, is that it is where the first Internet broadcast of a traditional religious ritual of one of the major world religions took place, on April 3, 1996. On that date, the congregation transmitted over its Web page a "cyber-Seder," which included a reading of the Haggadah, the traditional Passover text, as well as illustrated Haggadoth, images of the Seder ritual.

Jews in Prison (*http://www.sbchabad.org/sbchabad/prison*)

Though the Internet is global in reach, its content is often particularized toward specific audiences. This Web site, for instance, aims to "provide support, before, during, and after incarceration, to both the Jewish inmates and their family and friends." Produced by Chabad of Santa Barbara, these pages offer no amenities but plenty of sensible advice on how to cope in prison: dealing with anti-Semitism, what prison life is like, how to practice Judaism in prison ("with the appropriate planning and effort, many prisons will provide prepackaged freeze-dried meals for the eight days of Passover. Likewise, matzoh and grape juice will usually be given"), and so on. The site accepts e-mail for comments, suggestions, and criticisms.

Israel Ministry of Foreign Affairs (*http://www.israel.org*)

Sites devoted to Israel exist throughout the Internet. One of the most efficient ways to access them is via the well-organized official homepage of the Israel Foreign Ministry. Here, in addition to information specific to the ministry, webnauts will find information about the Israeli government, a detailed "Guide to the Mideast Peace Process," much information about Israel, and numerous links to nearly every aspect of Israeli life.

Ethiopian Jewry Home Page
(*http://www.cais.net:8o/nacoej/index.html*)

Not all Jews are white. Today thirty-six hundred African Jews, or Falasha Mora, languish in Ethiopia, their desired emigration to Israel tangled in both Ethiopian and Israeli red tape. This exemplary series of Web pages presents in simple yet elegant form the story of the Ethiopian Jews, through a poignant "slide show" that offers photos of these Jews, through links to assorted documents and relevant sites, and through an electronic newsletter, *Lifeline*. In addition, the site, sponsored by the North American Conference on Ethiopian Jewry, displays lovely color images of embroidered items—pillows, bags, matzoh covers, and so forth—made by Ethiopian Jews and given in exchange for donations. As Rabbi Kazen indicated, information disseminated through the Internet can effect sociospiritual change. In its effort to reverse one facet of the Diaspora, the Ethiopian Jewry Home Page is a sterling example of the use of the Net to hasten such change.

The Jewish Software Center on the WWW
(*http://members.aol.com/jewishsoft/index.html*)

Many of the Jewish sites on the Net offer free, downloadable software, though this is usually of an elementary sort, such as Judaic calendars. Some offer more complex software for sale, and other, strictly commercial sites offer items for sale only. One of the latter is the Jewish Software Center on the WWW, produced by the Jewish Software Company. The software available here ranges from screensavers (dancing Hasidim, a flying El Al jet) to CD-ROMs about Israel and Judaism, from digital Talmuds and Bibles to Hebrew/English word-processing programs.

soc.culture.jewish (and the soc.culture.jewish FAQ)
(*http://shamash.org/lists/scj-faq/HTML/*)

For all its splendor, the Web remains basically a one-way rather than an interactive medium. Give-and-take increases dramatically on the Usenet newsgroups, where serial postings allow discussion, sometimes heated, on every possible topic. Of the several Jewish-oriented newsgroups, including alt.music.jewish, alt.personals.jewish, soc.culture.israel, soc.culture.jewish.holo caust, soc.culture.jewish.parenting, and soc.genealogy.jewish, the most active is soc.culture.jewish. One typical day's postings included Hanukkah jokes, an intense discussion about whether circumcision is a form of child abuse, back-and-forths about the alleged use of torture by Israeli security forces, and a post by a man who wondered if he could be considered Jewish since his father was Jewish and his mother was a Catholic who converted to Judaism.

A FAQ is a list of frequently asked questions (with answers). The FAQ maintained by soc.culture.jewish and cached at Shamash, among other places, is an encyclopedic resource providing cogent responses to hundreds of questions relating to the Torah, Jewish thought, Israel, conversion, and nearly every other element of Jewish life.

#israel

Those looking for a real-time interactive exchange on the Net often turn to IRC, or Internet Relay Chat, which features "channels" on which people from around the world talk about all and sundry. The leading IRC channel devoted to Judaism is #israel. The level of conversation here, as on most IRC channels, oscillates from the elevated to the depraved. On an average recent day, #israel hosted conversations ranging from an exchange of Hanukkah messages to a flurry of quick asides about Jewish zombies. The majority of users of this channel are of college age or younger, most hailing from the United States or Israel.

 Cyberspace

An Annotated Conversation
with John Perry Barlow

*In John, you start out with the word, the word becomes flesh.
What we're in the process of doing is making the flesh
back into word.*

—John Perry Barlow

I'm in John Perry Barlow's bathroom and I can't get out. The knob rotates freely but the door won't budge. It's a hot day in the city, edging into the nineties, and the door, made of wood, must have swelled in the heat.

The air in the bathroom feels like wet wool. I wish I'd worn shorts instead of jeans. I lever up the knob, then bully against the door with my shoulder. No luck. I can hear Barlow's boots clomping in the kitchen. He's probably wondering what's keeping me, but what can I do? Anyway, when I showed up for our appointment he wasn't there. I spent fifteen minutes sitting on his front steps before I realized that I could reach him on his cell phone. He posts that number on his Web site, and I'd scribbled it into my address book a few weeks before. I walked to a pay phone and dialed, and Barlow answered from somewhere in the city—he didn't say where. We arranged to meet ninety minutes later.

It occurs to me, standing in the bathroom, sweat beading on my neck, that the earlier delay and what's happening now are metaphors for one of the most pervasive aspects of the online experience: the wait. Without a superfast connection, going online involves frequent pauses, especially on the Web, where each page much be loaded byte by byte into your home computer from the host computer. This seemingly small thing is, actually, no small thing. It breaks up the flow of the online experience, and tests one's patience time and again—two truths, I would learn, with considerable consequence for spiritual work in cyberspace.

Enough of this wait. I can't very well interview Barlow from inside his bathroom. I shelve my dignity and bang on the door. Barlow's boots approach, the door wobbles open with a pop, and there he is, smiling ruefully.

I can't see his eyes. Barlow scratched one earlier that morning, so he's wearing dark purple sunglasses. They strike me as appropriate gear for a man as famous for his songwriting for the Grateful Dead as for his stirrings in cyberspace. Everything about Barlow seems like a signifier. His black shirt seems emblematic of his status as a cool cultural icon. His purple neck scarf, like his shades, speaks of psychedelia. The blue jeans and cowboy boots appear to be a legacy of his roots as a rancher, of his childhood on a large Wyoming homestead, as does his deliberate, deep gravel voice. His slightly thinning, swept-back brown hair, his beard flecked with gray, his lined face—mementos of nearly a half century on the planet, including a college education at Wesleyan University, where I first met him many years ago.

I'm visiting Barlow in his funky one-bedroom apartment in Manhattan's West Village to talk to him about the nature of cyberspace and about the spiritual implications of that nature. Barlow's credentials as a commentator on digital realities are impeccable. He's a cofounder of the Electronic Frontier Foundation, an influential organization dedicated to the defense of civil liberties in cyberspace. His rare but eloquent writings, including "A Declaration of the Independence of Cyberspace," have helped to channel the political and spiritual discourse about the online universe. He is a man who understands that, in the long run, cyberspace will shape humanity's consciousness like a magnet shapes a pile of iron filings.

We settle at a wooden table next to the kitchen. A year ago, when I interviewed Barlow for a magazine article, we sat at the same table. (A small portion of that interview is included in this chapter.) His apartment looks just as it did then, but that's not surprising for someone whose true home base remains in Wyoming, and who spends most of his time on the road speaking about the virtual world.

On the table, and on shelves scattered throughout the apartment, books teeter in piles. A large Sony television rests against one wall. Near it stands a desk cramped with a computer monitor and other electronic equipment. Barlow's cordless phone rings often during our conversation, and he answers every call, sometimes typing in data on a keyboard as he speaks to the other party. Sounds of the city—the rumble of a truck, the yell of a boy—drift up through the fifth-floor window. As we talk, we sip coffee that Barlow brews extra-strong. Our talk, edited for clarity and brevity, as are all the interviews in this book, goes like this:

JEFF ZALESKI: How do you define cyberspace?

JOHN PERRY BARLOW: To the best of my knowledge, I'm the person who started defining it in its present way: Cyberspace is where you are when you're on the phone. Cyberspace is any information space, but it's interactive information space that is created by media that are densely enough shared so that there's the sense of other people being present.

You could say that cyberspace is also where you are when you're reading a book. The difference is that the ability to have real-time interaction with the author when you're reading a book is unlikely.

JZ: It's a space that's created when there's an exchange of information?

JPB: It's when there can be an interactive exchange between people in real or close to real time, and where there are a lot of people gathered at once. Not just the caller and receiver. A large social space.

JZ: Is cyberspace necessarily digitally mediated? When I'm sitting here and talking to you, is this cyberspace?

JPB: No, I would say not. It's not digitally mediated, but it's mediated. The big difference to me is that in cyberspace you don't have your body.

Trying to define cyberspace is like trying to tie a bow on a jellyfish. For that reason, definitions abound. *Wired Style: Principles of English Usage in the Digital Age*, by the editors of *Wired* magazine, defines cyberspace more broadly than Barlow does: "Information space.... The place between phones, between computers, between you and me." *Que's Computer and Internet Dictionary*, available on America Online, equates cyberspace only with "the virtual space created by computer systems." The definition narrows further in *The Grolier Multimedia Encyclopedia*, available through AOL on the Web, which says that cyberspace is "a catchword for the interactive computing and communications base available on the Internet."

The term first appeared in William Gibson's science-fiction novel *Neuromancer*, published in 1984. There Gibson described cyberspace as "a consensual hallucination ... a graphic representation of data abstracted from the banks of every computer in the human system."

For the purposes of this book, cyberspace is defined as the virtual space created through the activation of a computer. By this definition, cyberspace is created when, for example, a solo user activates the software adventure game *Myst* on a stand-alone computer, two or more human beings engage in computer-mediated communication, or two or more computers communicate automatically. Though the word *space* appears in this definition and others, this is not everyday, three-dimensional space. If cyberspace can be measured at all, it's by the number of sites that exist on it or the computing capacity of the machines that create it. Its potential size is, for all practical purposes, infinite. We will always be pioneers in cyberspace, for as we explore it, we create it, and as we create it, we explore it.

JZ: What do you mean by *information?*

JPB: Well, it's a little tricky because I've got two different notions of what information is. One of which relates to the idea of reality as a life-form, as the foundation of life, whereas the other is just that thing that Jaron Lanier referred to when he said that information is alienated experience. The stuff that is about something, that is usually a compressed and not particularly communicative artifact of the actual experience. [Jaron Lanier coined the term *virtual reality* and is VR's most important visionary; he is interviewed in chapters 6 and 8 of this book.]

JZ: Like words on the page. Or words on a screen.

JPB: Yeah. Words. It's not the thing itself, it's that which is about the thing itself, and can be easily communicated over a distance.

JZ: And then there's poetry, which is a thing in itself.

JPB: That's right. That's the other kind of information, because poetry is an actual experience. That's a good distinction to make. Reading a poem, or rather participating in a poem, is an experience.

JZ: What's the relationship between information and energy?

JPB: Well, in both forms of information, both the reportage and the reality, fundamental to it is relationship of difference. Now, if you take the Gregory Bateson formulation, which he essentially derived from Claude Shannon's information theory, information is "a difference that makes a difference." So if there is difference in whatever dimension—it can be difference in time, difference in space, spiritual elevation—information is that gap, the voltage of difference, the difference between one and zero.

JZ: So by that definition, energy is a form of information.

JPB: Yes, and vice versa.

Claude Shannon, born in 1916, founded information theory. In the late 1940s, while working as an electrical engineer at Bell Laboratories, he first described, by building upon the work of the nineteenth-century mathematician George Boole, the measurement of information through binary digits, by a one or a zero, a yes or a no. (Each one or zero, yes or no, is a bit of information. Eight bits equal one byte.) This binary presentation of information is the basis of all digital computing and of all digitally mediated communication.

Gregory Bateson (1904–1980) was an English anthropologist who applied cybernetics—the science that studies communication and control systems—to anthropology, and who in doing so came up with the phrase quoted by Barlow: "Information is a difference that makes a difference."

In his excellent book *Silicon Dreams*, Robert W. Lucky, executive director of research for Bell Laboratories, proposes that information be considered in terms of levels of organization, and be pictured as a pyramid. At the base of the pyramid lies what he calls

> *data....* the raw material from which information is extracted, which might include unprocessed observations, random sights and sounds, the "ones" and "zeroes" in a data communication stream, etc. This is the sludge of the information age.

Above data lies

> *information.* Now someone has taken the sludge—the raw data—and given it organization.

This is, Lucky points out, the sort of information we receive in newspapers, on television, and so on. When we ourselves store that information in our minds, we are, Lucky says, dealing with "knowledge." Finally, when we organize that knowledge in such a way that we can generate new knowledge from it, we are dealing with the peak of the pyramid, what Lucky calls "wisdom."

Employing Lucky's pyramidal grid, it seems that what is transmitted through cyberspace is, in most cases, information—not knowledge, and certainly not wisdom. What we do with that information, however, may transmute it into knowledge or wisdom. It's an old saw that mystical knowledge and wisdom—which may not be the sort of information and wisdom that Lucky is referring to—surpass logic and, by extension, don't arise from ones and zeros. This is said to be so because, reflecting what Rabbi Schneerson called the "inherent unity of the universe," mystical knowledge and wisdom are said to lie beyond the reach of logic and of binary computation, which divide unity into plurality.

A computer is a device that performs mathematical calculations, nothing more. Through these calculations, it can, with the right input, generate an output that simulates reality, as in a digitized photo, or that creates an alternate reality, as in a digitized photo that's been digitally manipulated. Only that which can be expressed through mathematical calculation, that which is computable, can be simulated by a computer. Many physicists believe that the universe itself is computable—that, as Paul Davies puts it in his book *The Mind of God*, there exists "a program or algorithm from which a correct description of the world may be obtained in a finite number of steps." (An algorithm is a rule or set of instructions for solving a certain problem.) If this is so, then the universe and everything in it may be simulatable with a computer, and the saw about mystical wisdom will be proved blunt as well as old.

Whether digital computers, which work discretely, could perform this simulation is another matter. Physicists have yet to determine whether the universe is continuous or discrete. Most of the evidence so far indicates that it is continuous. If the universe is continuous, it seems that a digital computer cannot simulate it with complete faithfulness. Quantum computers, however, which now exist only in the minds of futurists but which may be feasible, are capable of presenting information in units that are not only a one or a zero but a one *and* a zero at the same time. Perhaps someday a quantum computer will simulate the universe—that is, unless the Holy Ghost cannot be defined by an algorithm.

JZ: I've been asking these particular questions as a lead-up to my current driving question: What can be, or perhaps in the future will be, transmitted through cyberspace?

JPB: Right. Can you put *prana* through the wire?

Prana is a Sanskrit word sometimes translated as "life force," sometimes as "breath." It is equivalent to the Chinese concept of *chi*, and somewhat to the Judeo-Christian-Islamic concept of *spirit*. In all the major religious traditions, this force is seen as manifesting through the physical body of the human being. This view has profound implications for spiritual work in cyberspace, where the body is absent. This insistence on the sacredness of the flesh—the flesh animated with holy breath—surely lies behind Rabbi Kazen's injunctions regarding cyberspatial manifestations of a minyan and other Judaic rituals.

JZ: The Catholic Church has many Web sites, but they haven't yet put any of the sacraments onto the Net.

JPB: I wonder why that is.

JZ: Probably because a lot of religions believe that sacramental energy has an intimate and necessary connection with the body.

JPB: Ah. That's what it is. Let's take Communion. What Communion is really about is the experience of entering that metaphorical gap between the wine and the blood. If you don't have the grounding in the wine, the physical manifestation, I can see where they would think that there's no potential for that holy voltage between the physical symbol and the spiritual reality.

JZ: What do you think?

JPB: I think they're probably right, in a way. One of the reasons people have such a difficult time understanding metaphor now is because most people actually live in a metaphorical condition all the time. You know, they're living in this completely informational environment where there's no relationship to the physical world anyway, so what the hell would a metaphor be? Metaphors always have that grounding element. And so much of what the spiritual process is about is sliding up and down between those two poles of the physical and the immaterial.

JZ: There's an idea that is achieving common coinage on the Net: that the Net is somehow going to free us from the tyranny of the body, and of the material world in general—that we are souls trapped in physical reality and that by going digital we can break free of the prison of the flesh.

JPB: The line I keep coming back to, and how I always describe this to people, is "Now is the flesh made word." In John, you start out with the word, the word becomes flesh. What we're in the process of doing is making the flesh back into word. The flesh becomes immaterial substance by means that are available to us through nonspiritual techniques, or not explicitly spiritual techniques. That which lives in some kind of identifying manifestation can also live almost, maybe entirely, in cyberspace.

JZ: Is this a necessary, or even positive, direction for evolution to take? It's curious; it almost sounds like Descartes's "I think therefore I am"—as if the reality of the mind is superior to the reality of the body.

JPB: I don't think a human being ever gets completely free of the flesh except when he or she dies. And isn't supposed to. My own sense of why the soul is in the world to begin with is that the soul comes here and wraps itself up in the troubling prison of the body for educational purposes. You're here to learn about love in the presence of fear, and only by having a body does fear become real. Only by having something as fragile and as easily eliminated as the flesh can the soul experience fear. And only by having something as transitory as living in a world of so little certainty can the soul experience doubt. That's really all you're here to do.

What is love without fear? I'm assuming that on the other side of the real membrane—in real cyberspace, in the spiritual dimension—there isn't any fear, and there isn't any time, and there isn't any decay, and there isn't any doubt. So the soul has to come into the body to give itself context.

JZ: Again, it seems as if you and a lot of other people believe that there is this samsaric realm where we're caught in the flesh and then there's this transcendental realm, almost a Platonic realm, and what we're trying to do is to get more in touch with, or to be more part of, that transcendental realm.

JPB: Yeah, to inhabit it, at least in part. But there's something both blasphemous and futile about trying to leave the body altogether, and I wouldn't want to if I could.

JZ: You don't plan to be uploaded?

JPB: I have no interest in having my personality on a CMOS chip. And I also think that this will never happen because they just don't know what it is they're trying to capture there. [CMOS is an acronym for "complimentary metal-oxide semiconductor"—in other words, the stuff of a silicon chip. The "they" Barlow is referring to are the significant number of digerati who hope to upload, or transfer, their consciousness from their brains to computers, from organic matter to silicon.]

On the other hand, there are lots of creatures that are not human that can live in this kind of environment, and we are creating an ecosystem where those creatures will be able to grow more rapidly than anyplace they've had that at least was visible to us. I assume that the entire universe is teeming with that kind of invisible life and has been all along. All those little self-replicating loops of difference that just hang there in the space of possibilities. All the things that are weaving the nucleotides at the base of the DNA into those strands.

If you ask yourself, "What's down below the DNA?" it's the real life. We have never been able to see or experience that before, and now we're able to create an environment where we can see it, we can experience it, we can give birth to it, we can watch it grow.

JZ: Can you give me an example of that, from your own experience?

JPB: Well, there are a lot of different ways of looking at it, and one of the crude ones is computer viruses. Another is persistent ideas that kind of self-replicate across cyberspace. "A Declaration of the Independence of Cyberspace" is one thing that passed through me, and as soon as it got out there it took on a life of its own. Literally. And continues to cruise around cyberspace without my doing anything whatsoever.

JZ: So memes, cyberspace, may be the organisms that Tom Ray is creating.

JPB: Absolutely. And I think all this is fairly crude compared to the angels that will begin to develop here fairly shortly.

Tom Ray is the creator of Tierra, a network of virtual computers (software emulations of hardware computers) populated by executable machine-code programs that he considers self-replicating "digital organisms"—artificial life. He is interviewed in chapter 4 of this book.

Memes are self-replicating patterns of information—ideas or beliefs (say, the idea of one God) that engineer their own replication—but whether they exist or not is in question. Barlow believes they do. The concept that units of information are driven to replicate much as genes are was created—some might say "discovered"—by the British sociobiologist Richard Dawkins, best known as the creator of the selfish-gene theory, which postulates that it is the survival instinct of genes that drives evolution. Dawkins's selfish-gene theory has gained wide adherence among sociobiologists, though it seems to fail to account for some aspects of behavior, particularly altruism. Similarly, the meme theory is accepted by many information theorists and digerati, but not all. It is controversial because, by granting evolutionary capacities to nonorganic life, it seems to some to detract from the perceived specialness, even sanctity, of organic life.

In his essay "New Wine in Old Bottles" (available on his Web site), Barlow writes:

> I believe [memes] are life-forms in every respect but a basis in the carbon atom. They self-reproduce, they interact with their surroundings and adapt to them, they mutate, they persist. Like any other life-form they evolve to fill the possibility spaces of their local environments, which are in this case the surrounding belief systems and cultures of their hosts, namely us.

When I met with Barlow a year before, he said to me, "If you just accept sociobiology, what does that tell you? It tells you that the real motive force for everything is informational. It tells you that what's really being born into the world and trying to create more of itself is whatever loop of information that weaves the nucleotides into that precise arrangement, over and over again. It's not the nucleotides themselves, it's the information that lies inside them."

The concept of intelligent nonphysical entities, or informational entities, isn't at all alien to religious tradition. Neither is the idea that these entities are constantly coming into existence through human action. Consider "angels," the term Barlow used earlier to describe informational entities. As the great Talmudic scholar Adin Steinsaltz writes in his book *The Thirteen Petalled Rose:*

> There are also angels that are continuously being created anew, in all the worlds, and especially in the world of action where thoughts, deeds, and experiences give rise to angels of different kinds. Every *mitzvah* that a man does is not only an act of transformation in the material world; it is also a spiritual act, sacred in itself. And this aspect of concentrated spirituality and holiness in the *mitzvah* is the chief component of that which becomes an angel.

JZ: *Prana* is not a necessary complement to life, then.

JPB: Except that *prana* may be something that arises from there being a real ecosystem of these things.

JZ: Do you think it's an emergent quality?

JPB: Yeah, exactly. It's literally spirit. In a way, this is the fundamental unanswerable question of all spirituality—Whence cometh the spirit? Is it some sort of essence, or is it something that arises? The dominant religion of this moment, which is science, says that it's an artifact, just something that sputters itself into apparent existence in all the biochemical flickerings down there in the goo. It's not taken very seriously. I personally think that there is something else. There is a soul and a spiritual essence that doesn't simply arise from the body at all. The body arises not necessarily from, but with. Evolution does the rest of the work.

JZ: Regarding these creatures that Tom Ray is creating: Do you think they're tending toward something?

JPB: I think they are something, a very rudimentary something. Those creatures are like the blue-green slime of cyberspace. They're very low-grade evolutionary products at this point, but you can see what blue-green slime turned into eventually. Furthermore, blue-green slime had an evolutionary cycle, and everything between us and it had an evolutionary speed that was so slow that it took billions of years for this to happen. Information can metamorphose in this kind of an environment many, many, many times faster. You can get a billion years of evolution overnight.

JZ: Ray is dealing with very simple, basic units of information.

JPB: But they do evolve into things that are really quite different from what he started out with.

JZ: I wonder what sort of consciousness they have, or potentially can have.

JPB: I used to just snort at the whole idea of artificial intelligence—talk about blasphemy. The only good thing about the search for artificial intelligence was that when we started doing it, we thought we knew what intelligence was. And shortly we found out that we didn't, which I think is great. It's certainly worth the trip, right there. But I never thought that there was a way to actually do it, because there were too many elements of the *prana* sort that we couldn't understand or replicate.

I'm backing away from that a little bit, because I think that when you try to figure out how the mind works—and when I say *mind* I mean with a capital *M,* not just what happens here in the wetware but what happens in the space of all wetware, and however far that extends, into whatever dimensions—I think really what it is, is the operation of an ecosystem already, with lots and lots and lots of little tiny critters of the Tom Ray size interacting in societies, as

Minsky puts it, to create intelligence out of the field of all of those interactions.

Mind creates itself out of practically infinite little blips of response and perception. I'm starting to think that if you have a free-running ecosystem, it's not out of the question that intelligence will create itself in that dimension in the same way that it created itself in this one. Not to say that we will be designing it, precisely, but we will be creating an environment where it can grow into existence. I think that's a realistic possibility.

Then there's the question of consciousness, which is slightly different. And again, this is one of those things you think you know what it is until you start asking a question of it.

One question about consciousness—the question of whether it is an emergent phenomenon, arising spontaneously from a certain level of neural complexity—will when resolved press with great force upon the spiritual future of humanity in cyberspace. If consciousness is emergent, then when computers reach a certain level of complexity, they will display consciousness. Will they have what we might call a "soul" as well?

The "Minsky" Barlow refers to is Marvin Minsky, co-founder of the Artificial Intelligence Lab at MIT and best known for his theory of the "society of mind," which postulates that various phenomenon of mind emerge from the interactions of various brain mechanisms, or competing "agents."

JZ: Do you feel any sort of kinship with these entities that Ray is creating? I agree with Teilhard de Chardin, that mind is bound up in everything, including inorganic matter, and in fact my personal experience, including long ago with LSD, confirms that. But I wonder if that extends to artificial organisms. Do you believe that it does? [If cyberspace has an éminence grise, he's Pierre Teilhard de Chardin (1881–1955), a Jesuit paleontologist whose ideas about evolution have profoundly influenced many of the leading thinkers about cyberspace.]

JPB: Sure. I feel, and partly for the same reasons you do, a kinship with all that is because I know that I am inextricably and completely connected. That thing that one loosely and perhaps incorrectly calls *himself* is an area of the totality. It's not independent in any way, a monad unto itself. It's a region of the whole. I'd say I feel a kinship with it in the same way that I feel a kinship with my thumb.

JZ: A year ago you told me that you considered the Web more of a connecting force than a fragmentary force. Do you still believe that?

JPB: Yeah, I do. As I said then and continue to say, I evaluate technological change on the basis of whether it separates or connects. I would still say that overall what this technology is doing is connective. But nothing of this scale is going to be wholly one way or the other. It's just that the natural predisposition of the environment is to connect, whereas television, for example, even though you could say that connection took place, overall what you got was disconnection masquerading as connection in all kinds of insidious ways.

You have to be mindful of cyberspace with that earlier example in mind. A lot of people assume that it's somehow like television, that it bears many of the same perils. I think it's not. It's more like the reality inside the Talmud. It's alive in that sense.

Also, you are in a real back-and-forth, fully symmetrical exchange. The real difference between information and experience is, when you're having an experience you can ask questions in real time of everything that is going on around you. There's this continual sensorial telemetry that's taking place where you're monitoring the temperature, the sounds—God knows what all. We have no idea what we're monitoring in the course of having an experience. For all I know, we're able to detect our alignment to the galactic core in some subconscious way.

So that's what an experience is, where you've got that whole range of information coming in and being processed in real time by you. And I think that the thrust of things in cyberspace, though it's extremely rudimentary so far, is to what I call "re-experientialize" information, to create enough genuine interactivity so that you have a lot of the elements of experience even though the body is not present at the focal plane of the experiential phenomenon.

JZ: The most interactive experience I've had online is real-time live chat.

JPB: That's pretty dim.

JZ: Yes, it's dim. I wonder about where it's going, too. Now I can type words on a screen, some other people have CU-SeeMe so they have visuals, and so on. [The marvelously named CU-SeeMe is desktop video-conferencing software that allows both parties, if their computers are equipped with a camera, to see one another as they speak.] It seems like it's leading toward the point where it won't be much different than me sitting in front of you and talking like this, except for the lack of *prana*. But if, as its capabilities increase, the Internet offers simply a poor imitation of reality, it must not be fulfilling its potential. Its particular potential must lie in something other than as a simulation of the real world.

JB: Its potential is in realities as yet unexperienced. I spent a fair amount of time in virtual reality, in the early Jaron Lanier sense of the term. I probably have as much VR time as any civilian. I wasn't actually working in the field. I never thought there was much going on in there except for the ones that were not trying to be something else. The ones that were not trying to be a really lousy kitchen, but were in fact altogether different kinds of environments that couldn't have been done any other way.

JZ: I think of the quality of the experiences I've had on the Net, and especially on the Web.

JPB: The Web to me is a step backward.

JZ: Why is that?

JPB: I mean it's a step backward that has to be done in order to make the next step forward. But if you think that what you're looking for is an increased level of interactivity of conversation, that's not it. It's basically publishing where everybody has a megaphone. That's all. Now, I think the fact that everybody gets a megaphone is important. It's really important, because that has never been possible before. But the extent to which I can use my megaphone to directly react to yours, to what you're saying with yours, is still very limited.

JZ: So what is possible for the Web?

JPB: I think the Web becomes a substrate of a lot more interactivity. And obviously it is to some extent already. Here's a sort of crude example, but it's kind of interesting. There are quite a number of places where, if you've got a lot of bandwidth and a pretty good sized MasterCard account, you can get on the Web and dial up some girl who will do whatever you tell her to do. Play with herself or whatever, in real time, and you are genuinely interacting in that way. [Bandwidth is the data-carrying capacity of a communications network. The wider the bandwidth, the more data the network can carry.]

JZ: So that's one experience that's possible on the Web. Coming over here, I was thinking about words and about how it took a long time after Gutenberg, but eventually we got to the point where people were using words to write novels that would transform people's lives.

JPB: It took about 250 years for the novel to come into existence, depending on where and when you think it started. In English it was *Pamela,* and that was, I think, around 1750.

JZ: OK. So we're at a very early stage here, and it seems likely that it's in VR that this sort of transformative or transfiguring aesthetic will manifest.

JPB: If you're using *VR* in a fairly loose way.

JZ: There's VR on the Web now. I'm curious where you think that's going. I get on the Web, and my experience is mixed. I love doing it, but I feel that I tend to get hypnotized by it, like watching TV. I look for the possibility of a transformative experience there, and I don't find it.

JPB: I don't think it's quite there to be had yet. I think that the overall endeavor, the Great Work, will be transformative, and profoundly so, over the course of time, but I don't think that what's available at the moment is particularly transformative. In the same way that those very first attempts at a motion picture, of the naked man walking or the horse running or whatever—those were not *Citizen Kane.* It wasn't the kind of thing that would have a permanent effect on you. It was too early in human interaction with the technology for all of the possibilities to have been explored. We're just scratching the surface.

What it does to the attention, and to consciousness, to spend time in cyberspace is of great importance for religions moving online. If surfing the Web tends to hypnotize the surfer, as I state here, what does this mean for the online future of meditative practices, which depend upon freed attention? This question is approached throughout this book, most intensively in chapter 10.

The term *Great Work* is co-opted from its medieval use of referring to the building of the great Gothic cathedrals. By "Great

Work," Barlow means, as he put it a 1992 Teilhard-influenced essay of that name,

> the physical wiring of collective human consciousness. The idea of connecting every mind to every other mind in full-duplex broadband is one which, for a hippie mystic like me, has clear theological implications. . . . What Thoughts will all this assembled neurology, silicon, and optical fiber Think?"

JZ: You said somewhere that the first time you telnetted, it was a religious experience. Why?

JPB: Because I suddenly realized, in a direct and immediate way, that every computer that was connected to the Internet was continuously connected. That I could make a hard disk spin anywhere on this planet by typing in two words.

What happened was that I suddenly detected the nervous system of the planet. In its very germinal form—but I thought, God, this thing is now everywhere. And it's not like the telephone network, where you've got all this clunky switching going on, though it's emerging from it. It's something that is much more biological and organic.

JZ: Is it similar to our brain?

JPB: Well, it has the same basic structure. It's the same architecture. Internet architecture is much, much more like neurological architecture than a switched telephone network is. And the way in which it grows and adapts and sends messages through itself seems to be much more like the way in which the brain does it.

JZ: So though each of us is in our bodies, our brains are communicating together through a kind of *über*-brain.

JPB: I go back to Samuel Morse's great phrase from 1850, which was "I see no reason why intelligence may not be distributed throughout the planet by means of electricity." Intelligence is distributed throughout the body by means of electricity. And it's simply a matter of extending the wiring, so instead of these apparently isolated nodes in human crania, those become more like axons, or nerve bundles, in a much larger neurosystem.

JZ: Does it have a soul?

JPB: I think it does. But you know, that's a statement of faith.

JZ: How did you come to that?

JPB: Part of the way I come to that is by watching it try to get what it appears to want. I mean, I think the thing that wants everything to connect to everything else is that. It's saying, "Create me. Make me. Give me consciousness."

JZ: What differentiates this from HAL?

JPB: Well, I think that, for starters, it's already up and running and has been for a while. We're really just talking about making it a lot more tangible for us. Increasing the level of interaction between ourselves and it. An awareness on both sides of the spectrum. We've been in this condition where we're sort of like the mitochondria in our own bloodstream, which are independent organisms that are dimly aware of what we're thinking or doing. They're doing what they're doing . . . and I think that's been our relationship to them. But now, as it becomes more tangible, I think we can start to feel it in ourselves, start to watch it in its entirety.

JZ: What role do the new electronic media play in the Great Work?

JPB: I think they're fundamental. I think that suddenly the opportunity to take all of human thought, or at least expressible thought, including an awful lot of thought that was never before expressed, and to turn it all into a fluid that can be spread instantaneously around the whole surface of the globe, to all those parts of the planet that might find it of relevance—that's as basic in its transformation as anything we've ever done. I have a certain hyperbolic statement about this: "It's the most transforming technology since the capture of fire."

It may be that it doesn't actually change what it is to be a human being, because it may well be that human beings were always just a lesser part of that great mind that has been there thinking in ways that were completely invisible to us all along, in the same way that our thoughts are invisible to the mitochondria in our bloodstream. But I think that the big difference is that we become aware of that other body. For the first time, we have the means to detect that we are part of that other thinking. And we are for the first time aware of its thoughts.

JZ: What do you think it wants?

JPB: It wants to live. Like everything else, it wants to live and it wants to understand.

JZ: What is it, a kind of hyperhuman organism?

JPB: Yeah. The collective organism of mind. And I'm not even sure that it's appropriate to call it human. Since there are so many other organisms that go into making it up, both carbon based and electrical.

JZ: What kind of time scale are we dealing with here? Are we talking about centuries for this transformation?

JPB: The real question is in the definition and not in the result. It tends to be the case that one never arrives at transformations. They're always in process. One never says, "Ah, here we are." Because you never are. You're always coming, you're never getting there. And the extent to which the transformation has already taken place is usually invisible to you.

For example, last week I was with a bunch of Danes and Swedes up at a conference in Scandinavia, and, among other things, we were talking about the self, and about how technology affects what the self is, or what one's sense of the self is. Well, I went around this room of about twenty-five people, and asked each of them who they were and how they came to think that: What were the various coinciding spheres of selfness that went into making them?

The interesting thing that emerged, which I figured it would, was that all of those spheres of selfness that were critical were relating to one another and operating in fashions that would not have been possible—not all of them, but most of them—one hundred years ago, when technology gave you much less latitude for expansion and exploration of that sort. Whereas five hundred years ago, say, the self would not have been spheres at all, it would have been flat concentric circles starting with your body, and then there's your family, and then there's your village. None of these moved much. Now they're in free careen because of technology.

JZ: Are you saying that technology can elevate consciousness? Two thousand years ago, people were sitting on a meditation pillow, and after thirty years of doing that they probably had a very clear sense of what the self was and wasn't.

JPB: I'm not sure that I want to say that. All I really was intending to say was that technology had already done something profoundly transformative that was invisible. It wasn't until we started to discuss how all these things came together that people began to see that, "my God, it's already got us. Look where we are and look where we were."

For example, most of them still felt themselves to be part of an extended family, but the extended family was spread all over the surface of the planet. Most of them said, "Well, yes, my grandfather, my great-grandfather, my great-great-grandfather, they all lived in the village or such and such a place. And I visit there sometimes, my mother is buried there but she didn't live there most of her life." The sort of fixity that previously characterized European settlements was gone. People move all the time.

A good example in my own life is that because I went from one economic sphere that had one set of technological principles—agriculture—to another that is made possible by technology, instead of doing what I did before, which was entirely focused on one little slice of the physical world and that which was in it—my cows, the weather, the neighbors, tractors—now I am in continuous motion. I'm never in one spot for very long. My range of possible experiences is multiplied hundreds of times. And the possibility for depth of those experiences is reduced. Considerably.

JZ: How does that affect your sense of self?

JPB: It probably has the same effect on sense of self that attention deficit disorder does, in a sense. The self vibrates more. The self is dancing faster, it's a higher-temperature self. I'm not persuaded that it's necessarily a more advanced self. In some ways consciousness is increased, but I would say that it's a zero-sum game and it may be a zero-sum game always.

That may be part of the spiritual bargain—that if the world is here to teach the soul a limited set of things, all of which have to do with hardship and struggle and longing and desire and those kinds of things, then it's not going to improve, exactly. There's no such thing as progress. Because if we fixed it, if we took all of our tools and fixed it, the universe would have to go and find some other place for the soul to learn about these things.

JZ: Do you think the computer can be used as a spiritual tool? Comparing it, say, to psychedelics.

JPB: As I've said, it's going to be a long time before cyberspace has the price/performance ratio of LSD. We're far, far from that. But I also think that anytime you've got a large number of people going somewhere where they can't take their bodies, you are engaged in spiritual activity. It's that simple.

I mean, what have human beings been doing for most of their time on this planet if not trying to figure out some way to inhabit the immaterial? Well, we are getting there. It's not quite what we had in mind, but something is happening. I think it's very interesting that there would be monks blessing cyberspace, that they're sufficiently aware of the spiritual dimension of it that they would feel it's worthy of consecration.

JZ: The monks define cyberspace as "an extension of mind in a space where there is an absence of obstruction." So it's really the space between sites. [What Barlow and I are discussing here is a formal blessing of cyberspace conducted by Tibetan Buddhist monks in February 1996. The blessing is discussed in the conclusion to this book.]

JPB: It's not between minds? Because that's what it is for me. The informed space between minds. The notion that it's a place without obstructions, or relatively without obstructions, is critical, because ordinarily the body, acting in the physical dimension, has all manner of obstructions that you don't have in cyberspace. And a lot of other assets that you lose in cyberspace. Distance is an insurmountable obstruction for most human conversation, without technical assistance.

JZ: What exactly is it, again, that passes through cyberspace? If I'm on my computer, and in real-time chat, there's all this projection going on, and there may even be telepathy going on between me and the person I'm chatting with, but that telepathy is taking place through space-time and not cyberspace. Is there something that passes, or that can pass, simply through the wires?

JPB: Well, it's difference, in any case. And expressed in various layers of interpretation. I mean, what's really passing through the wires is a string of ones and zeros and the differences between them. But at the next layer up, it's the difference between what you say and how the next person responds to it. It's the difference of understanding between you and that other person, the difference of the language itself. What she says when she says such and such and what you hear are two importantly different things.

JZ: Again, what exactly goes through the wires? You say it's a string of ones and zeroes.

JPB: Voltage shifts. What's really going through the wires is differences in voltage.

JZ: Energy. It's energy that has a pattern

JPB: An interpretable pattern.

JZ: Which is the information.

JPB: It's not just difference. To use Bateson's formulation, it's difference that makes a difference. Noise is filled with difference. Noise is nothing but a bath of difference.

And cyberspace is filled with noise, as well as with information. It's a curious but telling and probably applaudable fact about Barlow that he doesn't spend a whole lot of time in cyberspace.

"You know," he said, "there's nothing like a lot of time in cyberspace to make you really love the grit and stench of meatspace. I think if you look at people over time, it has that general effect. I find that cyberspace is advantageous primarily in creating greater opportunity for me to do this kind of thing right now—which would not be taking place were it not for that. The interactions in my life are highly dependent on my ability to arrange and meet and schedule and all that in the virtual environment.

"Now, I suppose if I were staying in one spot, if I were still in the cattle business, I wouldn't need that, because everybody's relatively easy to find. You're all right there anyway. But that doesn't permit you the opportunity to have that kind of depth distributed over the entire planet. That doesn't give you broad experience, it gives you very deep experience. And what I'm looking for, having had seventeen years of deep experience, is broad experience. And the only way I can get that is by using cyberspace."

_____

John Perry Barlow's homepage is located at *http://gopher.eff.org /~barlow*.

CHAPTER 3

Islam

What is this Internet? This Internet is energy.
—SHEIKH HISHAM MUHAMMAD KABBANI

Five times a day, Muslims turn toward the Saudi Arabian city of Mecca, birthplace of Muhammad, for *Salat*, a series of prayers accompanied by sacred movements. To ensure that the devout know exactly when to pray, in every mosque on earth a muezzin climbs to the top of a minaret and calls out. These days, however, many Muslims live out of earshot of a mosque, particularly in the West. They can compensate by consulting any number of printed and electronic prayer-time guides, including several on the Web.

Muslim Prayer Times (*http://www.uwm.edu/cgi-bin/bashir /salat.cgi*) lists *Salat* times for dozens of cities, from Abidjan to Zurich. One prominent location is missing from its database, however: Mecca. No other Saudi Arabian city is listed either, and not just because in Saudi Arabia only the deaf can't hear a muezzin. A second Web-based prayer guide, World-Wide Qibla and Prayer Times (*http://arabia.com/prayer.html*), which will generate prayer times for any latitude and longitude, does present *Salat* times for Mecca. But it might as well not, for the irony is that, by law, few Muslims in Mecca are permitted to consult either database.

Saudi Arabia restricts Internet access. According to the Human Rights Watch report "Silencing the Net—The Threat to Freedom of Expression Online" (*gopher://gopher.igc.apc.org*

:2998/0HRW/r.852693792.4699.1), issued in May 1996, Saudi
authorities confine Net entry to universities and hospitals, with
all local accounts open to inspection by the Ministry of the
Interior. Similar restrictions—some looser, some tighter—bind
would-be cybernauts throughout the Islamic world. Dunya, an
Islamic Web site discussed later in this chapter, reports that "the
Netscape browsing software . . . may not be downloaded or
otherwise exported or re-exported into (or to a national or resident of) Iraq, Libya, Bosnia, Iran, or Syria. Apparently, it is considered national security software."

Nominally, it is government representatives rather than religious leaders in Saudi Arabia, Libya, Iran, Syria, Jordan, and
other Muslim nations who are limiting Internet access, but these
officials are in nearly every instance acting on behalf of the
state-approved religion of Islam, and in all cases are promoting
moral values espoused by traditional Islamic teachings. The
Human Rights Watch report states that in Saudi Arabia, "government officials have justified their reluctance to large-scale access on the grounds that there is a need to protect people from
pornographic and other harmful effects." Blockage of pornography is the most common reason cited by Islamic authorities in
defense of online censorship, but behind pornography looms the
source of these "other harmful effects": Western secular culture,
including its primary language, English.

In Islam, Arabic is considered a holy language, for Allah revealed the Qur'an to Muhammad in Arabic. Though the Qur'an
has been translated into English and other languages, as John
Alden Williams explains in his classic book *Islam,* "it is a matter
of faith in Islam that since [the Qur'an] is of Divine origin it is
inimitable, and since to translate it is always to betray, Muslims
have always deprecated and at times prohibited any attempt to
render it in another language." The reluctance of fundamentalist Muslims and their government representatives to embrace
the Net stems in part from a fear of contamination of Arabic by
English, the dominant tongue of the Net. Not only is English

considered secular, but as such it may be seen to carry within its structure and vocabulary, as all languages are said to do by some linguists, cultural biases, including spiritual biases, that collide with those inherent to Arabic.

Islamic groups aren't alone in calling for Internet censorship, of course. The federal government of just about every country on the planet, including that of the United States, actively opposes universal access, even by adults, to all the material available on the Net, with pornography as the prime target. In the United States this opposition has manifested through the Communications Decency Act, which is vigorously supported by numerous fundamentalist Christian groups, including the Christian Coalition. The Internet is fire to the world's major religions. It can warm souls to an acceptance of the sacred, but it can burn them too. The more orthodox the religious group, the more likely it is to balance any use of the Net to broadcast its own message with a reluctance to receive messages deemed inappropriate for its faithful. As Rabbi Kazen said, "Our setup was never for our own group. On the contrary, this was set up strictly to deal with the outside world."

Fundamentalist Islamic groups have scarcely dipped their toes in the online sea. The Net is a powerful proselytizing tool, however, and Islam is a religion that thrives on conversion. Further, because Islam posits no intermediaries between the individual and God, it seems well suited to expand within the ahierarchical Net. Nature and religion both abhor a vacuum. Although fundamentalist Islamic groups are nearly absent from cyberspace, more flexible Islamic groups—some equally traditional, some not—have moved online in force.

The following discussion of virtual Islamic resources is meant to serve three purposes. First, to highlight the resourcefulness with which Islam and, by extension, every major religion is embracing cyberspace by making use of every fold, bump, and valley in the virtual world. Second, to provide a map of that world, whose geography and topology are as complicated as those of the real world. Third, to vivify Islamic views of cyberspace. For the latter, I conducted telephone interviews with two leading Sufi masters whose groups have a strong Web presence. Perhaps inevitably, even these two masters display strikingly dissimilar ideas about the potential of digital spirituality.

INTERNET RESOURCES

The Internet is not a homogenous entity but a network of networks, as tangled as an orgy of octopi. Three representative networks on the Internet are CA*NET, the Canada National Network; SURANET, which connects the southeastern United States; and NSFNet, sponsored by the National Science Foundation. Islamic resources on the Internet can be found via the following:

Telnet

Telnet protocol was developed a quarter century ago, in 1972. It enables one computer to connect to another. Once upon a time Telnet ruled cyberspace, but the World Wide Web has usurped its throne. A peculiar mix of cyberspace resources still can be reached only through Telnet, however. Among them are many library card catalogs, MUDs (multi-user dungeons—virtual spaces for role-playing games), and BBSes. Telnet is an arcane Internet resource because it's necessary to know any computer's precise Telnet address in order to log in to it. The best Telnet address to know, then, is *Telnet: access.usask.ca* (log-in: hytelnet), the address of the Hytelnet search engine, which, perhaps to the dismay of grizzled digerati, is also available on the Web at *http://galaxy.einet.net/hytelnet/START.TXT.html.*

Key resource: The Carl Corporation Network and Uncover (*Telnet: carl.pac.org*) offers access to twenty commercial databases and more than 420 library catalogs that store a trove of listings of Islamic books and magazines, many obscure or out of print, making this a prime resource for scholars and students of Islam.

FTP

File transfer protocol, developed in 1973, was one of the earliest methods devised for transferring files from one computer to another. Many FTP files are included in the databases of gopher menus (discussed later in this chapter) and of Web search engines, but some are not. When I queried the FTP search engine named Archie (*http://archie.luth.se/archie*) for files containing the word *Islam* or the word *Muslim,* it dug up relevant files in 331 FTP sites cached around the world.

Key resource: A concise but well-chosen collection of Islamic files resides at the anonymous FTP service at Lysator Academic Computer Society, Linköping University, Sweden (on the Net, at *ftp://ftp.lysator.liu.se/pub/religion/islam*). Among the files here are the essay "Fundamentals of the Islamic Religion," by Sheikh al-Islam Mohammad Bin Sulaiman at-Tamimi; a partial excerpt of "A Conversation with Pir Vilayat Khan" (a Sufi master) from the *Monthly Aspectarian* magazine; and a collection of quotations from various sources about the prophets.

Mailing Lists

Mailing lists, also known as *listservs,* are discussion groups whose members communicate with one another through mass distribution of e-mail. They date back to at least 1979, when a group of science-fiction fans, never known to blush at high tech, started the list *SF-Lovers* (it's still around). Mailing lists tend to be focused, with subscribers often experts in the field under discussion.

There are perhaps two dozen Islamic mailing lists. The names (plus brief descriptions) of most of those that follow were obtained from one of the finest general resources on the Web, the World-Wide Web Virtual Library (*http://www.w3.org/pub /DataSources/bySubject/Overview.html*).

AMDA@TREEBRANCH.COM ("Islamic Education Network").

AR-RASSED@UOFTO2.UTOLEDO.EDU. News & analysis from
an Islamic perspective.

BERITA-L@UIUCVMD ("M'sia, S'pore & related SEA news [no
discussions]"). Has sublist ISLAM-NEWS, in English.

IMNET@STEIN.U.WASHINGTON.EDU ("Islamic Movement
Network"). News and views in English.

ISL-SCI@VTVM1 ("Issues on Islam and Science"). Natural &
social science.

ISLMECON@SAIRTI00 ("Islamic Economics Discussion List").

ISLAMIAT@SAKAAU03 ("ISLAMIC Information and Issues
Discussion Group"). Discussion of Islam by Muslims and
others.

ISLAM-L@ULKYVM ("History of Islam"). U.S., Saudi, and other
users.

MSANEWS@MAGNUS.ACS.OHIO-STATE.EDU. Muslim Student
Association News.

MSA-EC@WORLD.STD.COM. Mail Discussion Group.

MSA-L@PSUVM ("Muslim Student Association List"). U.S.,
Saudi, and other users.

MSA@HTM3.EE.QUEENSU.CA. Muslim Student Associations in
North America.

MUSLIMS@ASUACAD ("The Islamic Information & News
Network"). Weekly news; subsidiary of Pakistan News
Service.

NAHIA-L@MSU.EDU ("North American Historians of Islamic
Art").

POLITICAL-ISLAM@LISTS.UTAH.EDU ("Political Islam List").

SUFI@THINK.NET. Discussion of Sufi philosophy.

Key resource: Also housed at the Lysator FTP site are the
archives of *Tariqas*, a lively Sufi mailing list. *Tariqas* was started
in 1993 by Steve Habib Rose to focus "on spiritual paths/
ways/orders," as his welcoming letter to the list reads. "The
word 'tariqas' is Arabic, and literally means 'paths' or 'ways.' It

is applied to the various Sufi orders (e.g. the Mevlevi tariqa; the Naqshbandi tariqa). 'Tariqas' is intended for any person involved in any spiritual path, who is open to sharing in an open and honest way with others."

A recent day's postings on *Tariqas* included a discussion of the virtues and faults of the late Sufi teacher Idries Shah; a Q&A about whether Muslims may pray for dead non-Muslims; a request to help identify an eighteenth-century Islamic manuscript; and comments about the role of ritual in the spiritual life. To subscribe to *Tariqas,* or any other mailing list, you need to send e-mail to the list's electronic mail manager. For *Tariqas,* that's majordomo@world.std.com, with nothing or simply the word *subscribe* typed into the e-mail's subject field and, in the body of the letter, the statement, "subscribe tariqas [your e-mail address]" (e.g., "subscribe tariqas zaleski123@aol.com").

A perusal of *Tariqas* reveals that many of its subscribers are connected to the Haqqani Foundation, a worldwide extension of the Naqshbandi-Haqqani Sufi order. Sufism is the esoteric, mystical heart of Islam, as ancient as the religion itself but little known in the West until this century. (Islam, which means "submission," dates from the year 622 C.E., when Muhammad made his exodus from Mecca to Medina.) The Naqshbandi order, one of the most ancient of Sufi orders, takes its name from the Turkish sheikh Bahauddin-i Naqshband (1318–1389). Today, the Naqshbandi order sponsors centers around the world, as well as the Haqqani Foundation.

The Haqqani Foundation (*http://www.best.com/~informe /mateen/haqqani.html*) presents a homepage that is simply glorious—a tapestry of purple and gold that conveys a sense of something special, something sacred, and has won a number of Web awards. The page automatically downloads in English, but alternate versions of it, and of some others pages on the site, are available in Arabic, Bulgarian, French, German, Greek, Italian, Japanese, Polish, Russian, and Spanish, indicating the Naqshbandi order's global reach. Further pages include information on the foundation and its purpose ("to spread the Sufi teachings of the brotherhood of mankind and the Unity of belief in God that is present in all religions and spiritual paths"), its principles, and Sufism.

The spiritual presence behind the Web site and, though not officially, of *Tariqas* is Sheikh Hisham Muhammad Kabbani, "a scholar and Sufi shaykh from the Middle East," as his Web biography reads. A picture displayed on the site shows Kabbani to be middle-aged, dressed in black, his head topped with a white turban that's matched by the white beard that drapes down his chest. He holds degrees in chemistry, medicine, and Islamic law. In 1991, he was ordered by his own sheikh, or spiritual teacher, "to move to America and to establish the foundation of the Naqshbandi Sufi Order" there. Since then he has opened thirteen Sufi centers in the United States and Canada.

I contacted Sheikh Kabbani through the webmaster of the Haqqani Foundation, Mateen Saddiqui, who set up a telephone interview for me with the busy sheikh from a home in the Los Angeles area. I came away strangely giddy from my conversation with Kabbani, charged by the enthusiasm for life, the spirit, and the Internet that he manages to convey even over the phone. The sheikh speaks English in a high voice—well, but not perfectly. His baroque way of talking and Middle Eastern accent sounded, to my ears, as exotic as the Sufi path he teaches. Listening to him, it seemed to me that moving through the Net can be a kind of magic-carpet ride.

JEFF ZALESKI: Why was the decision made to bring the Haqqani Foundation into cyberspace?

SHEIKH HISHAM MUHAMMAD KABBANI: Because you know that always spirituality is high-tech. Spirituality is a kind of energy transmission from human beings to each other, if we are able to receive it, because human beings are receivers and transmitters at the same time. This is what we see also on the Internet and in the sophisticated equipment nowadays—that everything receives and transmits. So we want to show people that Sufism is a way of communication through energy that can move from one person to another through spirituality.

JZ: Do you feel that when people log on to your pages and read what you have there, they're receiving a sort of energy from you and from the other Sufi teachers you're presenting?

SHMK: Of course. Because in spirituality there are different levels. There is the ordinary level, and then you go up to higher levels. Not every person can receive without using an instrument. There are some people who can receive from each other, who can feel each other, who can sense each other even though they are very far from each other and not physically together. For example, you have this energy and the waves that are flying in the air or passing in air, so whenever you bring a television and you channel the waves correctly, then you see a picture. Or you bring a radio, then you hear a voice.

Not everyone in spirituality can reach this high level, so either through books or through Internet, people when they read and they begin to understand what is written or begin to see what is on the Internet, they can begin to take some of this energy and slowly, slowly build it up, and then they begin to communicate more through their meditation.

JZ: But it seems that what you're presenting on the Internet is just a first step. It's not enough for someone just to sit there and read Web pages, right? People have to take certain actions.

SHMK: If you go and study medicine in university, what they present for you at the beginning, for four years of studying or six years, they give you a theoretical knowledge. But later, when you finish this theoretical knowledge which you take through a book, through a picture, through an Internet or

whatever, then you have to go to an experimental knowledge, directly acting on the patient and checking him—
surgery and so on.

So this is the same. What we present to them now, at the
beginning, is something in writing that they have to build up
themselves. Later, they need a real connection, direct connection, with the guide or with the master of a Sufi order, to
meet with him and to sit and to take from him what is necessary for them as medication or whatever—as advanced
skills.

JZ: Is direct personal contact necessary for that? Is there a
level of teaching and learning that can't take place in cyberspace but that has to take place in the real world, face-to-
face with a teacher?

SHMK: This is very necessary. Through the Internet, we are
sending all this information on our homepage. And then we
are receiving a lot, lot of people reading it and contacting us
directly, and then we refer them to our centers which are all
over the world, to the nearest center to them. And then they
go there and they can be affiliated. They connect themselves
there and then later, when the master is free, or my master is
free, or whenever I am free, I go to these centers, or they can
come here.

JZ: On your Web pages I read an interview with you in
which you spoke about a new Age of Enlightenment that
might come within our lifetime or in the near future. Do you
think the Web, and your kind of activities on the Web, are
helping to bring that age about? Do you think the Internet is
a force for bringing people together and possibly helping humanity in that way?

SHMK: I think yes. Because these Web pages and the Internet,
anyone in the world can reach them. At the beginning they
manufactured or invented the car. Then they invented the

aeroplane, which went faster, then rockets. Now they have these very huge satellites, they go up to the outer limits. And you know also they were first speaking about the speed of light but they were not using the speed of light. Now this Internet is reaching easily every human being on earth, whoever connects from his telephone or wherever he is. You are reaching people more easily than faxes or telexes or whatever.

So now Internet is available in every home. This technology of life. What is this Internet? This Internet is energy. It's a kind of energy, it is coming up on that screen, but it is energy. For example, you go to that computer and take it out into parts and you find out that inside there is nothing except a silicon sheet, and on it small chips that are creating this huge energy. And they are putting it in a kind of way that you can read it. Every atom, if you bring it down and open that atom, you can see the nucleus, and around the nucleus these electrons or these neutrons that are swinging, they are turning around the nucleus in a speed that is so huge.

So you see everything is coming from energy. And that's why Newton said energy is not lost. Energy is always there. And that's why we believe that energy, spirituality, is always there. So we find spirituality and energy are twins. You cannot split them. And that's why we are going to see in the twenty-first century more advanced technologies that are slowly, slowly going to see everything come out, and everyone is going to say, "We believe in spirituality that is dominating and controlling this world." Because this is spirituality, and it is a kind of energy.

JZ: I hope what you're saying is right, but I have to say that I remain rather doubtful. Humanity has been around for a long time. Why all of a sudden is this going to happen in the next century—that humanity is going to wake up and say, "Yes, we want to be spiritually enlightened"? What about the forces of darkness and the forces of greed and the forces of sleep?

SHMK: Everything now is moving; you can find now spirituality is growing quickly, more than everything. Everything connecting with energy, you find it quickly growing, more than ever before. Now in the last ten years, you find that this using of energy is so huge. So all indications that we feel as spiritual people are that the twenty-first century is coming to a big change. Toward the best for a human being, and toward the good side more than the negative side. Goodness is going to be more toward people, for people. And that's what you are seeing now today even in the political world. You are seeing less fighting and more peace talks and more people coming to each other to speak with each other.

JZ: I don't know how much time you spend in front of a computer, but I spend a lot. I think that some of the people who will be reading my book also spend a lot of time in front of a computer, and when you spend a lot of time in front of a computer, you get kind of foggy, and you get zoned out, and you lose a sense of what you're doing. I'm wondering what advice you have for people who spend a lot of time staring at a computer screen. How can they remain aware of themselves and be more alive in front of that computer screen?

SHMK: We have a computer better than the computer that we are spending our time on. What I mean by our *computer* is our heart and our mind. Our mind and our heart are one of the best computers—that technology cannot compete with. So if we are going to spend our time in front of this computer and leave the main computer that is encouraging us, that is giving us life, to leave it to die without taking care of it, then of course we are going to lose a lot, and not to gain.

So we have to be fair. We have to spend a little time, or some time, for our own spiritual power by sitting by ourselves, as we spend time—eighteen hours, some people spend eighteen, twenty hours!—behind the computer screen. So we have to spend at least half an hour a day behind also our own computer, by which I mean in meditation and contemplation of our heart and our mind, in order to bring a balance and a harmony between the two poles, positive and negative. In every human being you have two sides, positive and negative. So to bring a balance and a harmony.

And when you bring that harmony and that balance, you find that you are so uplifted that you begin to feel that power inside you, you begin to see images, voices, and slowly, slowly, slowly you can begin to understand what's coming to you. Because you can detect the waves. As this computer detects through the lines that carry that whole information, and through these chips, also in our mind and our heart there are chips that, if you use them correctly, then you can find yourself in better position and more spiritually powerful and you see that you are so light that you can fly like a bird and you can see yourself, you are getting inspiration that never you imagined before.

And you feel sometimes that whenever you go and meet with some people, "Already I met these people. Where I met these people?" You begin to question yourself. So that's why spirituality is so important and that's why we are trying to reach maximum people through the computer—in order to bring that attention to the spiritual.

JZ: I understand what you're saying, and my experience shows me it's true. But I'm also wondering whether there's something that people can do while they're actually sitting in front of their computer at home or at work that can help them to remember God. And that can help them to remember themselves. Is there any sort of advice you would give them while they're sitting in front of their computers and doing their work—their office work or whatever?

SHMK: There is. What we are teaching our own people who are working or initiated with us, when they sit behind their computers for many hours, we tell them also to sit by themselves in their homes, not with the computer but in their rooms with the small light of a candle, at night, with no one around, and meditate. And slowly after this meditation, spiritual power begins to appear in them.

So what we advise them, after they begin to establish that in their heart, when they are sitting behind their computer, we ask them to put in the computer whatever comes in their heart, a feeling or a voice or a picture or a story that is being sent to their heart, an inspiration. And they begin to punch these keys and they will find themselves later what they have written. Because when you get something into your heart, if you don't put it immediately and save it, you lose it. So they begin to find that they begin to establish a true connection with their spiritual power. And when they want they bring it up from their computer and they find it up on their screen, and they find that they have lifted up so much that they begin to find that there is a new knowledge coming to them through this kind of spirituality, and through this putting information into the computer as soon as it comes into the heart.

Although it might not come, as you say in English, *fluently*—sentences behind each other. We tell them, "Whatever you think when you are punching keys," and they find out months later that they are putting complete knowledge, that it is a very good knowledge for them to learn and for others to be taught. And this is what we call spirituality.

JZ: That's fascinating.

SHMK: That will be very good for you.

JZ: Is there anything you'd like to add?

SHMK: As long as people are looking after spirituality and after their spiritual energy, power, and after balancing themselves in keeping their spirituality, not everything materialism, but looking after spirituality—as long as people are believing that, and they do good, and they follow any Sufi order or any spiritual teaching, they are going to be saved, they are going to be saved from the negativity that is found outside in this world. And they will be living a long life and they will have a good, happy life for themselves.

JZ: I say amen to that.

SHMK: May God bless you.

Usenet

The year 1979, in which the mailing list *SF-Lovers* came online, also saw the development of Usenet, the network of news-groups, by two Duke University graduate students. Numerous newsgroups host discussions pertinent to individual Islamic nations, but only two concentrate on Islamic spirituality. These are the unmoderated alt.religion.islam and the moderated soc.religion.islam.

Key resource: Soc.religion.islam, founded in November 1989. At present two moderators oversee this newsgroup. One is a woman. A brief but informative FAQ to soc.religion.islam can be found at *http://www.lib.ox.ac.uk/internet/news/faq/archive /islam-faq.intro.html*. On a recent day, postings on the news-group included discussions on adultery and the appropriate punishment for it; on the righteousness (or not) of the veil; on interfaith marriages; on whether genies can have "sexual abili-ties"; and on whether dogs are "bad for Muslims" as they might scare away angels.

IRC

Internet Relay Chat was developed in 1988 at the University of Oulu in Finland. Of the thousands of channels on IRC, only one, #islam, in my experience supports active discussion of Islamic is-sues (another, #islamicgateway, seems always to be empty).

Other Islamic chat venues exist on the Net. The Web hosts at least two, Muslim Chat on the Web Broadcasting Service (*http://*

pages.wbs.net/webchat3.so?cmd=cmd_doorway:Muslim_Chat)
and the ASFA Islamic Chat Café (*http://sunnah.org/chat.htm*).

Key resource: #islam, which on a recent evening hosted a
score of visitors hashing over the usual weird mix of subjects.
On this evening, opinions flew about the best books about
prayer, about gay Egyptians, and about whether it might be a
good idea to make a children's video about Barney the Dinosaur
visiting a mosque.

Gopher

Developed in 1991 at the University of Minnesota (whose mas-
cot is a gopher), gopher arranges Internet files according to text
menus. Gopherspace tunnels through cyberspace in a million
and one directions. A thorough way to search it for Islamic files
is to log on to the Web's All-in-One Search Page (*http://www
.albany.net/allinone/all1gen.html#General*), which links to the
gopher search engine Veronica (who, with Archie co-opted by
the FTP protocol, must make do in gopherspace with the company of a second gopher search engine named Jughead). When I
typed the word *Islam* into her entry field, Veronica harvested
more than twelve hundred gopher sites containing Islamic files.

Key resource: A lean but hardy Islamic gopher can be found
at *gopher://latif.com*, which, like the strongest gophers, tunnels
to other gophers, which tunnel to yet others. Among its file
headings are "LISTS and Summaries of Islamic Organizations,
MSA's, and Masjids," "Muslim Businesses and Educational Organizations," and "TIMELY ANNOUNCEMENTS—Conferences,
Conventions, etc."

World Wide Web

If Little Miss Muffet were around today, she'd be sitting not on
a tuffet but on a chair, watching that spider crawl up the World
Wide Web, the most popular way to navigate cyberspace. There
are more Web pages devoted to Islamic activities than anyone
might need. In early January 1997, Yahoo (*http://www.yahoo*

.com) indexed 250 Islamic sites. At the same time, the popular search engine AltaVista (*http://www.altavista.digital.com*) listed 35,634 separate Web pages that mentioned the word *Islam*.

Key resources: An especially companionable Islamic Web site and Net compass is Dunya (*http://www.ou.edu/cybermuslim*), "brought to you by the CyberMuslim Information Collective," which seems to be another name for Dunya's creator and webmaster, Mas'ood Cajee, who graduated in May 1996 from the University of Oklahoma with degrees in English and biochemistry. Dunya features a cartoon guide, Selim the CyberMuslim, who advises visitors on how best to negotiate the site. The information on Dunya runs wide and deep. It includes an "Activist Resource Center," links to online Islamic bookstores, electronic journals and news services, and connections to software repositories and educational facilities. Dunya's most ambitious project is its construction-in-progress of the first networked hypermedia Qur'an, employing text, illustrations, and audio and video files.

The Internet, including the Web, connects people to one another. In the course of writing this book, the Net connected me to three friends from my past: my college acquaintance John Perry Barlow; my ex-wife, Stacy Horn (interviewed in chapter 11); and a second college acquaintance, Ed Helminski, known these days as Sheikh Kabir Edmund Helminski.

Helminski is a Mevlevi Sufi sheikh, the chief representative in North America of the Mevlevi order, founded by the great Persian poet Jalaluddin Rumi. (This is the Sufi order renowned for its whirling dervishes). Like Sheikh Kabbani, he sports a beard, but his is still dark. Along with his wife, Camille Helminski, he directs the Threshold Society, "a non-profit educational foundation with the purpose of facilitating the experience of Divine unity, love and wisdom in the world," as the society's homepage (*http://www*
.webcom.com/threshld) states. Threshold's well-organized, text-rich site, which was created by Helminski, contains a gold mine of information about the Sufis and the Mevlevi order. Regrettably, it is self-contained, offering no links to other Web sites.

Sheikh Helminski, whom I interviewed by phone from his home in Brattleboro, Vermont, speaks with great care and thoughtfulness, and with a reserve about the Internet that I found unexpected and sobering after the enthusiasm displayed by Sheikh Kabbani.

JEFF ZALESKI: I'm curious as to whether you yourself spend any time on the Web or on the Internet.

SHEIKH KABIR EDMUND HELMINSKI: I go for long periods of time spending very little time there.

JZ: When you do go there, what do you go there for?

SKEH: I've gone there mostly for information. I've certainly explored spiritual Web sites, and I explored them quite a bit during the time that I was thinking of initiating a Web site, which was about a year ago. I created our Web site in December of last year. Since that time, some other people have come along to help me maintain it, to improve it.

JZ: When you say you "created" it, do you mean that you did the actual programming and design for it?

SKEH: Yes.

JZ: Did you have background for that, or is this something you learned in order to put up the Web site?

SKEH: I learned it in order to put up the Web site, although for years I was a graphic designer and I still do graphic design for our publishing company. It's one of the things that I like to do. I see graphic design as information design. That's always been an interest of mine.

JZ: I'm curious as to what you saw, or what you may still see, as the differences between designing, say, the cover of a book and designing a Web page.

SKEH: A Web page is much simpler. You have to design with a certain economy of information in mind. One thing I really don't like is the time it takes, generally, to be on the Web. One of the reasons why I don't spend that much time there is that I find it pretty slow.

JZ: That's a universal complaint. On the site, are you simply trying to present information clearly, or are you are trying to instill some sense of the spiritual in people who log on?

SKEH: Of course we'd like to give as much of a sense of the spiritual as we can. There are limitations of the very narrow band of reality that the Web site can convey.

JZ: What do you mean by "the narrow band of reality"? As opposed, presumably, to a wider band of reality that's possible in real life.

SKEH: The dimension of human presence is limited. I won't say it's nonexistent, because I believe that there's a connection beyond time and space that can be facilitated even through the Internet. But it's not like coming into a room with someone.

JZ: Why not? Perhaps if you're looking at a flat page of text you don't see the human being as clearly, but with virtual reality, with three-dimensional representations with stereo sound, it's possible to create a close simulation of a human being. So what's missing?

SKEH: Well, when we can get it up to six or seven dimensions, we'll get something closer to the virtual reality we're looking for. Why is it that sometimes more can be communicated in silence than with language? Why is it that more can be communicated when we close our eyes and turn inward than when we open them and focus on the images that appear on the screen of material existence?

JZ: Do you feel that something goes on between teacher and pupil that can't be transmitted in the electronic ones and zeros, the bytes, of a computer?

SKEH: I believe that there is a resonance that is possible. It is a physical resonance between or among individual human nervous systems. I know that phenomenon exists, and is very important. At the same time, I know the power of an idea, or an image, to awaken something. The power of a poem by Rumi to touch a heart. But most often that's either the beginning of further steps, or it's a confirmation by people who have made steps within that invisible reality.

The main function of the Internet today is that it reaches out across the whole world and can be available to people asking very specific questions. It's a search mechanism. I'll give you an example, an amazing example: I get a communication from a Sufi sheikh in Zaire, who has a group of Sufis who meet, presumably, in the jungle. Threshold Society has a monthly theme, usually a quotation with some commentary. And this sheikh from Zaire, who's not even of our order, asks permission to use our monthly themes in his circle in Africa.

JZ: So what do you see as the primary purpose of your site?

SKEH: The primary purpose of the site is to inform people about Threshold Society, and the Mevlevi order, and to share general knowledge about Sufism and spiritual transformation. To make very specific information or knowledge available to people who are seeing it in a way that's economical and efficient, and that would lead eventually to more complete contact.

JZ: How successful do you feel the site has been in achieving that aim?

SKEH: It's just successful enough in that I think we average more than one serious inquiry a day. One or more people per day asking for further contact, further information.

JZ: Has anyone joined the order as a result of first connecting through the site?

SKEH: Certainly. Quite a few people have formed a connection.

JZ: Do you think that God can manifest in cyberspace as elsewhere? And does?

SKEH: Oh, I'm sure God can. I think that cyberspace poses no obstacle to the Divine. Breakthrough can happen from any direction, anytime.

JZ: As you may know, some commentators about cyberspace believe that the Net is playing a part in a spiritual regeneration and perhaps even down the road a transfiguration of the human species—that it's beginning to bring all of humanity together in a certain way. Do you feel that the computer and cyberspace may have a kind of sacred role to play that way?

SKEH: I'm not sure it's all that positive. My attitude is more "Wait and see." I'm just not sure how much sitting in front of a computer screen is going to contribute to people's spiritual development, particularly if they do a lot of it.

JZ: That's interesting. I'm very curious to know what it did to you when you were spending a lot of time in front of the screen, putting up the Web site. Did you find that it posed a challenge to your attention?

SKEH: I recall meeting with quite a degree of frustration and stress in building the Web site. Of course, it was a time when one has to learn everything from scratch, and there really wasn't adequate information, and the tools were rather poor. I know it's getting much easier quickly. I spend a fair amount of time on the computer because I write, create, design. There are many times when I question how well spent that time is, even though it's productive time that allows me to design and create things I could not design and create any other way. I appreciate that, but I don't think it helps my inner state, and it appears that my inner state even suffers through this kind of work.

JZ: There certainly seems to be a difference between, say, building a piece of furniture or washing the dishes—doing something physical, where I'm more easily engaging my body as well as my mind—and sitting in front of this screen. I get kind of zoned out when I'm in front of the computer. I find it real hard to stay with myself—not that that's ever easy.

SKEH: You sort of forget that you have a body.

JZ: Yeah.

SKEH: You forget that you are a living, breathing creature. You enter a mental dimension, a mechanical and mental, technical dimension that is very absorbing and somehow pulls you in. This is a very interesting phenomenon. I don't pretend to understand it, and I've been trying to understand it for about ten years. There's something about the screen— it's mesmerizing, and it absorbs you.

JZ: Absolutely.

SKEH: And yet I don't feel any the better for it. I don't think working at the computer returns as much in the realm of quality as working in a garden, or painting, or playing music, or sitting down and talking to another human being. I don't believe that engaging in a conversation in the Internet on a keyboard brings us as much or as many levels of infor- mation and experience, touches our heart the way that being with human beings can touch our heart, and touch many levels.

I think its main use is in forming an initial connection among people that can later be developed in other ways. And it's great for when you have to reach somebody at a dis- tance. It's a great form of limited communication.

JZ: Do you have any advice to give to people who have to spend a lot of time in front of the computer, and who are confronting this absorption by the screen, this sort of glazing over? What do you recommend they do—during the course of their workday, for instance?

SKEH: Well, I would recommend that they periodically bring their awareness into their breathing, and periodically bring their awareness to their whole physical presence. In a non-analytical, nonmental way, simply to sense themselves. And to also periodically ask, "Where's the heart in all this?"

JZ: That's an interesting question. Can you explain that a little?

SKEH: Well, one way of understanding the heart is that it is the organ of perception for the qualitative world. It's a form of intelligence more complete, more whole, than our intellectual intelligence, but it is a form of intelligence. And it precedes a world of qualities, and by *qualities* here I don't just mean qualities of the sense world, but qualities of value, qualities of a spiritual world, the invisible world, which in fact is where all value and importance and significance lies.

A moment of feeling compassion, or kindness, or affection, or generosity, or forgiveness, or hope, aspiration, or yearning—these are the most significant human experiences. If my sitting at the computer is in some way an extension of my yearning, or of compassion, it may be useful. Do you know what I mean?

JZ: Yes.

SKEH: Making the heart primary, and technical things secondary.

Just in the last week or so, I've been reflecting whether I should have some kind of disclaimer right at the beginning of our Web page that says, "Please do not confuse this with spirituality. If it's spirituality you're looking for, go inside, look within."

JZ: My impression is that more and more people are looking for spirituality on the computer, and especially younger people. That may be more true in the cities. Certainly in New York, there's a large subculture of these cyberkids—late teens, early twenties, mid-twenties—who are just in love with the computer, and are looking for meaning through the computer and in cyberspace.

SKEH: I think that one of the great dangers of our time is the seduction of equipment, of technology. We are increasing our means so vastly while our end, our purpose, seems to be absent. We can do so much more, we can express so much more, and yet people who have developed themselves, developed their own inner resources, their own inner being, are fewer because we are attracted by, or absorbed in, this whole array of technological equipment. And there's always more of it. It's as if we're being presented weekly with more and more of this stuff.

Take something like the company Silicon Graphics. What is American culture good at right now? At creating spectacle. It's getting really good at that, you know. We have flying cows and tornadoes, and all kind of things.

JZ: You saw that movie too.

SKEH: I watched *Twister*. We have the means to create spectacles, and yet we really have very little to say.

I believe very strongly that, at this time, spirituality has to learn to do more and more with less and less. It's exactly the opposite of the trends we're witnessing. We've got to sit down, stop doing, stop thinking, stop consuming, stop filling ourselves, and instead start emptying and beginning the process of what I call *spiritual minimalism*—doing more and more with less and less in order to learn that reality, real reality, is not a matter of things. It's not a matter of material.

Our humanness is being eroded by our own cleverness in creating ever greater distractions for ourselves, and by a whole industry creating ever greater distractions. For maybe the first time in all of human existence, we have a culture that is being created by money, driven by profit and by little else. At some point maybe we will get so frustrated and so sick with this that we'll long for something else. Maybe human nature can survive this. I'm not sure. I'm a pretty hopeful person, but I'm not sure whether this sort of deluge of distraction will overwhelm human nature or not.

JZ: I think the place I have to look for an answer to that is in the young kids, again, and what's really driving them, because they are the future of the species. Even though these kids like the glitz of cyberspace, and the dazzle, they are still looking for meaning. The search for meaning is very strong in the young.

SKEH: It ought to be, because there's nothing else that is as satisfying, and there's nothing more terrible than the loss of meaning.

NON-INTERNET RESOURCES

Many Islamic resources in cyberspace operate apart from the Internet. America Online, for instance, and most BBSes exist as independent entities in cyberspace, although they often offer Internet access. In addition, many BBSes are linked through networks, like Fidonet, that allow communication between BBSes, primarily through e-mail.

Commercial Online Services

The lineage of the eight-hundred-pound gorillas of cyberspace— the large commercial online services like America Online and CompuServe—extends to near the dawning of the computer age.

CompuServe began in 1968 as Compu-Serv, the computer processing center of a life-insurance company. It and the other major commercial online services offer in-depth Islamic resources. America Online features vigorous Islamic discussion forums, live Islamic chat, and a library of downloadable Islamic files. All of the big commercial services, however, charge a monthly access fee.

BBSes

The first BBS software was written in 1978. Today the wires of the world hum with information poured out from approximately 60,000 public and 180,000 private BBSes. BBSes range from stand-alone computers with a single modem and a few files to huge information services that rival the large commercial online services.

The following list of Islamic BBSes is posted on Islam On Line & Mini Masjid's BBS Web Server (*http://hassan.hom.net*), which is an extension of the Islam On Line BBS:

Islam On Line 1. (912) 929-1073. Has Rip Graphics. 28,8K bps
Islam On Line 2. (912) 929-2873. Has Rip Graphics. 14,4K bps
American Islamic BBS. (202) 789-2527. Washington, DC. 2400
  bps
Imad-Ad-Dean BBS. (301) 656-4714. Bethesda, MD. 9600 bps
Mumineen Connection. (713) 597-8888. Houston, TX. 14,4K
  bps
Islam Lifestyles. (212) 679-0813. New York, NY. 28,8K bps
Shaykh's Oasis. (305) 662-1404. Coral Gables, FL. 14,4K bps
Islamic Bulletin Boards. (213) 937-9119. Los Angeles, CA.
  Books. 14,4K bps
Islamic Bulletin Boards. (714) 939-1633. Anaheim, CA. Books.
  14,4K bps

Key resource: Islam On Line BBS, which features access at both 28.8 and 14.4 kilobytes, full-color graphics, and a friendly interface.

Software

Islamic software, like Judaic software, is available for downloading and for free on many Internet sites as well as on the commercial online services and on BBSes. In addition, much Islamic software is available for a price. By far the most extensive listing online of Islamic software available both online and offline can be found on the SoftBase Web site, a library of freeware, shareware, and fee-ware. On one linked page, Softbase (*http://www .ummah.com/software/softbase*) lists 170 Islamic software programs, from electronic Arabic tutorials to an Islamic-law database to the interactive Islamic game *Journey to Mecca.*

CHAPTER 4

Artificial Intelligence/ Artificial Life

This creature lives in a digital informational universe, not the material one we live in. Its pleasures and pains will be completely alien to us. We will never mistake it for human.

—Tom Ray

There's a dog in my computer and she's a real cutie, a puppy with big black eyes and a sloppy grin. Right now Julia is frolicking in a fenced-off area of the screen called Julia's Playpen, wagging her tail, rolling in the virtual grass, barking as if to gain my attention. If I ignore her, she'll circle, plop down, and go to sleep. When I'm away from my desk she marches around the screen and will bark if anyone but me types on the keyboard.

Julia moved into my PC after I downloaded her from a Web site (*http://www.dogz.com*) maintained by her manufacturer, PF. Magic, Inc. Although Julia serves me, she belongs to my six-year-old daughter, Alexandra, who named her. Alexandra has taught Julia several tricks—to beg, to roll over, to walk on her hind legs—and she enjoys feeding the pup virtual bowls of dog chow and water.

Alexandra feels a bond with Julia. She says that she loves her. Others feel the same way toward their computer pets. As of

August 1996, more than one hundred thousand people had paid the $19.95 (plus shipping and handling) required to "adopt" a "dogz." The PF. Magic, Inc., site reprints e-mail from happy dogz owners. One woman writes, "I adopted my dog 'Max' 1 week ago today and to tell you the truth I can't stop playing with him. My husband thinks I'm crazy because I talk to Max while I'm playing with him. . . . I just want to extend a paw to those who made Max a reality. He really has brought us a lot of joy!" Another owner says, "My dogz Hunter hates being punished, after being sprayed he puts his paws over his head and whines. But he loves to play ball. I love you Hunter!"

Alexandra likes to play catch with Julia. Each time she uses the virtual white hand that came with Julia to toss a digitized ball across the screen, the puppy will rush the ball and return it to the hand. One day I got to talking to Alexandra about this.

"How," I asked, "do you think Julia knows to go after the ball?"

"Well, she wants to play ball with me."

"She does! Is she as nice as a real dog?"

"Yes, and she doesn't bite."

"Do you think she's smart?"

"Yeah!"

"Where do you think she goes when we turn the computer off?"

"I don't know. Maybe she goes to sleep."

Alexandra and other dogz owners speak of their cyberpets as if they were alive. According to the manufacturer, "dogz are the first pets to live on a computer" and "dogz are living creatures."

When I asked Alexandra if she thought Julia was alive, her answer was an emphatic, "No, of course not!" But after I pointed out that, in some ways, Julia acts as if she is alive, Alexandra thought some more. "She *is* alive," she said, "in the computer. But not in real life."

"What do you mean when you say 'She's alive in the computer'?"

"I mean she moves on the computer, so she's alive in the computer."

But movement generally is not considered a distinguishing characteristic of life. Cars move; coral doesn't. Tom Ray, the creator of the digital organisms mentioned during my talk with John Perry Barlow (in chapter 2), lists on his Web pages (discussed later on) only two necessary properties of life: self-replication and open-ended evolution. Most biologists accept these two properties, though many add others: metabolism, for example, and growth, adaptation, and, ironically, the ability to die. Julia exhibits some of these properties. She grows at the rate of a few pixels a day (a pixel, or picture element, is the smallest area on a computer screen capable of being manipulated; each screen contains thousands of pixels). She will "die" if I wipe her from my hard drive. But as Julia enjoys neither self-replication nor open-ended evolution, it seems fair to say that she is not alive, though she does simulate a living organism in some respects.

Alexandra's assessment that Julia is smart is accurate after a fashion. Julia isn't as smart as a real-life dog, but because she can learn to do tricks she may be said to boast a rudimentary intelligence. In fact, Julia is an example of applied artificial intelligence, or AI. Her software apparently employs a neural net, which promotes learning through experience (in Julia's case, by rewarding some behaviors with a digitized bone and punishing others with a spritz of water from a virtual spray bottle).

Among humanity's finer traits is our ability to feel empathy and compassion for other intelligent beings. And so one dogz owner finds her husband saying to her, "Why don't you let him out of his pen so he will have more room to run?" How far will this empathy extend?

One of the more popular singing stars in Japan, especially among technophilic young males, is the sweet-faced but sultry Kyoko Date. She reaches out to her fans not only through her songs but through the Web. Images of Kyoko, usually in shorts or miniskirts to show off her otherworldly legs, can be found on several sites—including her homepage (in Japanese, at *http://www.dhw.co.jp/horipro/talent/DK96/index.html*) and on another, English-language page (*http://home.inreach.com/macbain/dk96 misc.htm*) that contains brief, downloadable video clips from Kyoko's first CD single, "Love Communication," which presents a Windows data track that carries scenes of her walking through Tokyo and New York City. A third Kyoko page (*http://www.etud.insa-tlse.fr/~mdumas/kyoko.html*) explains that the singing sensation is seventeen years old, enjoys drawing, considers Christian Slater and Kyozo Nagazuka her favorite actors, and speaks a few foreign languages.

The site also lets on that Kyoko is composed of forty thousand polygons. Kyoko is a virtual star, created by engineers and designers of the Japanese model agency HoriPro. Even lacking artificial intelligence, she commands passion from many, but she doesn't engage computer users interactively the way Julia and her siblings do. Kyoko's descendants will, though—and much more fully. She is a harbinger of the virtual humans to come. Some time ago, I received a flyer for a "Virtual Humans" conference to be held in Anaheim in June 1996. The flyer described a "human simulation system" called MARILYN: "It includes facial animation, body animation with deformations, grasping and walking, and hair and clothes simulation. It also supports autonomy and perception, and can be used to create simulations in which virtual humans move around . . . and react to other virtual humans, and to real humans." MARILYN is impressive, but for all her abilities, she will one day, compared with the artificially intelligent virtual humans of the future, seem as primitive as *Australopithecus* does compared with us.

In the Judeo-Christian tradition, all that God created—mineral, animal, vegetable, the entire natural world—is seen as invested with the Divine and so worthy of reverence. Buddhism, Hinduism, and nearly all other religions also deem the natural world sacred. As artificial intelligences and artificial life grow in complexity, will we—should we—accord them like reverence?

The Web-based *Free On-Line Dictionary of Computing* (*http://wombat.doc.ic.ac.uk*) explains that "AI can be seen as an attempt to model aspects of human thought on computers." The sort of problems tackled in AI, the dictionary explains, are "computer vision (building a system that can understand images as well as a human) and natural language processing (building a system that can understand and speak a human language as well as a human)." Today, AI seems years, probably decades, away from achieving human-equivalent computer vision or natural language processing, for these are complex abilities that rely on intuitive reasoning and common sense.

Computers excel at logical reasoning and mathematical computation, however, which is why the IBM computer Deep Blue (which is in fact colored blue) won its first game against world chess champion Garry Kasparov in February 1996. Deep Blue is capable of searching up to 1 billion moves a second. Kasparov can search only an estimated two moves per second. It was Kasparov's very human ability to intuit patterns of flow on the board, and to select from those patterns, that allowed him to take the match. On a page about Deep Blue (*http://www.chess.ibm.park.org/deep/blue/dbphotos.html*), Feng-Hsuing Hsu, one of the computer's creators, is quoted: "Kasparov has a deep understanding of the game which is entirely different from Deep Blue's. Deep Blue does not mimic human thought—it reaches the same end by different means. Kasparov's advantages are his intuition, judgment and experience." To utilize these advantages, Kasparov, like any human, relies on the brain's ability to parallel-process information—to distribute the calculations necessary to solve any problem among a number of relatively independent processors (or, in the brain, neuronal configurations). Through parallel processing, the average human brain, which contains more than 100 billion neurons and trillions of interconnections, can make perhaps 20 million billion calculations a second, generating an ability to select and to evaluate sufficient to defeat Deep Blue's astonishing, if simpler, search abilities.

Computers and AI are forever, however. Like the Internet, they are here and they are not going to go away. Given the current vector of increase in the processing power of computers, it's likely that computers, even desktop models, will achieve human equivalence by the middle of the next century. By then, computers will consistently ace the world chess champion. Computers will recognize faces and carry on dazzling conversations in a legion of languages. Computers will do anything that human beings can do that depends on the calculations involved in information processing.

But we humans don't only calculate. We love, we hate, we fear, we worship. We have an inner life. When we recognize the face of a loved one, we don't just register it as familiar, we feel joy at the recognition. We experience *meaning*. Computers can calculate, and perhaps even reason, but would a computer have shouted "Eureka!" if it, instead of Archimedes, had watched a body displace an equal volume of bathwater? Do computers experience meaning? Will they?

Some scientists believe they do, and many believe they will. The question of a computer's inner life is answered by the nature of consciousness. The most prominent modern-day scientist to attempt to wrestle consciousness to the ground is Francis Crick, who in *The Astonishing Hypothesis: The Scientific Search for the Soul* stated, "You, your joys and your sorrows, your memories and your ambitions, your sense of personal identity and free will, are in fact no more than the behavior of a vast assembly of nerve cells and their associated molecules." If this is true, then once a computer is designed that exactly models these nerve cells and their associated molecules, that computer will experience joys, sorrows, memories, ambition, personal identity, and free will—and certainly will be worthy of at least respect, if not reverence.

Many scientists believe that consciousness is an emergent behavior, that an individual neuron in the human brain is not conscious but that the billions of neurons in the brain working

in a multitude of varied and interlocked assemblies, some cooperating, some competing, give rise to consciousness. By extension, they believe that consciousness will arise in a computer
that possesses a sufficient complexity of transistor-based interactions. It seems certain that in time, computers will success-
fully simulate most of the outward signs of an inner life. If in
fifty years my daughter's desktop computer tells her that it is in
despair because she violates its freedom each time she commands it to perform this function or that, on what grounds will
she doubt it?

The problem is that there is no way to determine with certainty from outside a mind whether that mind is conscious. In
1950, the British mathematician Alan Turing proposed an experiment to determine whether a machine was "intelligent," or
could "think." The experiment, which has come to be known as
the Turing Test, keys on the potential ability of a computer to
answer questions in such a way that the questioner can't tell
if the answers are provided by a computer or a human being.
Turing concluded that if the computer deceives the questioner,
it must be considered intelligent. The classic response to the
Turing Test was given by the U.C. Berkeley philosopher John
Searle in 1980. Searle proposed a closed room in which he,
Searle—who neither speaks nor reads Chinese—would receive
questions posed in Chinese ideograms. By consulting a set of
rules (a program) that directed which ideograms to associate
with which English sentences, he could answer the questions—
without, however, understanding the meaning behind the
ideograms. In like fashion, Searle contended, a computer merely
manipulates symbols according to a set of rules without understanding what the symbols mean.

The Turing Test and Searle's Chinese Room refer to intelligence and thought, not to consciousness, self-consciousness,
or higher consciousness. But Searle's lesson applies to the detec-
tion of consciousness as well. Consciousness can't be detected
with certainty by external observation. Science can't measure

subjective states. It's on the flip side of the coin that the hard question lurks: If a computer gives every indication of being conscious, by what measure can we be certain that it isn't? If in fifty years my daughter's computer tells her that it has just had a mystical experience, will she doubt it? How powerful will computers be in one hundred years? Ten thousand years? By then, we will be living with machines that will by every objective measure appear to be fully conscious entities. Kyoko Date's far-flung descendants will be identical in appearance (though presumably not in *prana*) to humans, capable of simulating, through the observation of external characteristics and cultural artifacts (and perhaps through the scanning of neuronal activity), the wisdom of a pope or a Dalai Lama. How, then, will we kiss the ring of a pope but not that of a seemingly identical robo-pope?

Traditionally, religions have taught that consciousness is primary to matter, and is not an emergent property. God created the world, not vice versa. Or as the Dalai Lama said to the physicist Jeremy Hayward (as reported in *Gentle Bridges: Conversations with the Dalai Lama on the Sciences of Mind*), "Matter can only be a cooperative cause, never the main or substantial cause for consciousness." The teachings of the great religious traditions have no argument, however, with the idea that various levels of consciousness ally at least to some degree with corresponding levels of neuronic complexity and functionality. Humans have more complex brains than slugs; humans are more conscious than slugs. Stimulation or suppression of various neuronal patterns affects consciousness, as anyone who has ever fallen asleep can attest. The Dalai Lama also said to Hayward, "I can't totally rule out the possibility that, if all the external conditions and the karmic action were there, a stream of consciousness might actually enter into a computer."

Correspondence needn't imply causality, and the correspondence of certain configurations of matter to certain levels of mind needn't mean that mind emerges from matter. This correspondence has, however, inspired a number of scientists to speculate about the possibility of uploading human consciousness into a computer, or re-creating human consciousness on a computer. The most visible spokesperson for uploading is Hans Moravec, director of the Mobile Robot Laboratory at Carnegie-Mellon's Field Robotics Center, who presented his version of mind transference from wetware to hardware in *Mind Children: The Future of Human and Robot Intelligence*. Moravec, who has been studying and building robots all his life, believes that robots will facilitate the transference of human consciousness into computers. They will scan the functions of each cell in the brain, then simulate them through a computer program until slowly the simulation duplicates the brain's entire contents and functioning.

The potentials of a software edition of the mind (*Jeff Zaleski 1.0*) are awesome. The computer running the software could be housed within a robotic body capable of superhuman sensory abilities, or in fact within any housing whatsoever—a biomechanical eagle, shark, or special edition of Xena, the Warrior Princess. Or we could dispense entirely with the natural world and exist within a computer-generated artificial reality—say, a re-creation of the Garden of Eden. As a rather big bonus, once our minds are transferred to a computer, backup copies can be made, rendering ourselves immortal, or at least viable for as long as the copies are preserved and hardware exists on which to run them. If we prefer to spend eternity in communion with other minds, we can network our software to someone else's—and, if we're narcissists, to copies of our own minds.

The range of human experience—thought, emotions, physical sensations—arises not only from the electrical activity in the brain. Chemicals play a part, too, through the endocrine system and neurotransmitters in the brain. But if all information can be digitized, then presumably chemical and hormonal influences can as well. Or perhaps, for the sake of ease, the computers running our uploaded minds—or whatever results from the attempts to upload our minds—will be wet ones. All this promise teeters perilously on two slippery assumptions, of course: that consciousness is emergent, and that it is computable. And what if consciousness is not local but universal, if the boundaries between minds are not rigid but fluid, and if, as attested to by mystics, we contain within our apparent individual minds the continuum of all minds? Try simulating that.

Frank Tipler, a professor of mathematical physics at Tulane University, has proposed a similarly universal simulation. In an audacious and increasingly influential book, *The Physics of Immortality: Modern Cosmology, God and the Resurrection of the Dead*, Tipler treats traditional theological concerns of the Judeo-Christian tradition—God, heaven, hell, the resurrection of the dead—in purely physical terms. According to Tipler, the human being is "a biochemical machine completely and exhaustively described by the known laws of physics." A person is "a particular (very complicated) type of computer program," and the soul is "nothing but a specific program being run on a computing machine called the brain." And so religion, he concludes, "is now a part of science."

Just as Thomas Aquinas based his theological arguments on Aristotelian physics, Tipler bases his on quantum and relativity physics. Tipler accepts the big bang theory of the creation of the universe and, as its counterpart, a big crunch that will end the universe as it collapses upon itself. In brief, Tipler proposes that, through the future invention of superintelligent space probes that are able to record all the information that exists and that ever has existed, the universe, including us, can and will be re-created in the form of a computer simulation that will activate during the last infinitesimal fraction of a second before the "Omega Point"—"the *completion* of all finite existence." Through virtual reality, we will experience heaven, hell, and purgatory. Through the workings of relativity physics, we will experience this last infinitesimal fraction of a second as an eternity.

Tipler borrowed the term *Omega Point* from Pierre Teilhard de Chardin, whom he credits. He takes the Jesuit to task, though, for embracing a "vitalism." *Vitalism* refers to the life force or élan vital—*prana, chi,* the breath of life. ("And the LORD God formed man [of] the dust of the ground, and breathed into his nostrils the breath of life; and man became a living soul" [Gen. 2:7, AV].) In today's science, vitalism is as dead as the dodo. So is, to many scientists, the idea that life must be confined to organic matter.

> Life on Earth is the product of evolution by natural selection operating in the medium of carbon chemistry. However, in theory, the process of evolution is neither limited to occurring on the Earth, nor in carbon chemistry. Just as it may occur on other planets, it may also operate in other media, such as the medium of digital computation. And just as evolution on other planets is not a model of life on Earth, nor is natural evolution in the digital medium.
>
> —TOM RAY

On January 3, 1990, Tom Ray changed the world by creating a new one. Ray's new world is called Tierra. It is a virtual world, actually a virtual computer—a computer emulated by a physical computer. On that date, Ray, then a thirty-five-year-old assistant professor of biology at the University of Delaware, inserted into the RAM, or random access memory, or volatile memory, of Tierra an executable machine-code program, a pattern of information able to perform instructions. The 80-byte program, which Ray dubbed "the ancestor," was instructed to self-replicate by allocating free memory space for its progeny, then copying its code to that space.

Ray wasn't expecting much when he inserted the ancestor into Tierra, but he was hoping for a lot. He'd designed the virtual computer in order to study by analogy the process of Darwinian evolution. The ancestor's code is analogous to, as Ray puts it on one of his Web pages, "the nucleic acid based genetic code of organic life." The virtual computer's CPU (central processing unit), which drives the execution of the machine code, is analogous to the energy that "drives the metabolism of organic life," whereas its RAM serves as an analogue to "the physical space of organic life." Further aspects of the virtual computer were designed as analogues to various methods of mutation, and to death. Once the ancestor replicated itself, it and its progeny would vie for CPU time and RAM memory space, just as organic entities vie for energy and space.

Within minutes, Tierra was home to numerous 80-byte replicants of the ancestor. It also teemed with codes 79 bytes long, no doubt because of a mutational device that called for a random "flipping" of a "bit" within the 80-byte machine codes. The great breakthrough came when Ray discovered the presence of 45-byte codes—"parasites," he soon determined, that borrowed the code from the 80-byte entities in order to replicate. Further parasites, hyperparasites, and other "creatures" of assorted byte lengths appeared, congregating in what Ray calls "diverse ecological communities."

The Age of Artificial Evolution had begun. Ray considers these entities not a simulation of life but an "instantiation" of life—not representations of organic life, but digital life. How will Ray's artificial life-forms evolve? Ray has speculated that they may undergo an analogue to organic life's Cambrian explosion, leading to a dramatic increase in the complexity and variety of digital life. To facilitate this explosion, he is currently testing the Tierra Network Experiment, which will create a global network of virtual computers swarming with digital creatures.

Ray demurs when asked to cite specific characteristics of these future organisms. He does suggest that what minds they possess will bear little resemblance to our own minds. "Imagine," he writes on one of his pages, "a machine intelligence living in the internet. Scanning a terabyte of data distributed globally over the net for instances of foolish predictions, and doing the job as a distributed process in a few minutes, would probably be very exciting for such an intelligence. . . . The data flow would be a direct sensory experience for this creature, not something happening in a separate information processing tool. This creature lives in a digital informational universe, not the material one we live in. Its pleasures and pains will be completely alien to us. We will never mistake it for human."

Expressing great caution in dealing with digital life, Ray insists that it be kept in contained facilities, because "given evolution's selfish nature and capability to improve performance, there exists the potential for a conflict arising through a struggle for dominance between organic and synthetic organisms." This may seem far-fetched, but others have echoed Ray's concern. In his essay "Virtual Catastrophe: Will Self-Reproducing Software Rule the World?" (included in the excellent *Clicking In: Hot Links to a Digital Culture*, edited by Lynn Hershman Leeson), the computer-virus expert Mark Ludwig imagines the possibility that, to ensure their survival, computer viruses may someday evolve to "become the electronic equivalent of highly addictive drugs." He speculates further that a virus could evolve that would, through the depiction of an alluring message on a computer screen, seduce humans into executing, or activating, it.

Digital life need not be conscious in order to affect our behavior, any more than a Venus's-flytrap is conscious when it seduces a fly. This isn't necessarily science fiction, and Ray is no mad scientist. His homepage (*http://www.hip.atr.co.jp/~ray*) presents charming color photographs of him; his wife, Isabel; and their daughter, Ariel Ivy. (The Tierra homepage is located at *http://www.hip.atr.co.jp/~ray/tierra/tierra.html*.) He is a dedicated and, by all signs, morally aware scientist whose work may yet shake the foundations of traditional moral and spiritual teachings. In the fall of 1996, I conducted an e-mail interview with Ray, who is currently based in Kyoto.

JEFF ZALESKI: Digital organisms don't seem to exist in three-dimensional space the same way we do; they occupy no volume, though they do occupy something—that is, their size and number is limited by certain parameters. Can you elaborate any thoughts you might have on this?

TOM RAY: They occupy RAM memory, which might be distributed over a network. So of course their size and numbers are limited by the amount and configuration of this memory.

JZ: And on how their particular medium of existence might affect their evolution?

TR: The initial results of Tierra are our first glimpse of this. I can't predict the future course of evolution, so I can't say any more about this.

JZ: Along the same lines, you quote your wife as saying, "I'm glad they're not real"; how does their reality differ from our own?

TR: I disagree with my wife about their reality. For my wife, they are not a part of her reality, the house. At least they don't exist outside of the computer in our study, so she doesn't encounter them in her daily life, so they are not real to her.

But this is a fairly parochial view of reality. (If you don't see it in your living room or kitchen, it doesn't exit, or it is not real.) Even so, it is a very widely held view. I think the majority of people consider the things that exist in cyberspace to not be real. However, cyberspace is every bit as real as the hardware that implements it.

Yet, perhaps a better comparison is with mental life. Our mental life is more that an element of our reality. We experience our private mental life firsthand, and it is absolutely real to us. However, we experience the mental life of others only indirectly, so it can seem very unreal. The information processes taking place inside of computers are a primitive and digital form of the same thing, and have the same reality properties.

JZ: You characterize the evolutionary possibilities of these creatures as being "open-ended." Do you see them, in this evolution, as tending toward ever greater complexity? Necessarily so?

TR: I am an empiricist. So far I have seen a few examples of small increases in complexity (by factors of perhaps two or three). In most evolutions, I have seen decreasing complexity, due to optimizations. I am speaking of the complexity of the individual algorithms, rather than the ecological community in which they exist.

Provoking a large increase in complexity is the main goal of the Tierra project. It has not been accomplished yet, and I don't know if it will be possible.

JZ: What are the implications for the evolution of the Tierran creatures of their not being bound by the laws of thermodynamics?

TR: They are bound by other "laws of nature," such as the logic of the instruction set implemented by the CPU, and the procedures by which the operating system allocates resources. It is just a different set of rules. The implications must be profound, and only a large amount of evolution in the medium will reveal them to us.

JZ: Do you believe that any of the Tierran creatures evolved thus far exhibit consciousness?

TR: No

JZ: Do you believe that they will do so sometime in the future? Why?

TR: If I am able to provoke a complexity increase comparable to the Cambrian explosion, then it would be likely to happen. But so far, digital evolution has not demonstrated substantial complexity increase, and we don't know if it can.

JZ: And if so, in what ways do you think their consciousness might differ from that of carbon-based organisms?

TR: See *http://www.hip.atr.co.jp/~ray/pubs/fatm/node44.html*.

JZ: You're a naturalist. You've spent a great deal of time surrounded by the richness of organic life, in the rain forest.

What do you think, and what do you feel, are the essential differences, if any, between organic life and digital life?

TR: One exists in a material medium, and the other in an immaterial logical/informational medium.

One has achieved a complexity increase of perhaps a dozen orders of magnitude through evolution, while the other has experienced virtually no complexity increase; thus the two differ in complexity by about a dozen orders of magnitude.

JZ: What is your emotional attitude toward the Tierran creatures, if any?

TR: They are still very primitive, as far as "life-forms" go, so I can't get emotional about them. Except that I created them. I am proud of that.

JZ: Do you think that the Tierran creatures might in time evolve their own emotional life? Love may be, as a lot of sociobiologists say, an attribute the purpose of which is to further the perpetuation of the gene; but we, and other animals, still feel love. What I'm really asking here is, do the Tierran creatures now, or will they, in your best estimation, have an interior life as well as exhibiting outer characteristics of life?

TR: This depends on how complex they become. If they become comparably complex to higher animals, then I expect that they will have a comparable interior life. But as I have said, we don't know if they will achieve such levels of complexity.

JZ: I'm curious as to whether the recent discovery of possible fossils of organic life on Mars has changed your thinking about the Tierran project in any way. Can you say?

TR: If it is true, then it must change our conceptions of the probability of life. It would make the emergence of life seem highly probable, almost inevitable. Also it provides us with another independent instance of life. Before Mars life, there has been one example of Earth life, and then some examples of synthetic life. It is good to have yet another instance of life on which to base our understanding of life.

JZ: Finally, I'd like to hear any thoughts you have about the implications of your work for humanity's seemingly endless struggle to understand itself.

TR: If the Tierra project is successful, it will teach us a lot about the process by which evolution generates complexity. This should help us to understand the processes that created us.

Static images of Tierra that were made using an "Artificial Life Monitor" appear on one of Ray's Web pages. They don't look like much—more like bands of confetti-colored interference patterns on a TV screen than anything else. Of course, appearances can be deceiving. Those wishing to observe artificial life in action can visit the Live Artificial Life Page (*http://www.fusebox.com/cb/alife.html*), maintained by Robert Silverman. This extraordinary page contains interactive presentations, either original or adaptations, of some of the most famous A-life simulations (or instantations, depending on your point of view; Silverberg refers to them as "simulations"). These include "Swarm," which looks like a school of sperm swimming against a black backdrop; "Morphs," evolving pixelated entities that take a variety of shapes; and "Life," the classic cellular automatons designed by the mathematician John Conway in 1968 at the University of Cambridge, in England. Cellular automatons are important tools in artificial-life research. They are simple devices that generate an infinite variety of forms by changing the state of a grid of cells according to a set of rules keyed to the state of neighboring cells. (In "Life," for instance, if a cell has no neighbors or just one, the cell dies of "loneliness.") On the Live Artificial Life Page, "Life" produces a digital fireworks display of red, blue, and gold particles.

Where will artificial life and artificial intelligence finally take us? One fanciful response to that question was given by the science-fiction writer Frederic Brown (1906–1972) in his 1950 short story "The Answer." In this story, for an event televised across the universe, a man—or perhaps he's an alien—throws a switch connecting all the computers on the 96 billion populated planets. He asks the central computer, "Is there a God?" A deep voice answers, "Yes, *now* there is a God," and a bolt of lightning jags down from the sky, fusing the switch shut.

CHAPTER 5

Christianity

This is who we are. Come in and learn about us,
but don't expect to change us.
—JAMES S. MULHOLLAND, JR.

If cyberspace is a digital ocean, then Christianity online is its tidal wave. As of early 1997, Christian Web sites made up more than 80 percent of the Web sites of the world's five major (i.e., most influential) religions. Yet the four other major world religions—Judaism, Islam, Buddhism, and Hinduism—together claim about 2 billion adherents, the same number that Christianity claims.

This discrepancy results from the domination of the Net by users from the United States and Western Europe, where Christianity reigns. According to the results of a recent study of the world's nearly 10 million Internet hosts (computers that provide information or services to other computers) by the research and executive advisory firm Killen & Associates (*http://www*
.killen.com), as of January 30, 1996, the number of hosts in Europe and North America outnumbered those in all other areas of the world (excluding sites classified as "transnational") by a ratio of nearly four to one. In years to come, this Euro-American dominance will weaken as Internet access penetrates the globe. It won't disappear for decades, however, if ever—and in the foreseeable future online spiritual seekers may be swept up by the surge of Christian sites. If information is power, then

during the next century Christianity, of all the major world religions, will benefit the most from Internet growth.

Though Christianity online is the tidal wave of cyberspace, it is a wave with a curious shape. Of the nearly 2 billion Christians in the world, about 55 percent are Roman Catholic. Yet Roman Catholic sites make up less than 25 percent of the sites indexed by Yahoo in December 1996 under the category "Christianity: Denominations and Sects." The Holy Roman Catholic Church dominates Christianity in the real world, but not in the virtual one. This is so partly for the same reason that Christianity as a whole dominates cyberspace: the majority of Internet users live in the United States, and the United States is predominantly Protestant.

There are other reasons for the relatively weak showing of Roman Catholicism online, as indicated in the introduction to this book. Any religion that relies on ecclesial authority and hierarchy, as well as on sacraments, is going to have a hard go on the Net. Much of this chapter consists of an exploration of the challenges faced by Roman Catholicism, and by Christianity as a whole, in cyberspace.

The majority of U.S. citizens are Protestant, but the single largest Christian sect in this country is Roman Catholicism, by a wide margin. As of late 1996, Roman Catholic sites online outnumbered those of any other religious denomination, Christian or non-Christian. At that time, Yahoo indexed 762 Catholic sites, whose variety testify not only to the many facets of Roman Catholicism, but also to the flexibility and responsiveness of cyberspace, where everyone can have a voice and where human interests in all their shadings manifest. These sites included, among others, 96 homepages for individual churches, 261 outposts of Catholic educational institutions, 194 links for Catholic organizations and 21 for individual dioceses, 6 sites devoted to Pope John Paul II, 7 to the Shroud of Turin, and 12 to saints. But these numbers are deceptively small. Of the 12 Yahoo-indexed sites devoted to saints, one is itself an index that lists 101 Web pages for individual Catholic saints—more than eight times as many as listed directly on Yahoo.

The immediate problem facing anyone seeking spiritual information online isn't the paucity of information, but the plenitude. The Internet is the new library of the human race, and a proper card catalog is sorely lacking. The challenge in creating one is staggering. AltaVista now searches more than 60 million Web pages. By the year 2000, it may have to search a billion Web pages to do a thorough job. This is equivalent to searching not just the title of every book in the Library of Congress, but every page of every book. For this reason, a general index like Yahoo must be selective, and rely for finer or more complete charting on specialized subindexes.

The task of indexing Roman Catholic sites has been taken up by numerous clergy and laypeople. One of the most ambitious of Roman Catholic indexes resides on the Catholic Information Center on Internet (CICI), which in August 1996 received an award as the top-rated Catholic site from I-WAY 500 (*http://www.iwayonline.com/iway/index.html*), one of several Web sites that in turn rate other Internet sites.

CICI "has as its mission," as one of its pages proclaims, "to make the truth of the Gospel of Jesus Christ, of the teachings and the activities of the Roman Catholic Church, and of the statements of the Popes readily available to as many people as practicable. . . . CICI is a central directory and repository of all data on the Internet that reflects the Magisterium or authoritative teaching of the Catholic Church."

A tall order, that. To fill it, CICI calls on the talents of many people. Twenty-one names—an extraordinarily high number for a religious Web site—appear on its main credits page. The crowning name is that of Archbishop Renato Martino, Permanent Observer of the Holy See to the United Nations (or, the Vatican's ambassador to the U.N.); his e-mail address is martino @catholic.net. CICI is also supported by a general staff of five and a technical consulting staff of twelve, plus a three-man board of directors, including a priest, Monsignor Eugene Clark, and the site's founder, publisher, and editor, James S. Mulholland, Jr.

These faithful have generated a smooth site that emphasizes substance over show. CICI features few graphics, although its homepage does present a beautiful color image of Mary and the risen Christ. Further pages on the site offer, in addition to a "Catholic Internet Directory," the text of various Catholic periodicals, papal encyclicals, and pronouncements; links to other Catholic media; information on the Pope and on the Holy See mission; an extensive directory of pro-life resources; and a "Catholic Issues and Facts" forum that features position papers on assorted Catholic hot potatoes ("What is Papal Infallibility"; "Pius XII & the Jewish Holocaust"; "Abortion Facts & Figures") and the opportunity to discuss the issues in sequential postings.

To find out more about CICI, I telephoned Mulholland at his suburban New Jersey office. Mulholland is cordial but reserved on the phone. His businesslike presence is sweetened, however, by the lilt and tenor of his voice, a melody of Irish America that sounds uncannily like the voice of the late film star James Cagney.

JEFF ZALESKI: Will you please tell me a bit about the history of CICI? How it came to be, and how you came to be involved in it?

JAMES MULHOLLAND: I'll give you a quick background on myself first. I'm a general engineer, graduate of MIT in 1944. In the navy for a couple of years, came out and went into publishing, and in 1952 founded Hayden Publishing. They publish magazines like *Electronic Design, MicroWaves, Computer Decisions, Systems and Software, Personal Computing.* We also had a Hayden Book Company, which published a lot of books in the computer field, particularly in the early days of personal computers. And we had Hayden Software, which was at one time the leading software company for Apple products.

I sold all that in 1986. But from 1981 to 1986, I had been developing radio programs for Radio Free Europe on the subjects of monotheism, Christianity, and Roman Catholicism. We were pretty much the only religious group supplying material to Radio Free Europe and Radio Liberty. We'd supply them in thirteen-week segments, and the programs might be as short as ten minutes. Each would be repeated several times during one week. At the end of five years, we were working in five languages regularly—Russian, Latvian, Lithuanian, Ukrainian, Estonian.

Then I started a Freedom, Justice, and Peace Society to conduct world days of prayer for human rights, picking up the idea from Pope John Paul II, who had assembled in Assisi on October 26, 1986, the leaders of the major religions of the world. There were 180 religious leaders assembled at Assisi, to pray for peace.

Like Chabad-Lubavitch in Cyberspace, which evolved from the efforts of Rabbi Menachem Schneerson and his followers to spread the holy word through radio, telephone, and television, Mulholland's Internet activities grew out of his evangelizing via earlier media. The marriage of spirituality and technology is an ancient one, reaching back to before the first cave paintings. Humanity first entered into a relationship with the sacred through a dawning awareness of the inner self, but also through our taming (or "capture," as John Perry Barlow put it) of fire, a technological advance that put us on an equal footing with the gods—hence the myth of Prometheus. Millennia later, the invention of the book, albeit in handwritten form, helped propel Christianity around the world. When Gutenberg first cranked up his printing press, it was a Bible that he printed. In our century, Christian evangelists like Billy Sunday, then Billy Graham, seized upon radio and television to broadcast their messages.

Information specialists—particularly those, like Mulholland, with a background in earlier technologies and in broadcasting to a multinational audience—play important roles in digitized spirituality.

It's notable that Mulholland came to the Internet as an expert in book and magazine publishing. Today's Net works primarily on a publishing model, as a print-oriented medium. That will change as computers gain in speed and power, allowing visual simulations of reality to supplant textual ones. Meanwhile, the brief radio segments that Mulholland produced can serve as a template for most parcels of text presented on the Net, which tend to be brief, partly to accommodate computer-monitor screen sizes but also in response to the limited attention span that the Net—the Web in particular—seems to foster and to thrive on.

JZ: How did this translate into CICI?

JM: So I went through that long iteration—when does it start? Perhaps when you're born. There's a certain momentum, and my momentum is somewhat in the direction of evangelization. My son and I had invested in MecklerMedia when it was a very small company. They had a couple of newsletters, and they wanted to convert them into magazines. So we invested and the magazines were produced, one of which is the magazine *Internet World*.

The operation was prospering and then, about two years ago, Alan Meckler came up with what was a revolutionary idea at the time, one that's been picked up fairly generally since—of having a virtual shopping mall where companies would have their storefronts, actually homepages. As he was describing this new idea to me, I said, "Alan, how would you like to give this operation a little class, and have as one of your early tenants the Roman Catholic Church?"

He said, "Oh, that's a great idea." And I said, "Of course, rent-free." What I was doing there was picking up the idea from the Christian Scientists of a reading room, a walk-in reading room. Except that this would be a Roman Catholic reading room on a global scale.

To be that, you begin to take on some of the characteristics of a library, but you also have to bring people in. So currently we have a variety of periodicals, about a dozen. Back issues can be searched, and current issues can be read. The publishers get the reward of cooperating and participating by having people easily sample their wares, and subscribe to their magazines.

It's the rare Web site that's meant to be a hermitage. Some Internet services, particularly professional or academic mailing lists, restrict access (such as Priest-L, a mailing list restricted to Roman Catholic priests), but even they must scatter some sugar to attract visitors. For most spiritual Web sites, garnering hits is of crucial importance if they are to fulfill their evangelical mission. This can be done in several ways. Rarely, a religious site will advertise. More often, a site will attempt to draw the curious by linking to other sites. A parish homepage linked by hypertext (a coding system by which documents are connected via clickable keywords) to one hundred other sites is going to receive more visitors than a homepage linked to fifty sites. Most important, a site will draw visitors by providing rich and fresh content that earns publicity through word of mouth, through winning awards or by being listed in a "best of" index like that offered by I-Way 500, and through coverage in Web news and review services, as well as in other media.

The Web is a Janus. Its threads tie together through hypertext, promoting cooperation among sites. Yet by offering links, sites invite visitors to leave, to move on to other sites. It's impossible, given the limitations of current Web browsers, to use the same computer to log on to two sites at the same time. So even as the Web promotes cooperation, it encourages competition. In the real world, moreover, religions are often protected through legal means (blue laws) or by custom against competition from secular seducements. Most stores, movie theaters, and bars in America are closed on Sunday mornings, when Christian churches hold services. The Internet is a round-the-clock affair, however. No site shuts down on Sunday morning.

To thrive among competitors spiritual and secular, online and off, a well-constructed site must consider its entertainment value—whether the digitized information it offers is pleasing to the eye and ear, and to some extent whether it incorporates the latest innovations in online technology. This challenge isn't new to religion. Michelangelo painted the Sistine Chapel not only to elevate the souls of those within but also to quicken their attention, to keep them coming back. But the danger of the medium subverting the message—of cyber entertainment supplanting contemplative encouragement—increases in lockstep with technology's power to dazzle.

JZ: How else do you bring in visitors?

JM: We also did have, and we're going to have again, a daily news feed as another attraction. And the most startling one, I think, is that we're going to have a central directory of all Roman Catholic activities on the Internet.

AltaVista now lists about ten thousand. To deal with that, we've developed software that enables us to have a package that's relatively automatic. We have librarian personnel who will process the data as it goes through. So we're looking forward to being a central directory where we would list categories, subcategories, and sub-subcategories of various directories, various homepages.

JZ: Let me go back to something you said before. When you were talking to Alan Meckler you asked, "How would you like to have the Roman Catholic Church on your site?" What makes this a site of the Roman Catholic Church? As opposed to a site from a lay Catholic?

JM: This is a site of primarily lay Catholics. We are not an official Catholic outlet. But we carry only material that reflects, and is in agreement with, the Magisterium of the Church. [The Magisterium is, as a page on CICI puts it, "the Church's divinely appointed authority to teach the truths of religion."]

JZ: Who decides that it reflects the Magisterium?

JM: I do. I also have the aid of other people. One of our directors, Monsignor Eugene Clark, is pastor of Saint Agnes Church in New York. He was the P.R. director for Cardinal Cooke many years ago. [Cardinal Cooke is the late former archbishop of the Diocese of New York.] So he's a man of wide knowledge and aegis in the area. We have reference to a large number of theology personnel.

JZ: I see that on the Web page where you list people connected with your site you have at the top Archbishop Renato Martino. Does he take an active hand in what goes on at the site?

JM: It's a sponsorship. He sponsors us. He does review the site fairly regularly. He leaves the responsibility for the site in my hands, however.

JZ: Do you have any official sort of standing in the Church?

JM: The highest standing I have is that I'm on Archbishop Martino's board of directors for the Path to Peace Foundation of the Holy See Mission to the U.N. I'm also a Knight Commander in the Order of Saint Gregory. That's the highest honor that the Catholic Church awards to a layman who is not a head of state. I'm also a Knight of Malta, and a Knight in the Equestrian Order of the Holy Sepulchre.

So I do have a good access and a cooperating arrangement, but I'm careful to make clear that our pronouncements are not official pronouncements. We *carry* official pronouncements.

The distinction is important, but the relationship between CICI and the Vatican is an intimate one. Funds from the Path to Peace Foundation helped launch CICI. The president of the foundation is Archbishop Martino, who made the official announcement about the debut of the site with the words, "For the Church to fulfill her mission of teaching and serving all mankind, it is appropriate she make use of a technology that offers the possibility of immediate, in-depth communication with the entire world."

> JZ: What sort of response have you been getting to the site? How many people log on daily?

> JM: We get about fifteen hundred a day. I think when we're carrying those sites that are Catholic sites that are conforming to the Magisterium—and we'll look for them to make some statement; we won't police them, but we'll look for them to make a parallel claim that what they're carrying reflects the Magisterium—we'll have a multiple of attendance.

Religions and spiritual movements always have to contend with the question, or problem, of who makes "official" pronouncements for them and who does not. Historically, religions with a strong central governing authority, like the Roman Catholic Church, have both declared their official positions on spiritual matters (for instance, in the catechism) and monitored information from any and all sources to gauge its accordance with that official position. As recently as January 1997, the Vatican's Congregation for the Doctrine of the Faith excommunicated a Sri Lankan priest, Father Tissa Balasuriya, for writings that challenged basic Roman Catholic tenets like the Immaculate Conception and original sin. As public information sources multiply through the Internet, it's likely that the number of sites claiming to belong to any particular religion but in fact disseminating information that the central authority of that religion deems heretical also will multiply.

JZ: Here's a theoretical question: Do you think religious ritu-als—and in the case of the Church, any of the sacraments—will ever be offered on the Internet? For instance, the sacrament of Confession?

JM: I have to first confess an ignorance. I don't know enough about the ecclesial requirements for that particular sacra-ment to speak. I would think that some of the requirements of the confessional are possible, one of which is confidential-ity, with the various security systems that are abounding and will be even more possible as time goes on. They'll be more readily available, easier to use, so confidentiality is possible. We've had the telephone for a long time, however. It has never to my knowledge been used for Confession. So per-haps this new form of communication may not fully qualify.

I think certainly Communion is impossible. And I don't think we're going to cure the shortage of our priests this way.

JZ: So it's a matter of being able to fulfill certain ecclesial re-quirements.

JM: I think so.

JZ: I want to ask you about the "Catholic Issues and Facts" forums, or discussion groups, you have on the site. What's the purpose of those?

JM: There are many issues that in the public media get dis-torted for one reason or another, and this is an opportunity to have a position presented, and then an interactive ex-change. We need to have more of that. But the purpose is really that the truth be exposed, and that through the ex-change of pros and cons an even better understanding of the issues be developed.

JZ: I was surprised not to see any discussion of the ordina-tion of women, or at least of the role that women might play in the future in the Church. Do you think you might create a discussion group about that at some point?

JM: No, I don't think we will, in the manner that you might be thinking. It's an issue that's out there. But I do think that if we took a position and presented it as a position paper, we'd be presenting it as the Church's position, which is fairly clear at the moment.

JZ: Yes, but it's clear on abortion and the other issues discussed in the forum as well, isn't it?

JM: Yes. If you're getting your information from the general press, you get the impression that it's an ongoing discussion. But if you get it from the Pope and a few of his allies, there's no discussion. And there's not likely to be. The Church does not take a position that it has to back off from sometime in the future. When it says, "No, this is all over," it's all over.

I feel sorry for the people who are persisting in thinking that we can deal with it in a democratic fashion. Of course, we Americans are steeped in the democratic position from our birth, and we begin to think that everything lends itself to that.

JZ: That raises an interesting question. America is a democracy, or at least a republic, and the Church is not a democracy. It's a spiritual hierarchy. The medium you're using to disseminate the Church's teachings, the Internet, is generally perceived as being, if not democratic, at least very antihierarchical. Do you see any tension or problem arising from that?

JM: No. I see some issues arising, but I don't think they're problems for us. This is who we are. Come in and learn about us, but don't expect to change us.

We're just about to announce the active effort of getting all of the dioceses online. As the Pope said to me when I made a presentation to him, "In the world?" And I said, "Yes, all twenty-four hundred." I think there are approximately twenty-four hundred dioceses in the world. I said, "You will be able to communicate with your bishops—all of your bishops—simultaneously."

JZ: How do you think that's going to change things?

JM: Well, it will strengthen the central organization and weaken, perhaps, the power of the national organizations. It will not weaken the power of the bishops. Most people do not appreciate the great power of the bishops. A lot of people view the Catholic Church as a dictatorship where the Pope decides every issue. That's an impossible task, which he doesn't do at all. The bishops have the power and are very influential on the statements that are part of the Magisterium. So I don't think it will weaken them at all. But it might weaken that in-between group, just as it has in industry, where it has somewhat attrited the importance and power of the middle level of management.

The Web is organized laterally rather than vertically or radially, with no central authority and no chain of command. (Individual webmasters have power over Web sites, as do sysops, or system operators, over bulletin board systems, and moderators over Usenet groups, but their influence is local and usually extremely responsive to the populations they serve.) Moreover, on the Net, at least as of this writing, freedom rules. The Internet is anarchy in action, a libertarian cyberland, and it nurtures direct (albeit virtual) contact between individuals, without hierarchical intermediaries. Stewart Dalzell, one of the judges who initially ruled on the constitutionality of the Communications Decency Act, stated, "It is no exaggeration to conclude that the Internet . . . has achieved, and continues to achieve, the most participatory marketplace of mass speech that this country—and indeed the world—has yet seen."

Because the medium influences the message, it's possible that in the long run the Internet will favor those religions and spiritual teachings that tend toward anarchy and that lack a complex hierarchy. Even now, those who log on to cyberspace may tend to gravitate to religious denominations that emphasize centrifugal rather than centripetal force, just as the medium that is carrying them does. Authority loses its trappings and force on the Net, and not only within Roman Catholicism; it remains to be seen whether the guru-student model of Hinduism, for instance, will withstand the leveling effects of the Net.

Mulholland may be underestimating the effect the Net will have on the flow of power within the Roman Catholic hierarchy. When individuals are able to communicate directly with Rome, and have their voices heard en masse, without being filtered through levels of ecclesial bureaucracy, it stands to reason that the "power" that Mulholland speaks of will settle closer to the grass roots.

It also seems likely that if women gain greater access to the Vatican's ears through e-mail and other means of digital communication, they will increase their leverage and perhaps in time achieve clerical standing. This may take many decades, even centuries, but, as stated before, the Internet is forever—or at least for as long as humanity rides the technological juggernaut. Information technologies, particularly radio and television, surely played a hand in promoting the global social changes of the past century, including the Church liberalizations wrought by Vatican II. The Roman Catholic Church is ancient, but even two thousand years don't count for much in the face of eternity. The changes the Internet and other technological developments will bring to human spiritual affairs over the next thousand years, or ten thousand years, or 1 million years, will be radical, almost beyond imagining.

Whatever eventual effect the Net has on ecclesial pathways, it's certain that today it stands unsurpassed as a networked medium between human beings. Through no other means can a multitude interact so directly among itself. Because of this ease of interaction, the Internet over time will strengthen organizations even as it stirs their internal structures. The sort of organizational communion the Net promotes is exemplified in how, through one Web site, it has facilitated the transfer of information among members of one Roman Catholic order, the Order of Saint Benedict.

> Great care and concern are to be shown in receiving poor people and pilgrims, because in them more particularly Christ is received.
>
> —*RULE OF BENEDICT* 53:15

This quotation appears under the legend "Cyberspace Pilgrims" on the welcoming page of the Order of Saint Benedict (OSB) Web site. It comes from the influential *Rule* written by Saint Benedict between A.D. 530 and 560 as a guide to the inner and outer aspects of the monastic life. The OSB Web site reflects Benedict's admonition in every particular. Though dotted with pleasing graphics, its pages rely primarily on text, for easy downloading. They are written in HTML (hypertext markup language, the standard computer formatting language for creating World Wide Web documents) in such a way that they can be viewed by any Web browser, thus allowing universal access. The site actually encourages the creation of such universally readable documents by offering information on their design in an area called "The Scriptorium," and through that name links the creating of Web documents with the ancient monastic tradition of producing illuminated manuscripts.

If the light of Saint Benedict shines brightly over the OSB site, it's because it's reflected off the particular personality of one monk, Brother Richard Oliver, the site's webmaster, a resident of Saint John's Abbey in Collegeville, Minnesota. Through his efforts, the OSB site—which sprang into existence on April 1, 1995, and is sponsored by the College of Saint Benedict and Saint John's University, also located in central Minnesota—has become one of the most appealing Catholic sites in cyberspace.

In addition to proffering much information about the order and its *Rule*, as well as about related orders (for example, the Cistercians and Trappists, and including Anglican Benedictines), the OSB site provides other services. A revealing one is the "Readers' Comments, Questions and Suggestions" arena, where Brother Richard reprints e-mail to the site, as well as his answers to that e-mail. The postings give a taste of the variety of reasons why people use the Net. Among the posted e-mail from late fall 1996 were a message from someone in the Philippines reporting that the site has inspired him (or her) to inquire about affiliation with a local abbey; requests for the e-mail addresses of various monastics; a query about whether there exists "any method to train the memory power and concentration ability"; and a plea for information for a grade-school research assignment.

Of all Net-mediated communicative tools, e-mail is the most popular by far. The majority of Americans with Internet access use the Net only for sending and receiving e-mail. What e-mail provides above all is speed of access and, if desired, range of access. The same e-mail can be sent to any number of people simultaneously. The OSB site contains a "Monastic E-mail Directory" in which scores of Benedictine monastics, including oblates—laypersons living in the world according to the spirit of Saint Benedict—list their e-mail addresses. On this list I looked for, and found, the e-mail addresses of my twin brother, Philip, and his wife, Carol, both of whom are Benedictine oblates. Unfortunately, e-mail also fosters speed of disposal. One tends to scan e-mail rather than to savor it as one does a handwritten (or even typed) letter, and its broad reach encourages the proliferation of junk e-mail.

Several of the interviews in this book, such as the interview with Tom Ray in chapter 4, were conducted by e-mail. In each case, the person interviewed chose that method, likely because responding in writing permits a fully considered response. E-mail interviews lack the give-and-take and organic unity of interviews conducted face-to-face and over the phone, however. Lost is the opportunity to ask on the spot for an amplification, or to challenge a statement.

For the following interview, I sent a list of questions to Brother Richard's e-mail address. The next day, he e-mailed me his answers.

JEFF ZALESKI: What is the purpose behind the OSB Web site? Is there what you would consider a sacred purpose, and if so, what is it?

BROTHER RICHARD: The purpose of this site is to provide information about the Order of Saint Benedict and the monastic order of folk. Pretty straightforward. My master's degree is in library science. What is the purpose of a book? I do not consider the fact of the OSB site itself especially sacred, but it treats an organization that takes the Sacred very seriously.

JZ: I was fascinated how you related the HTML and other information available in the Scriptorium to the *Rule of Benedict* 53:15. Can you please elaborate on this, and on in what ways you feel your Web site perhaps shows "great care and concern" in receiving "pilgrims"?

BR: I used to have a link at The Scriptorium that quoted *RB*'s "Your way should be different than the world's ways." My concern about writing good HTML is based on my experience with Lynx, a nongraphical browser. I use Lynx a lot from my cell, where my only connection to cyberspace is a dumb terminal and a 2400 modem. It is possible to write HTML documents that will display some form of helpful information, but few are careful or considerate enough to do so.

I suppose I am bothered by an image that came to me of a catechist in poorest Africa who saves .25 liters of gas to run a generator that powers a 286 that connects to the Internet for about half an hour. If she has to wait for graphic-intensive

pages to download, then discovers that all she gets is
[INLINE]s and [LINK]s, that's sad. I try to insure that every
image includes an <alt=""> tag so that either some information is displayed or at least the [INLINE]s are suppressed.

HTML code, when written carefully, can be converted
into audio for the blind. These are the kinds of "pilgrims"
who might find an encouraging or enlightening word at the
OSB site for whom as a Benedictine I can give at least a little
"care and concern."

JZ: What has the response been to your Web site among
members of the Benedictine order, and among the public at
large? Do you feel that you're accomplishing what you wish
to accomplish?

BR: The response from other Benedictines has been uni-
formly positive. Saint John's, the largest monastery in the
Western Church, has been graced with many gifts, material
as well as spiritual. Through Saint John's University and the
College of Saint Benedict in cooperation, we are engaged in
a multiyear, multimillion-dollar upgrade of the computer
network on both campuses. This splendid resource was there
for the using of it, so I did.

In the seventeen months of its existence the OSB site has
become the de facto source of information about Benedictine
life. This was not intended; it happened. So, in effect, I have
accomplished much more that I had hoped to accomplish,
mainly because of the number of monastics and laity who
collaborate by editing sections of the site or by sending information for inclusion. Whatever accomplishment has been
achieved is the result of collaborative effort. I look forward
not so much to any further development of the OSB site itself, but the development of individual communities' own
WWW sites. I think of the OSB site as a kind of Christmas
tree that supports the more attractive and interesting sites of
the individual monastic houses.

As for nonmonastics, the Comments, Questions and Suggestions have come mainly from them. There is a lot of trash on the Internet, and I am heartened when visitors to the site are able to find something worthwhile—either of a practical nature, like a Sister's e-mail address, or of a spiritual nature, such as a passage from the *Rule* that moves them to reflect or pray.

JZ: It was so interesting to come across the documents relating to *lectio divina*. [*Lectio divina* is a traditional way of reading, practiced not only by the Benedictines but by most Christian contemplatives, in which one absorbs written words slowly and carefully, with full attention, allowing the words to resonate in one's heart.] The Web, with its onslaught of information, and in particular with its linkages that invite—persuade?—readers to move from one link to the next, seems to encourage a sort of rapid, nondiscriminatory intake of information that is the very opposite of what's intended in *lectio divina*. Will you please comment on this?

BR: Benedictines are so lucky that our Founder decided that when we weren't eating, sleeping, or working, we should be reading! I think monastic life attracts the kind of person who can stick to a good book from beginning to end. In our refectory, we have read some books that have taken months if not a year to get through. Monasteries, of course, have their share of people who would rather listen or view, but, in general, I would say monastics are a literate bunch of humans.

Liz Knuth has done a great job of assembling in the Lectio Divina section a fine collection of really solid spiritual works that lend themselves to the kind of slow, ruminative, meditative reading of them that Benedict seems to intend in the *Rule*. I find it not impossible to read great chunks of interesting or well-written material on the Internet without feeling a compulsion to click and move on. But then, I am a librarian. Our national test scores prove that the art of reading with comprehension, let alone enjoyment, is not what it used to be. I would hope that the Internet would continue to provide something for everyone.

JZ: How do you feel that your Web activities have helped— or hindered—you in your own spiritual life?

BR: Definitely hindered in some respects. I have always been a night owl, but it is so easy to let time pass when it is very quiet, and one can concentrate on writing good HTML. Saint John's is a very active monastery, and always has been. Still, I sometimes must make an effort to walk away from my computer to join my brothers at prayer and community functions. On the other hand, I have lucked out by finding a kind of employment that does lend itself to the interruptions of a monastic schedule, and has been very rewarding and satisfying personally in that I have found a use for my some- what unfocused, general liberal-arts education.

JZ: There's a lot of talk around about the Net, particularly the Web, being a force that is helping humanity to bind to- gether. As you may know, a number of high-profile cyber commentators, especially in the *Wired* magazine crowd, have talked about the Net in the sort of evolutionary terms that Teilhard de Chardin wrote about: as a major step to- ward global consciousness. A Lubavitch—ultra-Orthodox— rabbi I interviewed lately postulated that the Web was a holy tool, intended by God to help unite humanity. What do you think about this?

BR: I have read as much of this kind of rhetoric as I could stand. Where is the evidence of it? One can find the most an- tithetical and virulently opposed camps represented on the Internet. I see absolutely no evidence of the kind of "conver- gence" Teilhard imagined.

JZ: One question I'm looking at in my book is just what sort of spiritual activities cyberspace lends itself to. Clearly, there is a form of interpersonal communion that goes on. But I do wonder: (a) how you personally conceive of cyberspace;

BR: A bunch of electrons temporarily congealed into meaning.

JZ: (b) whether it is possible to feel the presence of God in cyberspace. I'm curious if you ever have, and, if so, what the circumstances were. Does God manifest Himself in cyberspace?

BR: Not yet to me, thank God.

JZ: Along these lines, I've noted that while every established religion has posts in cyberspace, none has so far tried to extend any of the sacraments online. I wonder (c) whether you think that the Roman Catholic Church will ever offer sacraments online. Say, Confession, which would seem to be the easiest technically, as it could take place in a virtual manner in, say, a live chat room. Will there ever be a Mass conducted online? This may be a question of Presence. (FYI, I've read, but I can't remember where, that there was some debate after the invention of the telescope whether one could be said to have attended Mass if one viewed it from miles away through a telescope. Of course, there's a world of difference, perhaps literally, between viewing a Mass while in one's body, even from afar, and attending a "virtual Mass.") What are your thoughts about this?

BR: I await with horror the day Mother A. or another will focus a camera on the Reserved Sacrament and make it available at a WWW site so people can have "Jesus" with them on their desks at work. I prefer my sacraments live, please, in the flesh, as Jesus Himself seemed to prefer them to a life apart from the blood, sweat, and tears of humanity.

JZ: I was intrigued to see that one of your links is to Partenia. What do you think of Bishop Gaillot and his Web activities?

BR: What little content there is there, I do not find especially interesting or captivating. It takes all kinds of threads to make a good Net.

Roman Catholic sites thread the Net in a lush embroidery. The basic fabric of the Net, though—the majority of all religious sites online—is Protestant. The three most populous Protestant denominations in America—in order, Baptist, Methodist, and Lutheran—host the most Web sites, in like order. Behind them are arrayed the virtual counterparts to just about every non-Catholic Christian denomination, including Presbyterian, Seventh-Day Adventist, Unitarian, Episcopalian, Mormon, Branch Davidian, Calvinist, Christian Scientist, Society of Friends, Jehovah's Witnesses, Plymouth Brethren, and many more. Only two influential Christian denominations seem to shun cyberspace: the Amish, because they eschew the use of electricity as an unwanted connection to the world, and the Shakers (a handful of whom linger on in Sabbathday Lake, Maine), who, of all Christian groups, would benefit most from the Net, as they are celibate and gain new members only through conversion. (The Net hosts many sites about the Amish and the Shakers, but these are sponsored by non-Amish and non-Shaker groups or individuals.)

One of the longest and most colorful threads of Protestantism online unspools from the group known as the Church of Christ. This denomination dates from the turn of the nineteenth century, when preachers from Methodist Episcopal, Baptist, and Presbyterian congregations in Maryland, New England, Kentucky, and West Virginia broke away from their traditional practices to embrace what they envisioned as a purer Christianity based strictly on New Testament practices and edicts. Today, about fifteen thousand individual Church of Christ churches spot the globe, most of them in the United States, boasting a total membership of perhaps 2 million.

Each Church of Christ church stands autonomous. No person heads, and no governing body rules, this evangelical movement, although Church of Christ churches cooperate in charitable and missionary work. To a remarkable degree, the anarchic yet cooperative structure of the Church of Christ thus mirrors the structure of the Web itself, where independent sites link cooperatively. Perhaps this is why so many faithful of the Church of Christ have seized upon the Web to cast their message around the world.

One of the several hundred Church of Christ sites on the World Wide Web is ChristianWeb. In addition to presenting its own information about the history, beliefs, and practices of the Church of Christ, ChristianWeb, which presents its homepage against an electric-blue backdrop, serves as a depot for other Church of Christ sites. Noting the generosity of its offerings and links, I decided to learn more about the site. Like most other spiritual sites on the Web, ChristianWeb includes a field on which to e-mail its webmaster. And like the webmasters on so many of these sites, ChristianWeb's webmaster maintains an anonymous presence on his pages, where he is known only by his title. As I learned from his e-mailed response, the man behind ChristianWeb is Nick Ragan, who, after a brief flurry of e-mail, consented to an e-mail interview.

> JEFF ZALESKI: What is your background? How did you come to be involved in the Church of Christ, in computers and online activities, and, finally, in online activities for the Church of Christ?

> NICK RAGAN: I am thirty-four years old. Though my real name is Nimit Ragan, I usually go by Nick. I am originally from Bangkok but grew up in Singapore, where I spent all my junior and high school years. I had been a Buddhist all my life but was converted while I went to college at Texas A&M University. I attended the curriculum in biblical studies at the Bangkok Church of Christ school of preaching and graduated in 1986.

I am now living with my family in South Bend, Indiana. Currently I am an independent computer consultant.

JZ: What is the (brief) history of the online activities of the Church of Christ? Of ChristianWeb?

NR: In 1995 I began this ministry with the goal of reaching out to people in the Internet community, to provide the basic information about the church and its biblical teachings. The main goal is simply to generate interest in visitors who may want to know more about the church, to provide counseling to those who may be intimidated and feel uncomfortable in the real-life church surroundings, to make friends, and to invite visitors to visit a local congregation near where they live.

The site that I maintain is never meant to be a site devoted to theological discussions, nor is it meant to represent the official Church of Christ view on any doctrines. It is an attempt to plainly and simply explain to people what the church is all about, and hopefully to generate enough interest in visitors that maybe they'll visit our local members and give us a chance to answer all other questions in person.

Since then there have been several congregations of the Church of Christ who are maintaining their congregational Web site as well. Several church members have also engaged in other Internet ministries such as Bible correspondence courses, family counseling, etc., so the site has been adding links to these other sites and by doing so has evolved to become somewhat of a central link to many of the Church of Christ sites on the Internet.

In 1996, several members of the church got together and formed an online user group of church members interested in serving in this Internet ministry. The group is known as Church of Christ On Line Ministry (OLM for short).

JZ: How many people have come into the Church of Christ through the ChristianWeb sites? Do you have a story to tell of one or more such people?

NR: Yes, we get stories periodically from church members. Here is an example of a note we recently received from a brother in Alabama about a baptism in Australia:

"I'm John [name changed, as are the other names in "John's" story]. Thank you for your interest in Jane, the student who was recently baptized. Actually, I met Jane on IRC. I was sending lessons to a college student from Russia that I had met on the Church of Christ chat channel. He told Jane about the lessons and she asked to "meet" me. He introduced us and I offered to send her the lessons. She was very interested in meeting Christians like those in the New Testament. She started the lessons, but very slowly. We began trading e-mail and visiting on IRC. When questions about baptism came up, Bill sent me the texts he has on that subject, and after reading them she said she wanted to be baptized.

"I asked Bill to help us find some Christians close to her, and he did. I think he also had some of his deaf members there write to her. (She is also deaf.) Once she had names, then other objections started arising. We just kept talking, and she did a few more lessons. Then after I had been out of town for a week I came home and found she had contacted the people Bill had found for her, and was baptized! It was very exciting especially since we have talked so much and she is a friend even though we've never met."

This is a classic example of the proselytizing power of cyberspace. The initial contacts between "John" and "Jane" took place in digital reality—on IRC and via e-mail. Jane didn't meet a Church of Christ member in the flesh until after deciding to be baptized. The networking was global. A college student in Russia contacted Jane, who lives in Australia; the story was told by a man in Alabama to Ragan, who lives in Indiana. It's notable as well that Jane is deaf, a trait that proves little impediment in cyberspace.

JZ: How many hits do you get a week, a month?

NR: Not sure, but last monitored it was approximately 150 hits a day. Other OLM sites may also report similar hits.

The figure of 150 hits received daily by ChristianWeb seems about average for a religious Web site. That number may not appear large, especially compared with the 30,000 a week logged by Chabad Lubavitch in Cyberspace, but over a year it translates into more than 50,000 hits, which adds up to a lot of information going out from just one Church of Christ site.

JZ: How is it decided what will be put on ChristianWeb? Who decides?

NR: Me.

JZ: In an e-mail to me, you mentioned the Cyberspace Church of Christ site. Is this the same as ChristianWeb? I'm confused on this point.

NR: ChristianWeb is presented as a nondenominational presentation. It is meant to draw all Christians and non-Christians alike. Cyberspace Church of Christ site, however, tends to be more explicit about the Church of Christ and to present the church as the New Testament Church to visitors. Many people who visit this particular site are church members who use it as a resource.

In fact, Cyberspace Church of Christ is hosted by the ChristianWeb site (its address is *http://www.christianweb.com/cyber space*) and duplicates much of the information contained on ChristianWeb. Both ChristianWeb and Cyberspace Church of Christ present information about the Church of Christ, including essays about the history, practices, and beliefs of the denomination, and both feature numerous links to other Church of Christ sites, some of which are identified as such, some not. Both sites link to the online magazine *Christian Computing*, which serves up news and articles on such subjects as Microsoft's discounting policy for church groups, biblical software, tips on installing various Windows applications, and reviews of software products. ChristianWeb links to *Christian Computing* through a host site called gospelcom.net, however, whereas Cyberspace Church of Christ links to it through a host site called website.net. The editor of *Christian Computing* is none other than Nick Ragan, who clearly delights in weaving his own tight but very tangled web.

JZ: On a more philosophical note: In what way do you feel that your Web activities are complementing real-life activities of the Church of Christ? How may they be supplanting them in some ways?

NR: Internet ministries are never meant to be a replacement for real church. It is impossible for anyone to develop a personal relationship with God without being around His people, His church. These Internet works are nothing more than something to draw in people who may otherwise not want to know anything about Jesus or not want to visit a church for fear of the unknown. For some reason, people find it less intimidating if they can sit at home in the privacy of their own room asking questions about the church and Bible and God that they have always wanted to ask but never quite feel comfortable enough in the real church to do so.

JZ: I note as well that there are certain functions—baptism, the partaking of the Lord's Supper—that are not offered in any form on the Web. Do you think that sometime in the future, perhaps the far future, these can be offered in a virtual form?

NR: No. Again, Internet ministry is *not* a substitute for the real relationship that must be developed between Jesus and his family, or between church family members.

JZ: Do you think cyberspace itself can be sacred space? Why or why not?

NR: No, there is nothing "sacred" about space or cyber-space. Just another tool, another medium through which we can spread the good news about Jesus Christ.

Ragan copied our e-mail interview to the rest of the Church of Christ On Line Ministry, inviting supplements to his answers. Ten days after that copying, I received e-mail from Michael S. Cole, M.D., the webmaster of a Church of Christ church in Arkansas. Here is the partial text of that e-mail, which takes up the question of what constitutes an "official" site for any religion:

> Since December 1995, I have served as the Webmaster, as well as the original designer, for the Web site of the West-Ark Church of Christ in Fort Smith, Arkansas. Churches of Christ are unique in the religious world in that we have no earthly headquarters or leadership which controls more than a single congregation. The various congregations are loosely united by our common doctrine, which we believe is an independent, simple interpretation of the Scriptures.
>
> There is no Web site which any of the Churches of Christ consider to be an official Homepage for the church. Around 300 different congregations have their own sites on the World Wide Web. These sites are as different as they are similar. Most have been "authorized" to be placed on the Web by the leadership in the individual congregation being represented. Some are merely the creation of a single individual who has put together what he considers to be appropriate. (I don't know of any created and maintained by women, but this is possible.) Nick Ragan's site is an example of a site that is maintained independent of any particular congregation. No particular Church of Christ Web site can be taken as representative of all the Churches of Christ. The Web site I maintain, however, can be viewed as representative of the beliefs and practices of the congregation which meets at the location we call West-Ark.
>
> To really see my own philosophy of how a church Web site should be constructed, please feel free to explore URL: *http://church-of-christ.org/west-ark.*

As Cole indicates, in cyberspace the word transmits from numerous sources, in many ways. The more secular among us may thank the fecundity of the human imagination for this blizzard of communications. Others may want to nod toward the Archangel Gabriel, who (according to Charles Panati's book *Sacred Origins of Profound Things*) was always known as God's messenger and who in 1951 was declared by Pope Pius XII as the patron saint of telecommunications—and thus of cyberspace.

The homepage of Catholic Information Center on Internet is located at *http://www.catholic.net*.

The homepage of the Order of Saint Benedict is located at *http://www.csbsju.edu/osb*.

The homepage of ChristianWeb is located at *http://www.christianweb.com*.

KEY SITES

The Holy See Vatican Web Site (*http://www.vatican.va*)

The original Vatican Web site went online on Christmas Day 1995. Within two weeks, more than 1 million people had logged on, two hundred thousand in the first twenty-four hours. The biggest draw was no doubt not the site's visuals, which were rudimentary, nor its papal messages, but the chance to e-mail the Pope. By summer 1996 the site had shut down in preparation for a new site that would include a "complete database of the documents of the Church." The remodeled home for the Vatican in cyberspace promised to be stunning, as it was to be designed by the monks of New Mexico's Monastery of Christ in the Desert, renowned for the superb quality of their HTML work, displayed on their own site at *http://www.christdesert.org*.

On Easter Day 1997, the Vatican opened its new site to the public. It is a masterpiece of Web art. Presented as a virtual index folder comprised of sheets of parchment, these pages employ rich tones of brown and gold, as well as simple icons drawn from images of classic art, to convey a powerful sense of authority, dignity, and restraint. Available in German, Spanish, English, French, Italian, and Portuguese, the site divides its holdings into six areas: "The Holy Father," "The Roman Curia," "News Services," "The Vatican Museums," "Jubilee 2000," and "Archive." Each area is in-progress, but when all are complete they will together offer the intended extraordinary database of documents.

The Holy See Web site is wonderful—but it also commits what, in cyberspace, must be considered two cardinal sins. It offers no links to other sites, and so gives lie to the terms *Internet* and *Web*. (It is not alone in this transgression, of course. Both the Threshold Society Web site discussed in chapter 3 and the Mormon Web site discussed below also fail to link to other sites.) The Vatican's site also uses the Net strictly as a broadcast medium. The e-mail facility provided on the original Vatican Web site has been removed from the new site, and no other form of interactivity—of turning an eye or an ear toward those who log on—is offered. This is cyber religion as if from a mountain-top enclave, and it does not bode well for the future of the Roman Catholic Church online. (Again, others commit the same philosophical and strategic error. The Mormon site discussed below also fails to understand that the Internet is not a fancy form of television.)

The Church of Jesus Christ of Latter-Day Saints (*http://www.lds.org*)

The official Web site of the Mormon Church is as clean-cut as most of the religion's adherents, as impeccably groomed as the streets of its geospiritual center, Salt Lake City. Crisp rectangular and square images, icons, and legends fill this site; no circles, ovals, or fuzzy lines mar its pin-neat pages. The homepage features a painting of a muscular, broad-shouldered Jesus sporting Fabio-like locks and a trim beard, as well as an invitation to call (not e-mail) for a free copy of the Book of Mormon. Other pages offer "a selection of official Church policy statements on selected issues" and a "Global Media Guide" that presents articulate information about church finances and history, the Tabernacle Choir, the church's missionary activities, and so on. This site is so user-friendly it makes you want to pet your mouse, but it suffers from the two errors made by the Holy See Web site: It is entirely self-contained and invites no response from visitors. This is what the Web would be like if each strand were torn from the other. It's not a happy sight.

The Catacombs: A Christian Community
(*http://www.mindspring.com/~tentmaker/pphp/landlord.html*)

The Catacombs, in contrast to the Latter-Day Saints site, offer a true web, a variety of voices and links. "This is a community for Christians who share the same faith in God and His Son, Jesus Christ," reads the welcoming page of this digital meetinghouse maintained by "landlord" Margaret Carlock. The Catacombs contains within its virtual chambers dozens of homepages of "members of the Body of Christ"—individuals as well as organizations. Among the members are the First Baptist Church of Pleasanton, California; Mal Stewman, who styles himself the "Mighty Morphin' Man of God"; the Alliance Bible Seminary, based in Hong Kong; a "teenage Christian"; and an illustrator who is "addicted to Jesus." Further links connect to the words and images of scores of Christians who reside outside the Catacombs, to a church locator with more than three thousand churches in its database, and to other Christian resources. This excellent site exemplifies what the Christian Internet, at its best, is all about.

First Church of Cyberspace
(http://www.execpc.com/~chender)

"Let There Be Light!" proclaims the opening page of this cheerful, techno-savvy site that claims to house the first religious group "to organize within cyberspace itself: making connections, constructing links, dropping clues that point to the presence of the Creator within the creative chaos of the Internet." The site reflects that chaos through an exuberant but scattered mix of text, images, icons, links, and reviews. The man behind the happy mayhem is the Reverend Charles Henderson, a Presbyterian minister. On the site, which was founded by the Central Presbyterian Church of Montclair, New Jersey, he offers such electronic amenities as RealAudio and Java applets. Webnauts with advanced browser capabilities will benefit the most from these pages, which have won numerous Net awards.

The Prayer Page
(http://www.nb.net/~snoopy)

The ability of the Internet to promote heart-to-heart communication glows on this wonderful site, one of several on the Web that allow visitors to post requests for prayers. The Prayer Page, which has a sponsor identified only as Mike, is an exceedingly well-organized online arena played out against a blue sky scudded with puffy white clouds. Mike groups the prayer requests he receives each month according to subject ("Finances," "Physical Healing," "Blessed Repose," etc.). Among some of the requests posted in late 1996 under the category "Inner Healing" are one from "Steve" for others to pray that his wife return to him; a request by "Lisa and Steve" that others pray that their adopted children "awaken to the way of the Lord"; and a plea by "Unknown" that people pray for his wife and him to "get over the death of our child and her two pets." The site links to a few other Christian support resources.

Christian Spotlight on the Movies
(*http://www.christiananswers.net/reviews/reviews.html*)

At its best, the Net promotes interactivity among many participants. This information-intensive site, sponsored by Eden Communications, a "worldwide, evangelical media ministry," publishes reviews of scores of recent and classic films that give each movie's "Christian Rating" and grade its "Moviemaking Quality" on a scale from one to five, with no necessary correlation between the two. Thus, *The Island of Dr. Moreau* receives only a "1" on the Christian Rating scale but a "4" on the Moviemaking Quality scale. The reviews, always lively and often eccentric, provide a detailed synopsis of each film, as well as a discussion that may center around the film's moral tenor. In *Braveheart*, we're told, "homosexuality is strongly implied. Nudity is briefly shown, as is adultry [*sic*]. The 'F' word is used twice (however, the Scottish brogue is very thick and it is missed by most people)." *Waterworld,* meanwhile, presents "a blatant acceptance of the *theory* of Evolution." The interactivity is made possible by software that allows visitors to post their own follow-up reviews, which often veer from the originals. An enjoyable and useful if extremely conservative Christian and family resource, Christian Spotlight on the Movies helps to make the Internet the human exchange it is.

Brethren/Mennonite Council for Lesbian and Gay Concerns
(*http://www.webcom.com/bmc/welcome.html*)

As this plain and simple Web site shows, just about every conceivable religious grouping, no matter how focused, seems to find its way to the Internet. That Mennonites are on the Web will surprise only those who confuse them with their techno-resistant cousins, the Amish; in fact, Mennonites have a powerful Internet presence, with scores of Web sites, mailing lists, and discussion groups. What is surprising, perhaps, is that this intensely traditional religious denomination includes an organization dedicated to the spiritual rights of gays. The site links to supportive congregations, a newsletter, and other resources.

Bible Shareware Collection—Games, Studies, Tools (*http://www.pc-shareware.com/religion.htm*)

Batter up! It's the Sadducees versus the Pharisees. To hit a double, you must correctly answer this multiple-choice question: "Whose food consisted of locusts and wild honey?" If you pick "John the Baptist," you're on second base and on your way to winning another round of the slightly gooney and definitely cheesy *Bible Baseball for Windows,* one of many Christian shareware or freeware programs (the former ask for a small fee to be paid voluntarily to the creator; the latter are entirely free) available for downloading on this generous site sponsored by Softword Technology. Other programs among the many available are *Bible Concentration,* a King James dictionary, and *Bible Botany,* "an exhaustive online index of plants of the Bible, from Algum to Wormwood."

alt.religion.christian/soc.religion.christian

Usenet discussion groups are classified according to "hierarchies" such as alt., rec., soc., and talk. The groups in alt. tend to be free-wheeling, anything-goes affairs, and are generally not moderated, whereas those in soc. often are moderated, with inappropriate (generally, offensive or commercial) postings refused or expelled. Alt.religion.christian and soc.religion.christian reflect the standards of their respective hierarchies. A recent typical day's postings in alt.religion.christian included a plea for "$ to fight abortion," a sale of "angel prints," some obscene comments about the death of the astronomer Carl Sagan, a diatribe against Freemasonry, and a rant about the Pope as the Antichrist. By contrast, on the same day, soc.religion.christian, which is moderated by an elder in the Presbyterian Church, contained postings on such subjects as why the Virgin Mary doesn't smile in most depictions of her, notes on Christian-Muslim dialogue, and commentary on tithing, exorcism, and the Magi.

Christian Chat
(http://pages.wbs.net/webchat3.so?cmd=cmd_doorway :Christian_Chat)

One of the liveliest chat rooms devoted to Christian talk is sponsored by the WebChat Broadcasting System (which also sponsors Muslim Chat; please see chapter 3). The conversation here tends to be more sincere and friendly than on many IRC channels, with people sometimes engaging in searching debate about faith, and sometimes just kidding around.

CHAPTER 6

Virtual Reality

An Annotated Conversation
with Jaron Lanier, Part 1

What is transubstantiation, if not virtual reality?
—JARON LANIER

If Gene Kelly were in this rain, I bet he wouldn't be singin'. It's sheeting down, soaking my trousers despite my umbrella, sweeping soda cans, cigarette butts, scraps of newspaper along the sidewalk, darkening the buildings on this block in Manhattan's fashionable downtown area of Tribeca into a muddy smudge. As I walk, I keep a wary eye on the street. It's filled with puddles, and if a car speeds through one just so, I'll be in for a splashing.

It's the sort of gloomy day that makes me yearn for a bit of virtual reality, where the rain won't get me wet no matter how hard it comes down. It's appropriate, then, that I'm on my way to visit Jaron Lanier to talk about VR, particularly as it bears on our understanding of consciousness. Lanier is one of the great seers of cyberspace. A visiting scholar at both the Department of Computer Science at Columbia University and the Interactive Telecommunications Program, Tisch School of the Arts, New York University, Lanier, who's in his mid-thirties, achieved global renown in the late 1980s for his coinvention of fundamental VR components like interface gloves and VR networking, for his coining of the term *virtual reality,* and, above all, for his energetic promotion not only of VR but also of himself. His penchant for self-promotion is a blessing, for Lanier, as I know from scanning his Web pages, has an expansive mind whose insights into digital reality are original, vital, and oriented toward what really matters.

At last I reach the building where Lanier lives in a loft perched high above the street. Opening his door, he peers at me through blue eyes so bright they shock. Suddenly he smiles as if I'm the best thing that's happened to him all week. He invites me in with a voice that, high-pitched and soft as mink, seems to belong to a smaller man than this heavyset, red-bearded imp clad in an overshirt and white baggy pants. He takes my coat and umbrella, laughs as they drip water on his floor, and leads me to a black velour sofa. Lanier settles nearby, half-reclining into a matching armchair that might be a La-Z-Boy.

I look around. Exotic stringed musical instruments are pinned like butterflies to the walls of the loft. Except to brush his dreadlocks off his forehead, Lanier moves little as we speak, but his eyes scan constantly, sometimes settling on those instruments as he searches for the right word, the precise phrase. He is an accomplished musician who has performed with Philip Glass, Ornette Coleman, and Terry Riley, and he talks as if exploring a jazz riff, emitting a swirl of words, boosted by firm opinions, that soar from his theme into startling places before returning home. His energy seems irrepressible, erupting into gales of laughter and giggles that give our talk a happy, dizzy feel.

JEFF ZALESKI: What do you think of what you see on the Web? How do you think it affects people?

JARON LANIER: The Web has gotten to be quite a big place. It's an ocean. And that's very much the point of it. For me, the foremost thing about the experience of the Web is that it's the first time in history we've had a working anarchy. I think

most of us went through some idealistic phase when we
thought maybe anarchy would be possible. Then when you
searched for evidence that it might be possible, you'd end up
looking at a five-minute period in 1936 Barcelona. But it
turns out that the human spirit is capable of this kind of remarkable cooperative behavior if we remove ourselves from
the constraints of divvying up limited physical resources.

If you look at how the Web happened, it was something
that was unplanned, lacked authority figures, lacked
celebrity figures, lacked public relations, lacked money.
None of the traditional structures for motivation—neither
hierarchy nor finance nor need, for that matter—were there.
The Web wasn't something that was needed, it was something that was wanted. Here you have millions of people cooperating to create this vast thing because they want it.
That's new. That's a new piece of evidence about the capability of the human spirit.

In 1993, the year the Web browser Mosaic was released, the
Web proliferated at a 341,634 percent annual growth rate of service traffic, according to the classic time line of Internet history,
Hobbes's Internet Timeline (*http://www.handshake.de/infobase
/netze/internet/hit.htm*).

JZ: What about your experience of surfing the Web? My own
is that it's difficult to keep my attention for long on any one
site. I always want to go on to the next site.

JL: That's what I call the *erotic* quality of the Web. That
whatever you're looking at right now might not be that interesting, but there's always this draw that if you remove the
next veil, there might be something that you need to see.
That's the energy source that propels the Web.

JZ: Do you think the fluidity of the mind can be experienced
on the Web?

JL: Not yet. A little bit. If you compare what's happening with information technology to previous revelations—I was going to say *revolution,* I think *revelation* is a better word—in the history of human culture, this one has a different character. What we're used to is a culture based on ideas and human practices, and that can change very quickly. So when Saint Augustine publishes a work that expresses the ego for the first time, suddenly the ego is just there and all of a sudden everyone has one. We're used to these sudden changes.

This is different. Instead of being an expression of a new idea or a new paradigm, this is a step-by-step construction process. This is a slow-release revelation. I think it spans over many generations. I find it necessary to think in terms of centuries into the future. There's a lot of talk about instant cultural change because of the Internet, and there are some aspects of cultural change that are instant, but I think the important ones will be much slower to come. Just because we happen to have one aspect of technology, which is the computer technology, that happens to improve at exponential rates, that doesn't mean that everything else moves that quickly.

You're starting to see in children a way of using computers in which they are creating an objective version of the contents of their imagination in a rather quick turnaround and at an earlier age than people have ever experienced—and especially as a mass culture. You see it especially in kids that create these multiple-user dungeons, the MUDs and the MOOs. And you see it on Web pages, when people create this little fantasy life on the Web. What I see happening eventually is a new culture emerging in which children, as they grow up, just naturally assume that whatever goes on inside their heads is turned into an objective reality in a huge, oceanlike, simulated world that's shared with everyone else.

This notion of an inversion of imagination, turning it objective and having this vast shared dream existing and supported by information technology—that's where the real cultural revolution is. The reason I'm convinced that people are excited about the Internet even when a lot of the stuff on it is rather dull is because they can sense this aspect of it.

JZ: That sounds very similar to your ideas about virtual reality.

JL: Sure.

Virtual reality, like cyberspace, attracts many definitions. Most commonly, the term refers to a computer-generated artificial environment that is relayed to (or, depending upon your point of view, generated within) the recipient by means of interfaces such as head-mounted displays, which present trackable, three-dimensional images and stereo sound. In turn, feedback into the virtual world is provided by interfaces like the data glove, which detects hand motions and allows you to manipulate virtual objects—for example, to point a gun at a rampaging pterodactyl in the popular VR game *Dactyl Nightmare*. In time, human participation in VR environments probably will take place through direct neural stimulation, through a direct interfacing between the human brain and a computer, perhaps of the sort imagined by William Gibson in *Neuromancer,* where cybernauts "jack in" their nervous systems to the "Matrix," the global communications infrastructure. According to the August 1996 issue of *Wired,* Peter Fromherz, the director of Germany's Max Planck Institute for Biochemistry, has succeeded in stimulating leech neurons with transistors—an important first step toward this goal.

Also like cyberspace, virtual reality is young. It dates only to the early and mid-1960s and the computer scientist Ivan Sutherland's development first of Sketchpad, the first interactive graphical computer interface, and then, three years later, in 1965, of the first head-mounted display. Lanier entered the VR field in the early 1980s. He quickly drew attention for his idea of creating a visual, as opposed to an alphanumeric, programming language that would be accessible to computer novices. Called Mandala, it was featured in mock-up form on the cover of *Scientific American* in 1984. Lanier went on to design further VR software and hardware, but his most important contribution to the digital world lies in his bringing, as a trained scientist, through his speeches, writings, and presence, a deep humanity to a field too easily swayed by scientism.

JZ: Let's look at this idea of human beings as information processors. There's this idea that what goes on in our heads is simply a form of computation. This idea sits parallel to the idea that eventually artificial intelligence will evince consciousness. I gather that you have a problem with both of these ideas. Why?

JL: There are two fundamental ways to think about what a computer is. And it's not a question of which is true or not, because this is all a fantasy.

Computers don't exist, to put it bluntly. Computers are just a bundle of matter, and they act as computers by virtue of cultural ability to recognize them acting as computers. So we can make of them what we will. And the various interpretations are just as valid as different interpretations of symbols if we were making up a new language. It's up to us to decide what the word *apple* means, and in the same way it's up to us to decide what a computer is.

We have a choice here. One way to think about a computer is that it's a conduit between people. It's a communication technology in which people can create miniature worlds that are models of things inside themselves in order to have a new form of communication in which they make up a shared objective reality in simulation instead of passing symbols between each other exclusively. Which is what we've done with language. I think that's the right way to think about computers, and I believe that in every case in which computers act effectively, even on the most practical level, that ultimately is what is happening.

Another way to think about computers is to think of them as being other entities that are like people. Now, the problem with that cuts very deep. The real issue here is whether you notice the magic of life or not. The experience of life happens to be a very mysterious, magical thing. And the most magical thing about it is that we experience it at all. There's no need for experience to exist. We can have exactly the same universe with all the atoms in exactly the same position and all the same things happening, precisely the same history, precisely the same future, and no experience. And who would care? Why would that be any different? So the existence of experience is a profoundly mysterious, odd little bonus, like a little Cracker Jack prize in reality.

The fact that experience is here makes day-to-day life into a profound mystery. It means that we don't have the methods to fully understand what's going on. The methods that we have for understanding the universe involve empiricism, and the use of logic—both things I love and respect greatly and am utterly devoted to, and yet they're clearly not complete. So I think if you fail to notice experience, if you decide to ignore it . . .

JZ: I can't believe that people like Dennett don't notice their experience.

"Dennett" is Daniel Dennett, a professor of philosophy at Tufts University and a leading proponent of the theory that mind arises from brain. He is a favorite target of Lanier's ("Only a zombie like Dennett could write a book called *Consciousness Explained* that doesn't address consciousness at all," crows Lanier on his Web site). In *Consciousness Explained*, Dennett posits that what we generally acknowledge as consciousness actually consists of "multiple drafts of conscious-

ness," all arising from the brain's distributed network of unconscious neural circuits. This understanding of consciousness is
similar to the "society of mind" approach to consciousness,
mentioned later by Lanier and touched upon earlier by John
Perry Barlow, that has been promulgated by the MIT computer
scientist Marvin Minsky.

Empiricism is, in its broadest definition, the philosophical
doctrine that all knowledge derives from experience. Within the
Western scientific tradition, empiricism usually refers to the der-
ivation of knowledge from measurable observation. Empiricism
and logic, which is the systematic study of valid inference, com-
bine in the scientific method.

JL: Oh, it's true. People like Dan Dennett either simply are
missing it, or, as I suspect strongly, although he'd never
admit it, he has a psychological motivation to pretend not to
have it in order to annoy other people. I've tried to corner
him on it. He keeps on insisting he doesn't have it—or it's
just that he does have it but it's not really there, which is the
same thing. But anyway, we can't worry too much about
Dan Dennett, because that's just what he wants us to do. It's
a smart-aleck thing. It's like some kid telling you, "Oh, you
have some goober on your lip," and you look for it. "No,
no, it's really there."

On a deeper level, it's a new form of death-denial culture.
The old style of death denial was that you did notice experience and you said, "If I experience, therefore that's all the
evidence I need to believe in this host of other things. That
means there's an afterlife, that means that the afterlife has a
specific heaven, and that heaven is this form and that form
and these people get into heaven and these people don't."
And of course you know no such thing. The mere experience
of existence doesn't say at all what happens after death. It
simply is a mystery.

There are consequences to believing that computers are people. This belief has a percolating effect. First of all, you design poor computer products. If you believe that computers are smart, it's effectively the same thing as making yourself stupid. Furthermore, it creates this nerdy, weird, bland culture. That is the aspect that concerns me the most, because I think beauty is fundamental. Right now, probably the biggest problem in computer culture is that on the whole it has not been beautiful. It's been bland, one of the most bland cultural changes in history. I mean, it's on the level with Bolshevism or something in terms of ugliness.

JZ: Let's return to VR for a moment. From what I understand about your ideas about VR, you posit two factors: sensorial input, this virtual reality coming into the body, and then the mind. It seems to me that you leave out the internal sense of the body of the person who is experiencing VR— say, the internal energies of the body as experienced in meditation. This relates to the issue of *prana,* whether it can be transmitted or re-created digitally.

JL: Do you remember when I said a while ago—that computers don't exist? That they're like symbols of a language, that we make up the meaning of them? The same is true for virtual-reality equipment and for the experiences. It's a thing that exists only within a certain cultural context. If you drop a virtual-reality system from a helicopter into some tribe somewhere, it would mean nothing, though you might be able to make boomerangs out of the goggles. It wouldn't have that context.

I conceive of and understand virtual reality specifically within the Western framework, and I talk about it using the framework of Western ideas. I live in a larger framework, especially musically. I don't particularly extend virtual reality into that framework because I'm not sure it's meaningful in the larger framework. I think of virtual reality as a Western idea, I make sense of it within the Western framework. I feel very comfortable with that. I think that the quest for the universal cultural framework that can contain everything is futile. So I don't feel a need to try to explain *prana* in virtual reality. I use a different set of categories to explain virtual reality that don't include *prana*. In my life, I certainly think in the larger framework that does include it.

This becomes a problem of empiricism once again. It's very important to remember that we can never know everything about nature. That the way science works—this was Karl Popper's clarifying insight—is through ever-better falsifiable theories, and they get better because previous ones have been falsified. So it's a tentative construction. And since we're part of nature, we can really never know everything about ourselves. So if you talk about building a perfect virtual-reality machine that can utterly represent another person's body, it's by definition an impossible task because we don't have the epistemological tools, we don't have the empirical abilities, to know if we've ever gone the whole distance. There's always going to be room left over, no matter how good the technology gets, for some aspect that we haven't gotten to.

The scientific method posits that knowledge may be gained by defining a problem, collecting data pertinent to the problem, creating a hypothesis, or plausible answer to the problem, and testing the hypothesis through experiment. This method relies upon inductive reasoning, in which a supposed fact (the hypothesis) is proved true if repeated observations confirm it. Sir Karl Popper (1902–1994) rejected this method of reasoning in the empirical sciences, insisting that any hypothesis or theory can be considered scientific only if one supposes that it is false and can in fact attempt in a practical way to show it false. This proving a theory false necessarily leads to new knowledge, and Popper held that science advances through the progressive falsification of theories.

JZ: That's why? Not because there's something that can't be captured?

JL: What I'm saying is that within the Western framework, there's that gap between what we can pose as a falsifiable question and what we don't know that we haven't posed yet. In that gap is the room where *prana* can exist. From a Western mind perspective, I'm too well schooled to get caught in the trap of dualism and to say that there's an alternate level of reality that has the *prana* in it. That would be the equivalent of saying, "Well, that's just another empirical universe that we can eventually develop sensors for." So my Western mind is utterly unimpressed with such things.

Now, as I say, I can think in another framework. From a Buddhist perspective I would say something utterly different.

JZ: Please do.

JL: From a Buddhist perspective, I would say that the thing that's obvious is ultimate reality. And another thing that's a little less obvious is samsara—the tentative, practical reality. In order to experience at all, you have to be in some samsara or another, so it might as well be this one. The moment you break samsara you lose experience, right?

JZ: I wouldn't know.

JL: The reason you can experience is that you're surprised by the next moment. So the ignorance that comes from being trapped in time is what makes experience possible. It depends upon a limitation, a narrow scope. And that's what this stubborn, practical everyday reality is. That's what samsara is. Samsara is a straitjacket that lets you live. It's a straitjacket that lets you perceive. Without it, you turn to gas that perceives nothing. I mean, you turn into everything.

The most mysterious thing, though—the thing that we can't know, the question that you can't really ask—is how many levels there really are between your particular samsara and the ultimate. In all the religious traditions, there are different layers. In Christianity there's one, called heaven. In Buddhism there's a series, which are called *bardos*.

Virtual reality is like the build-your-own-*bardo* kit. You can make your own sublevel samsara.

JZ: What's the point of doing that?

JL: Because it creates awareness. When you go inside virtual reality, you have a very interesting experience, which is experience itself in a sense. You become a floating-point-like angel. You have only your own experience.

In everyday life, all of us are aware that there is something out there that is objective. That samsara is stubborn enough to be really there. It's stubborn enough to make the Western empirical process work. We're also aware that none of us perceive it identically, or perfectly. That our own perceptions are always qualified, are always partial—are always crippled, really. And we don't know what the balance is. We don't know how objective we are when we perceive the world. None of us know if we can trade minds. If we could trade heads, if I could see out of your eyes, we don't know how similar what I would see would be. It's an unknown.

When you go into virtual reality, however, the world that you see there is a construct that was made by a computer. It's very precisely defined. So all of a sudden the edge is sharp. What you perceive in virtual reality was made up by somebody; it's no more than that, and no less. For the first time, you have a sharp edge as opposed to the fuzzy edge in the everyday world, and so whatever is on the near side of that sharp edge—that's you. That's you! You can never feel yourself in physical reality to the same degree that you can in virtual reality.

JZ: It's true also that I don't know if you experience the virtual reality in the same way that I do.

JL: Of course not. But the point is, whatever you're experiencing, it is you. Whereas in the real world, the boundary's fuzzy. Part of it is you, part of it is the couch you're sitting on. But in virtual reality, you know.

JZ: I don't quite get why it's sharp in virtual reality. Because of the straight lines and planes?

JL: No, no. Let me slip back to the Western terminology for a second. In the physical world, there's this empirical limit where you can't really know what's here. You say there's a table there, but what is the edge of the table? Which atom is in it, which isn't in it? We don't have any methods available to figure out how objective the table is, but we do know that we have a similar-enough perception of the table that everything functions. The boundary between our perception of the table and the table is always going to be a little fuzzy.

JZ: Is that because we're made of the same substance as the table while virtual reality is digital?

JL: The physical world, and simulated worlds in computers, are built of fundamentally different things. This is a very, very important concept. This is the way that they're most different from each other. The physical world is built out of nature stuff, whether you think of it as particle/wave things or however you wish to think of it. It's the stuff that physicists are constantly trying to get a better handle on, and probably will never quite succeed. We have limited knowledge of the physical world because of the limits of empiricism. We're always getting closer to it but it's never perfect.

Simulated worlds are built out of computer programs. Computer programs are built out of ideas. So the atom of a virtual world is not like the atom of the physical world. It's actually an idea, and a very precise idea.

JZ: What do you mean by an idea? Do you mean a one and a zero?

JZ: No, no, no, an idea that's embedded in a program. A better way to explain that particular point is through some of the criticism I've made of computer art. I'll make a claim that musical notes never really existed until computers, and the reason why is because before computers, musical notes were only an interpretation of what someone did. After computers, the note was actually built into the process, it was objectively there for the first time, because it was mandatory and because it was not only a mandatory organizing principle but really the sole one. It's really what the thing is made of. The process is made of this idea of the representation of the note; therefore it's really there—unavoidable, unopposable, permanent.

I sometimes use an off-color metaphor to talk about this: When you try to do creative work by playing with computer programs that embed your own ideas or someone else's ideas, it's a little bit like hooking up a tube between your anus and your mouth to get nutrition. What you're doing is, you're recycling ideas instead of contacting nature and exploring it. That's the real difference between playing with musical instruments and using computers.

This reflects back to my distinction about the way to think about the computer. If you think of the computer as only a conduit between people, you don't run into this problem at all, because then you're dealing with it as a conduit between minds. As soon as you treat the computer as an objective thing—as a real instrument, like a real person, as something that stands by itself—you run into this problem, you connect the tube to the wrong hole.

JZ: What about artificial life? What about these "organisms" that Tom Ray is creating, that are undergoing the process of evolution?

JL: Making a computer simulation is a form of representation. If somebody painted a great fresco that depicted evolution, you wouldn't treat that as empirical evidence that evolution is real. You wouldn't treat paintings of organisms as being real organisms. Simulated organisms on a computer are no different. They're a representation crafted by a person, both consciously and unconsciously, just like a painting.

JZ: Well, he would say, and he has, that they're not representations. That they are things in themselves.

JL: I think it's the same fallacy as the person playing with a music program and ending up with very dull music because they're just exploring the ideas that have been stuck in the music program. Essentially, if you try to do science without going back to nature, all you're doing is reexploring human ideas that have been set down in a computer, and amplified by the simulation. So what you're really doing is, you're self-glorifying your own ideas that have been set down. It's a little bit like taking a little poem that you wrote and then putting it up in a huge marquee in lights and saying, "Oh, wow, that's really wise." It might be, or it might not be, but the point is that you're blinding yourself. Essentially, a simulation takes a starting human idea that somebody had and amplifies it, and it looks more impressive.

JZ: Regarding simulation, on my computer at home, I use mostly text, which allows me to communicate with people through e-mail, or through forums or live chat. I could get CU-SeeMe, and then I could see these people. But it seems to me that still I'm going to end up with a simulation of a face-to-face encounter that's not quite up to snuff to meeting someone in the flesh. The potential of VR clearly doesn't lie in this sort of simulation. Where does it lie? And what excites you that's out there?

JL: The potential does not lie, ever, in simulating something in the physical world. Because it will always either be done poorly, or if it seems it's not being done poorly, it means you're fooling yourself, as in the case of the music example, or this evolution-simulation example. If it seems like the computer is simulating the real world, well, it just means that you've lost touch.

The right way to use computers is to use them to simulate alternate worlds, together with other people, as a form of communication. That doesn't necessarily mean virtual reality, which is not economically viable at this point at the level that it would need to be. It can be something that's just text, or text plus images as you see on the Web. This is what all media does. This isn't fundamentally new, but it's new in its method and its timing.

What are some of the things that excite me? There are some things that probably seem banal to you that kind of excite me because of what I think they mean. Everybody's sort of dumb and banal personal Web pages where they list their record collections and pictures of their dog and all that kind of stuff? To me there's something exciting about that. People becoming individuals in the media world instead of just receptacles. I actually find that a sign of hope even though— this might be an example of that erotic quality I was talking about—I'm more interested in what it means for the future than what it is right now. I have a feeling the Internet's always going to be like that, even in five hundred years. Whatever's going on is going to be exciting because of its sense of promise rather than what it is. And I think that's fine. This is a media with velocity.

We're so used to a culture based on static artifacts that result from cultural activity that in a real dynamic culture it almost seems as though nothing's happening. The right way to think about the Internet is not as a metaphor to a musical score—"Where are the great symphonies?"—but rather to the process itself. When you're listening to music, it's not any note that matters but that it leads to the next note. If you look at the Internet as something that happens in time instead of something that's leaving a trail of artifacts, it's a great symphony.

But it's not necessarily positive. The Internet is a giant mirror being held up to mankind that we've never had before. It reflects all of our flaws and our embarrassments as well as our best qualities. It's an honest mirror. So there's a lot of dreadful stuff, but it's really us. It's really who we are.

JZ: What do you think of Richard Dawkins's idea of memes?

JL: Poor, poor idea.

JZ: Why? Doesn't it helps to explain certain phenomena?

JL: You know, coming up with explanations for things is not all that hard. The meme idea is kind of dumb because, first of all, its formulation—the whole point of it, the reason why it has any zing, the reason why it appeals like a worthy idea—denies the weird, subjective complexity of life. It denies the observer, it denies the thinker, it denies experience. It just says that the idea's out there as an objective thing.

Is it a viable framework? Sure. So is Marxism. Marx wasn't actually wrong about anything, he was just incomplete. He was a smart guy who tried to come up with a total theory of everything and couldn't. And then people took him way too seriously. I think if we think back on how we wish people had treated Marx, people should have said, "This is a clever guy, he's a nice-spirited guy, has an insight." I think in a balanced way it's kind of a nice thing to stir into the mix, it's worthy to think about it. But for God's sake, don't design a government after this, that would be insane!

I think exactly the same attitude should prevail toward ultra-Darwinism right now. People like Dawkins and Dennett—they have an interesting perspective, they have a lot of energy. They're plainly right in a certain framework. But we shouldn't allow that framework to rule our lives. In balance, taken with the appropriate dose of salt, it's a perfectly interesting way to think. And it's a nice extra perspective to have, among others.

But you know, Dawkins's psychology is a little different than Dennett's. Dennett is the smart-aleck kid who's saying, "Nah-nah-nah, you don't have experience." Dawkins is different. He has Galileo envy, in the sense that his problem is that he really wants to be the bearer of the news of a scientific revolution and he wants to be in the position that a lot of scientists have been, of saying, "Well, all these sentimental people don't want to see it, but this is the truth."

This battle about ultra-Darwinism is kind of strange because it is not a battle about the objective makeup of the universe. It's not a battle about how science works. It's a battle about how people should properly think of themselves. It's a battle about whether ideas exist independently of people—whether experience exists, ultimately. And that's a philosophical issue, not a scientific issue. Unlike real scientific revolutions, unlike what Darwin went through, unlike what Galileo went through, this is not in the service of a better understanding of the real world. It's really sort of a religious battle between two different forms of death denial.

I think the real core disagreement between Dawkins and Dennett, people who feel uncomfortable with death, and all these other ultra-objectivists—I call them "information positivists" sometimes, or "zombies"—and others is often a conflict between two different forms of death denial. The old-style death denial is to imagine that there's some other kind of reality that we can graduate to upon death, and that there's some continuity. Then there's a new style of death denial, which is that technology will conquer all and so either through cryonics, or through nanotechnological repair of the body, or through transferring the mind to a computer, you can overcome death. And that we have to all not believe in experience, because if you believe in experience it screws up our new fantasy of how to get around dying.

Cryonics is the practice of freezing an organism, and sometimes just the head of an organism, in the belief that eventually medicine will come up with a cure for whatever killed the organism. The hope is that when the body, or head, is thawed, fixed, and recharged, the mind will also spring back to full life. The endurance record for frozen humans belongs to the Californian James Bedford, who has been on ice since his death from cancer in 1967.

The sort of medical repair work that will be needed on thawed bodies may be carried out through nanotechnology. A nanometer is equivalent to one-billionth of a meter, or about four atoms. Nanotechnology deals with the manipulation of matter on this scale, through computers or robots miniature enough to do atomic reconstruction. Nanotechnology is coming and, in theory, promises a godlike dominion over matter, for through it we may be able to build anything whose atomic structure we can describe—including, in time, brains of any and every sort.

JZ: Why would it screw it up?

JL: Because if experience is real, it's a very mysterious thing. If experience exists—and I'm experiencing right now, so it does—how does it connect? If you back up your mind to a computer, why should it connect to that thing? In fact, there's a good argument that says it wouldn't. There have been a lot of formulations for how this mysterious experience can bind to parts of the universe or can connect to it. Why is it stuck in my head and not over by the piano right now or something? If you believe that it's because of a particular organization of things in my head, well, why aren't there a cluster of millions of similar consciousnesses? Why isn't there a separate consciousness that's my head plus the phone? There's a lot of talk about subconsciousnesses, like the society of mind idea that there are subconsciousnesses inside your brain. Why aren't there super ones?

JZ: You tell me. Why do you experience your experience as being in your body and not your body plus the piano's?

JL: Well, there could be another experience entity that's me plus the piano floating around. But if you imagine that consciousness just shows up where there are certain patterns, you end up with the superset problem where all the combinations of patterns have to produce yet separate consciousnesses, and the complexity of that is overwhelming. It violates Ockham's razor. It's just a ridiculous way to think. [Ockham's razor, a principle attributed to the fourteenth-century English philosopher William of Ockham, states that "plurality should not be assumed without necessity"—in other words, make only the minimum number of assumptions necessary to explain any phenomenon.]

JZ: When the Dalai Lama was asked whether consciousness could settle within a computer, he thought possibly so. He didn't see any reason why silicon-based matter wouldn't do instead of carbon-based matter.

JL: Well, who knows? I'm not making any claim that it can or can't do anything. I'm saying that we don't know. I could drop an orange from the top of the World Trade Center and say, "That splat will be my consciousness when I die." That would make absolutely as much sense as measuring my neurons and backing them up to a computer disk. It's all completely senseless, if you believe in experience, which is ultimately sort of a mystical thing, because it's not empirical, it's a-empirical. If you don't believe in experience, if you can make it not exist, and you only believe in objective process, the things that actually happen in the movement of particles, then the problem goes away and then certainly you can make up whatever. If you believe in experience, experience serves as an enormous uncertainty as to whether any of these technological schemes for avoiding death mean anything. And it puts the whole pursuit into the same category as any other religious endeavor, which indeed it is.

JZ: Let's look at the religions going online. The chief question for me here is, What about ritual and sacrament? Take the Catholic Church. There's no way right now that they're thinking about putting the sacraments online—say, Communion, or Baptism.

JL: There are really two questions here. One is, What will be the adjustment made by traditional religions to this new situation? That's an interesting question. And then there's the more general question, which is, Syncretically, what will happen? So I want to treat those as two utterly different questions.

On the first question, I think it will be different with different ones. The Catholic Church, the Western religions, have the most difficulty here because of our sense of literalism. That's a tough bind; that's just going to be hard.

JZ: What do you mean by "our sense of literalism"?

JL: That Mecca has to be located in a specific physical place; that it has to be physical wine. And it's not just the physicality, it's this specifying that is a holdover from a different era. That's going to be rough. I think that if new media technology eventually forces a little bit of a weaning of the Western religions from this tie to very specific things, it would be very healthy. Because a lot of the violence in the West has been from fighting over these particular things. It takes a few centuries, but the Catholic Church usually gets around to creating some structure of ideas to adjust to times as they change. Presumably they will here, and I'm sure that it will be ingenious.

Jews kind of seem to split in two. I'm Jewish myself. Ever since Spinoza, we've maintained both a secular and an ultra-Orthodox front that somehow seem to keep talking. I imagine we'll just keep on doing that. It seems to suit us perfectly well.

JZ: The director of a Lubavitch site I spoke with raised the same reservations that Catholics raise. He told me, to paraphrase, "Look, you can't have a kosher meal on the Net.

There are some things that depend on the body. That's part of our religion."

JL: You know, religion is sort of like a theme park of the past. And it's an important theme park. We're going to maintain the Lubavitchers, and we're going to maintain the Hasidim. They'll always be here, I'm sure. It's an important link, and it's an important role, but at least in Judaism, as I say, we for centuries have had these two faces and that's just what Judaism in fact is. The secular part of Judaism has got to be treated as part of it by now.

And then Islam—boy, that's interesting. Islam has sort of a different split between a state religion and a mystical religion. The mystical religion I think should have no trouble. State-oriented Islam is going to have a problem, because of the issues of the Internet violating national boundaries. And so, you know, that's going to be very interesting and, I think, quite tumultuous.

Buddhism?

JZ: Buddhism has a very strong presence on the Net. It seems to lend itself easily to the Net.

JL: Tibetan Buddhism in particular has had to live as a diaspora culture for quite a long time because of the Chinese regime. The Internet can be very, very important to it.

JZ: There also is an emphasis on mind in Buddhism, as well as emphasis on visualization.

JL: Let's go to the syncretic side of things. I've often believed that Western culture has this bizarre power of foresight. For instance, Western culture created a music that was based on discrete notes and a discrete notation that nobody else in the world had ever created, and in advance of the computer showing up. If some other culture had invented computers first, they wouldn't have been able to represent the music in computers the way we can because we happen to have a notation that already fits. It's bizarre. Why did that happen? I think that there's a similar thing going on here with Catholic liturgy and the Internet.

I mean, what is transubstantiation, if not virtual reality?

JZ: I don't think you're right, but it's a good line.

JL: I'm not proposing that the Catholic Church would ever accept that idea. I'm sure they'd find it horrible and heretical. But on the syncretic level, the set of beliefs that allow the Internet to feel like a real and meaningful thing are precisely the beliefs that have shaped Western religion and been shaped by it for two thousand years.

JZ: Can you give me an example?

JL: Well, what was it you brought up before? Communion and . . .

JZ: Baptism.

JL: I see all those things on the Internet all the time. I see syncretic versions of them. I see the Internet as a syncretic version of Christian ritual, I really do. There's this sensibility and transcendence that's applied to computers, regularly. Where did that come from? That's a Christian idea.

JZ: Perhaps syncretic versions do exist, but syncretic versions may not be sanctified. Can a sanctified baptism take place on the Net? In cyberspace, baptism would involve virtual body and virtual water. Traditional Christianity holds that you have to have an actual body and actual water. It's not just a form, an empty ritual. People believe, certainly the Catholic Church holds, that there are actual sacred energies involved. Can they manifest in this sort of imaginary or hallucinatory or whatever-you-want-to-call-it space of cyberspace?

I was talking about this with Barlow, and we were discussing what it is exactly that goes through the wire. He pointed out that it's voltage shifts. Can shifts in voltage carry sacred energy?

JL: This is not an empirical question. I'll share with you my old slogan, which is that information is alienated experience. So, nothing goes over the wires whatsoever. But it can be whatever we wish it to be. This is exactly the same question as whether the computer is conscious or whether you can survive death by backing up yourself or any of these things. They are for us to decide. They are not empirical questions. They are not questions with any reality to them. These are things we make up, like language.

JZ: That's a very relativistic point of view.

JL: It's not relativistic. It's really a very harsh empirical analysis. It's pointing out what you can build a meter for, what can't you build a meter for. You can build a meter for temperature, but you can't build one for the amount of language present. You could have a physical theory that describes all of the motions of all the particles through the rest of time that doesn't include language.

JZ: But is there an internal meter of our experience? It may not be quite accurate to say that experience can't be measured. You have your own subjective measurement of your own experience.

JL: No, you only have your experience of your thoughts, which is different.

JZ: Not just your thoughts. You have experience of something beyond, or behind, your thoughts. Of the space between the thoughts.

JL: Well OK, from a Western point of view you have an experience of whatever your neurons are doing, which is the totality. If you want to have a duality, if you want to have some other level that's the magic in the water of baptism or the *prana* or whatever, that's completely fine. It does not change the fundamental argument. You're still experiencing only either the neurons or the dualistic neurons of *prana*. It's the same thing, it's all just other mechanisms.

You know what I have to do, as long as we're talking about the body? I have to pee. The body intervenes.

———————————

Jaron Lanier's homepage is located at *http://www.well.com /user/jaron.general.html.*

CHAPTER 7

Buddhism

My shit-stick is cyberspace.
—ABBOT JOHN DAIDO LOORI

In late summer 1996, Tracy, Alexandra, and I drove up to the Catskills for a long weekend. We planned to go horseback riding, hike a country trail or two, and also stop in at Zen Mountain Monastery, which maintains a vigorous site on the Web.

The monastery is located in the town of Mt. Tremper. So was our room, at an inn that a friend had recommended to us as "quaint." That was one way of putting it. The room turned out to be musty and the furnishings worn. Still, we were glad to hear from another guest that the monastery was just across the road, and after unpacking we spent a carefree afternoon roaming its green grounds, where high on a hill we found ourselves amid a herd of deer. Some places have good vibrations, and Zen Mountain Monastery, we agreed, was of them. Before we left, I stopped by the monastery's office, where the director, Geoffrey Shugen Arnold, agreed to set up an interview for me at some later date with the abbot, John Daido Loori.

Returning to the inn was like entering a cave after a day in the sun. Our gloom increased when Alexandra, who had caught a cold, decided to take a bath and all that poured from the spigot was ice water. We felt trapped, and wished we had booked elsewhere. We decided to ask for another room. I went to look for the owner and found a man wiping down the bar. He let slip that they had known when we'd checked in that the boiler was broken. None of the rooms had hot water, nor would they that day. "Why didn't you tell us?" I asked. As so easily happens, question led to protest, then to argument—and, after the owner arrived, to some hard words muttered in my direction. Within minutes we were hustling out of the inn, our clothes sticking out of our bags every which way.

Back in the car, we looked at each other and began to laugh. We laughed and laughed. We felt free again, just as we had at the monastery, ready to head out for destinations unknown.

Soaring through the Internet can give that same feeling of freedom, of cutting loose and taking to the open road. It was on one such journey that I first came across the Zen Mountain Monastery Web site. What caught my eye was an icon on its homepage for "Cybermonk," identified as "a senior monastic available through e-mail to answer your Dharma questions." What convinced me that I should interview Abbot Loori was the transcript posted on the site of "Dharma Combat On-Line: 7 August 1996, 4:30–5:30 pm EDT," with an explanatory note that read:

> Dharma Combat is an unrehearsed dialogue in which Zen practitioners test and sharpen their understanding of Zen truths. With the tools provided by the Internet, it is now possible for such an encounter to occur between people in separate geographic locations. On this particular occasion, Internet Relay Chat (IRC) via a channel on an RRC.DAL.Net server was used. The koan chosen for this Dharma Combat was posted on the ZMM Web site as well as e-mailed to registered participants at 3:00 P.M.

I was as excited as a kid in a toy store when I read these words. As far as I knew then and know now, this transcript records the only attempt ever made within any of the major world religions to duplicate online and in full a traditional religious practice. (The "cyber-Seder" presented by Congregation Emanu-El of the City of New York and discussed in chapter 1 of this book was a broadcast of a ritual, not the ritual itself.) Truly, John Daido Loori would be someone to talk to.

It's six weeks later. A Trailways bus has just dropped me off beside the inn. Remembering the trouble we had there, I'm tempted to hurl my copy of the *New York Times*, its pages splayed for maximum littering, on the lawn, but my conscience twinges at the thought. Instead I head for the monastery, which lies down the road, on the other side of a gorge. Once across I walk up a small rise. At the summit a young woman kneels, playing a flute. The notes pierce the air with a brittle, mournful sound. She sees me. I wave. She stops playing, waves back, and retreats into a stand of trees.

I slip past the monastery's gate and climb another hill. Dry leaves crunch beneath my shoes. The treetops look like over-turned bowls of Fruit Loops, jumbles of reds and yellows and greens and purples. The sky is blue, nearly cloudless, and a wind blows fresh and cool. Ahead rises the monastery's main build-ing, a peaked Tudor mansion built of bluestone quarried from nearby cliffs and of white oak cut from local groves.

The building's main door opens onto a narrow staircase that leads down to the offices. There I spot a group of youngish men chatting with a handsome older man leaning against a wall. He doesn't resemble any Zen abbot I ever imagined—he's Ameri-can, not Japanese, and he's wearing a red-and-blue checked flannel shirt, blue jeans, and a blue utility vest—but his age and manner tell me he's in charge. Somewhere in his sixties, rangy, with soft, luminous brown eyes below a shaved head that mag-nifies his already sizable ears, Loori looks like Yoda might have looked before the years shriveled him into the mite who taught Luke Skywalker the way. With an easy smile and a firm hand-shake, the abbot ushers me into an inner office where we make small talk and I tell him about my book. He offers me a tour of the grounds.

Set on 230 acres along a slope of Tremper Mountain, Zen Mountain Monastery (ZMM) harbors wide lawns, a pond, streams, fields, rocky areas, and forests. It serves as home to any number of porcupine, deer, owl, fox, hare, and coyote, in addition to maybe two dozen male and female monks and lay residents. Speckling the grounds at irregular intervals are buildings of all sizes. Some of these house branches of Dharma Communications, the nonprofit, educational outreach arm of the monastery.

As Loori shows me around, he lights a cigarette, one of many he'll smoke before our time is up. He seems heedless of the mud that sucks at my shoes (he's wearing hiking boots) as he leads me along wet paths that loop from one building to another, through a video studio, an audio recording studio, and a publishing center stacked with copies of the books he's written and of *Mountain Record,* the monastery's quarterly journal (portions of which are available on the Web). Loori walks more slowly than I, and I suspect more deliberately, with a straight spine but head bowed as if in prayer. Between buildings, I ask him about Cybermonk. "It began on a whim," he says in a relaxed, cultured voice that carries undertones of a youth spent on the street. He explains that one day he received a piece of e-mail and was inspired to sign his response "Cybermonk." Further mail to and from Cybermonk followed—enough so that these days he delegates the duty to other senior monastics.

We reach a small building whose main room corrals a few desks and computers. This is command central for ZMM's online activities (which include a BBS). Loori settles in at a terminal and taps briskly on the keyboard. He couldn't look more at home, and no wonder. Loori has been around computers since the early 1950s, when he worked in chemical spectroscopy. He may be the most wired spiritual teacher in cyberspace.

Loori brings up the transcript of "Dharma Combat On-Line." He tells me a bit about the participants in the event, three of whom, including himself, were logged in from the monastery, with nine others scattered at seven locations including Canada and England.

"Since we were doing it for the first time, we decided that we would restrict it to students," he explains. "All of the people involved were familiar with the language of Zen. And while we had a time restriction, there was a lot of time. It was the one thing that I didn't like about it. Because I would give an answer, and then I would just sit here waiting. Two or three minutes would go by before the response came. Part of what Dharma Combat is about is instantaneous response. So that's one of the weak points in doing it this way. Usually when we do a Dharma Combat, it's done publicly, and the *zendo* [meditation hall] is filled with maybe a hundred people. People come up one at a time, face-to-face, and deal with a question. It's back and forth, very, very, very rapidly. Here, there was a lot of time to reflect, which tends to make responses more intellectual."

Loori begins to read aloud from the transcript, commentating as he does ("Shosanshi" is his handle):

SHOSANSHI: Very well then, DaveTap, you're next.

DAVETAP: Shosanshi, I AM NOT KNOWING, HOW CAN I TALK TO YOU?

SHOSANSHI: Who just wrote what you said?

DAVETAP: The self at the keyboard, but not the no-self which does not have to recite the poem.

SHOSANSHI: You lost me.

DAVETAP: How is that possible?

SHOSANSHI: Guess.

DAVETAP: With no separation, you are never lost. In answering, I separated. I shall turn to the wall.

SHOSANSHI: Good move. May your life go well.

"What he's doing," Loori says, "is putting a very intellectual notion of what not-knowing is about. So if he's not knowing, who wrote what he just said? He's juxtaposing a self and no-self, and that's where he lost me. And I said, 'How it that possible?'"

As the abbot speaks, I am struck again at how much richer a face-to-face meeting is than one conducted online. I ask Loori to comment on the difference between Dharma Combat in person and on the Net.

"Big, big, big difference. In *dokusan*, that's the face-to-face teaching that takes place every day—when I'm in a room off the *zendo,* sitting in *zazen* [Zen meditation], and they come in and prostrate themselves and either present their koan or ask a question and a dialogue ensues—there I know what's going on with the student. I see their face, I hear the trembling in their voice, I can almost smell the fear. And somebody who's frightened, I won't push. I'm a little more gentle with them. When a monk comes up who's been practicing a long time, I kill him."

A startling choice of words, but I let it pass. So what was it like, I ask, for Loori to engage in Dharma Combat online? What sort of connection did he make with his students?

"The students that I know, it was par for the course. We've had very similar dialogues. With the people that I didn't know, no real connection at all. You know, it was as if I were talking to a computer."

A woman dressed in light cottons enters the room and says that she needs to get to work. She's Victoria Hosei Cajipe, the solid-state physicist who maintains ZMM's Web site. Loori tells her that we'll soon be finished, and she obediently departs. "She's high-tech, super-super-high-tech," he says after she leaves.

In "Buddha's Digital Flower," an article she wrote about ZMM's Web site with two other practitioners for the fall 1995 issue of *Mountain Record,* Cajipe makes three provocative claims: that the Net is "forming the tissue for a Teilhard de Chardinesque cerebralization of the globe—the planetary mind";

that "the bits of multimedia information on the Web and their flow patterns are very much like the contents and movements of the mind"; and that Loori "has embraced the digital duality of 1 and 0 as skillful means for communicating the Dharma." Loori's take on his online ventures seems more down-to-earth. When I ask him why he experimented with Dharma Combat online, he says, "Basically to find out, to push the envelope. To see what are we able to do with cyberspace. One of the things that motivated the creation of Dharma Communications to begin with was that there are a lot of people in this world who, for various reasons, can't study with a teacher or go to a monastery. Some of them are housebound, some of them are incarcerated, some of them live as far away as Alaska or Montana. So the question always in my mind was, How can I reach those people? And the Age of Communication is here, you know, so why not use first audio-tapes, and then videotapes, and then cyberspace?"

"Why not use these media?" I ask, tossing the question back to the abbot. "Because maybe what's offered through these media is an incomplete experience. On IRC, what people get is words, not the presence of the flesh. Is it possible that they are being given just enough to satisfy but not enough to really nourish?"

Loori gazes at me as if taking my measure. I get the sense that, as with so many spiritual teachers, on his home turf his words are rarely questioned. But though he seems surprised at my modest challenge, he doesn't seem to mind it. "I guess the same thing applies to books," he says. "And, you know, books have been working fine for a long time—for thousands of years, in a sense, if you go back to scrolls and people chiseling things out of stone. There is a sort of communication that takes place. And what's the difference between a student who is sitting in the *zendo*, in *zazen*, listening to me give a discourse, and looking at a video of me giving a discourse—the very same discourse? In the video there are even additions. There are cutaways to what else is going on, to the students who are listening. You can't do that in the *zendo*, because if you start looking around in the *zendo*, somebody will yell."

"You asked a question again. I'm going to answer it. What's the difference? No *prana*."

"No what?"

"No *prana*, in the videos. The Hindu term—life force. The videos are only a representation."

"That being the case," Loori responds, "we'd have to say there's no *chi*, which is what we call it—breath, life—there's no *chi* in a work of art. And I don't buy that for a second. I feel that art can be transformative, has been transformative. Maybe not narrative in written word, but sure as hell poetry is. I don't see how anybody could read Whitman's *Leaves of Grass* and not come away from that in some way touched very, very deeply. Whether they will become transformed is another question. But people become transformed from all sorts of things, you know? A pebble hitting bamboo. The sound of it: click. The sight of peach blossoms in the spring."

"Of course," he continues, "the pump was primed before that, in order for that to happen. But, you know, one of the characteristics of the dharma has always been that you use whatever's at hand. I use the example of Master Ummon, who in his koan, somebody asked him, 'What is Buddha?' and he answered, 'A shit-stick.' Which was a stick that was used to push turds out of the roadway so people wouldn't step in them. Master Mumon, commenting on that, says, 'Ummon didn't know what else to do, so he used a shit-stick to prop open the dharma gate.' Well, my shit-stick is cyberspace."

I smile at that, and Loori smiles with me. "If the Buddha had access to a computer," he continues, "I'm sure he would use it, you know. *Skillful means* means whatever is at hand. Now, true, it's still not the intimacy of being face-to-face, present, feeling the energy. But you know, one of the characteristics of Chinese painting is that if you haven't captured the *chi*—if you're painting a mountain, if you don't have the mountain's *chi* in the painting—then your painting's dead. And it's the same with a photograph or a drawing. A work of art must have *chi* to be alive. So the same is true for words. And we call words with *chi* 'live' words rather than 'dead' words. The live word is a turning word, and a turning word can happen by voice, typed on a computer keyboard, or written as a word in a book."

I like Loori's response, so fresh and unexpected. I do wonder, though, if words are less likely to "turn" when digitized on a screen than when spoken. "The computer seems to me to have greater hypnotic, or at least soporific, powers than a book does," I say. "Its samsaric powers seem that much greater."

Loori concurs. "They do. And you know, the samsaric powers of the written word are great, and that's why we have poetry, the Bible, sutras [discourses of the Buddha]. It's a counterpoint to that. Because we have pornography, it doesn't mean that we destroy books. The media leave much to be desired. They keep feeding the abuse of women, abuse of children, guns and murder and so on. That is the imperative behind Dharma Communications. The media are not going to disappear. So, how do you use them in a way that nourishes? Cyberspace is here to stay. How can we use it to nourish?"

An important question, but its answer must wait because Cajipe needs to use the room and Loori and I need to stretch our legs. We leave the building and meander a few hundred feet to Loori's small house, where his big friendly dog leaps at me and nearly knocks me down before I can grab a seat on the porch, which overlooks a pond. Loori shoos the dog inside and sits parallel to me across a small table supporting an ashtray. We're sitting directly in the midday sun. During the bus ride up from the city, I contracted a headache that hasn't faded and has made my eyes as sensitive to light as a mole's. I suppress a powerful urge to put on my sunglasses, and instead ask Loori for a cigarette. When I'm done with it I stub it out in the ashtray. Loori lets his own butts fall to the deck, where he grinds them out under his boot.

"About the hypnotic effects of sitting in front of the computer," he says, "I agree. The same can be said for sitting in front of a TV set, a CD player, anything else. Actually, I probably don't spend more than two hours a week online. My day starts at three fifty-five in the morning and ends at ten in the evening. Four hours a day routinely is meditation and then one week out of every four weeks we meditate from four o'clock in the morning until nine o'clock at night, every day for the whole week. So that provides a balance in a situation like this. The time that I have, or anybody else has, to sit in front of a computer is five hours a day, maximum. But even if I had the time, I don't think it's any more interesting than a magazine is."

"You don't, but a lot of people do."

"It's a novelty. I think it will wear off. People will get used to it and realize it's a tool. I've got a student who's paraplegic. When he's here, we need to provide twenty-four-hour maintenance because of the medical things that happen. So he connects with us through cyberspace. We have another student who's in residency right now who's deaf. He was born deaf, his parents are deaf. What we do is, with the talks, we set him up in the back of the room with a fast typist, and he sits in front of the screen and he looks from the screen to me to the keyboard. That's how we did the beginning of the Zen Training Workshop, the Dharma Combats—all of the things that he participated in. Full participation for the entire month, because of a computer. So it's that that I'm most concerned about."

"As a communicative tool."

"Yeah."

Loori tells me that one way he plans to communicate with computers is through a CD-ROM. It will, he hopes, "come reasonably close" to re-creating digitally the flesh-and-blood experience of attending the monastery's Zen Training Workshop. Users of the CD-ROM will "walk" up to the front door of the monastery, enter, and be greeted by a receptionist, who will ask them to fill out an application just as in the real world. They'll continue on to the *zendo,* where they'll find animations depicting proper meditation postures; to the monastery's Buddha Hall, where they'll hear sacred chants; and to the library, where they can access various readings. The CD-ROM will connect to ZMM's Web site and to Cybermonk, allowing for real-time interactivity.

Although the CD-ROM will presumably carry pictures of Loori, perhaps video clips of him speaking, it seems unlikely that the air of authority he manifests through his personal presence will carry with full force into cyberspace. "In cyberspace," I say, "every voice is equal, and a lot of people, especially Americans, don't like dealing with authority. It cuts against the American grain. So I'm wondering whether cyberspace, which is by nature egalitarian, might be beginning to undermine some of the more traditional religious structures based on hierarchy, like that of the teacher-student relationship."

'It might, and it might not," Loori responds. Before he elaborates, a phone rings from inside the house. "I'm going to let that ring," he says. "Hierarchy is a fact of life. It exists from the simplest microorganisms to a complex creature such as ourselves. There's no way to avoid it, and there's no reason to think that it's going to go away. And there's a good reason for it, you know? If you've got five people in a lifeboat, and one of them is a navigator, and you want to get to shore, you don't take over the boat, you ask the navigator how to get to shore. Right? But in Zen, it's not a guru relationship. A Zen teacher will never tell anybody how to live their life, or what they should or shouldn't do. That's a guru, and that exists in Buddhism, but not in Zen.

"In Zen, the training starts with the teacher-student relationship. At most Zen centers you just arrive, you pay your dues, and you're a member. Most churches are like that. Here, it's not like that. Anybody's welcome to participate in anything except the teacher-student relationship. I don't see people other than students. In order to become a student, when they come to their first meeting with the teacher, they must do nine bows and ask for the teaching. That's very important: 'Please teach me.'

"So it begins with a kind of a parent-child relationship, where the student is very dependent on the teacher. After a period of time, usually not very long, the teacher becomes more of a spiritual guide, pointing rather than directing, trying to get the student to take the lead. That evolves into a relationship that's a spiritual friendship. That evolves into a relationship where they're spiritual equals. And that finally evolves into a relationship where there's transformation, where the parent becomes the child, the child becomes the parent. That's actually part of the transmission ceremony, when the training is finished. The teacher becomes the student, the student becomes the teacher. And then the teacher disappears."

This all sounds a bit pat to me, the sort of neatly packaged theory that tends to unravel under real-world stresses, and I tell Loori so. "Once someone takes the transmission ceremony," I ask, "does the learning stop? I mean, who teaches *you?*"

Loori looks at me steadily. I have the sensation, as I have had all along, that he is giving me his total attention—a rare gift from anyone.

"Well, when the teacher disappears, what's left is the whole universe. And that's where the teachings then come from. But as far as I'm concerned, my biggest teacher has been my students. Because there's a heavy sense of responsibility to do it right. When I was working with my teacher and I was half-assed, he would stop me. But now there's nobody to stop me if I'm being half-assed."

It occurs to me that in the sort of spiritual work Loori is engaged in, there is at least one distinct possible advantage to online communication. The early stages of work with a spiritual teacher are inevitably fraught with fear, for desire gives rise to fear, and the teacher possesses knowledge that the student wants. This fear may be magnified by the trappings of a teacher's office—in Loori's case, by the ceremonial robes he wears and the platform he sits on during Dharma Combat, elevating him above his combatants, as well as by the deference shown him by his many students. These all reinforce the idea that "I have it and you don't." Perhaps online, where these trappings are less visible and where hierarchy loses sway, the fear can lessen. Perhaps online, a student could even, if necessary, work up the courage to tell Loori that he's being half-assed.

"It's been my experience," I say, "that one of the main blocks to the student-teacher relationship is fear. At least when you're dealing with people in cyberspace, and it's true with books too, that fear is less."

"Sure," he responds. "It's a loss, not having that. I mean, it's a setup. When people come, they walk into the *dokusan* room, and there's an altar lit behind me, I'm sitting there in full robes, cross-legged. They have to prostrate themselves. They come forward, and the ball is in their court. They have to start by hitting it. And, well, Daddy's in the *dokusan* room. Whatever problems you have with authority, they're going to immediately come up. That's the first thing that's settled. The teaching can't happen until that's settled."

"It's settled? Really?" I don't try to keep the doubt out of my voice.

"Oh yeah. It's a big difference with my seniors. When they come in, they need to be aggressive. When they make a presentation, they need to be really clear. And once they do their bows, there are no rules, until the bell rings. Until I ring the bell, we're in the middle of the universe. There's no protocol, there are no rules, anything can happen, anything goes. And when that bell rings, it puts an end to it."

I shake another cigarette out of Loori's pack. The sun shines off the surface of the pond as if off beaten metal. "Would you ever consider conducting a sacred ritual online?" I ask. "Say, a transmission ceremony?"

"No, definitely not. Nor can I envision ever doing on the Web the equivalent of the thirteen years of training that I just did with these monks, transmitting the dharma to somebody that I've never seen. Absolutely not."

"And why not?"

"Because the teacher becomes the student, the student becomes the teacher. It has to do with an intimate relationship. So much of it has to do with being on the firing line. That's one of the most difficult aspects of lay practice. I have lay practitioners who have been practicing with me for seventeen years, and they're not yet ready for the transmission, just because the amount of time they spend in direct contact is less. You don't really see a person until they're in the pressure cooker."

"That goes two ways, right? I mean, they have to see you just as you have to see them."

"Sure. People have all these idealized notions about what a Zen teacher should be. You know how many times I hear about smoking cigarettes? That somehow this is against Buddhism, you know? I went to a conference of ministers, prison ministers. There were about sixty or seventy ministers there, and I was asked to talk about Buddhism. So the rabbis were smoking, the Catholic priests were smoking, the Protestants were smoking, yet everybody took issue with the fact that I was smoking. That somehow Buddhists shouldn't smoke. You know, I was supposed to be pure."

Loori grins, displaying big white teeth. "So it gives the students that chance to see the bumps and the pimples, and at the same time to understand that it's possible to lead a moral and ethical life in harmony with the universe, bumps and pimples included. And when I say 'bumps and pimples,' I'm talking about, for example, yesterday morning. Once a month, every Friday morning, whoever is in residence comes over here for breakfast. They come to my house. They see me in my own environment. We eat together, we talk, we hang out. That's something that's hard to do in cyberspace. And what's communicated during that time is hard to communicate in cyberspace."

I suspect that Loori is referring to more than just seeing what he calls bumps and pimples. "I'd like to get my finger on that. Are you speaking simply of your students observing how you are, or are you also talking about some sort of energy transmitted from teacher to student that can't be transmitted through cyberspace?"

"There's no doubt about it. Take *dokusan*. It happens during long periods of meditation, and it's pretty hard to keep your masks on in a situation like that. It's very direct, it's very honest. That's the pivotal thing in Zen, because Zen is a special transmission outside the scriptures. It's not about words and letters. It's a direct realization of what it is. It's an ancestral lineage, and it's been transmitted mind to mind, person to person, for twenty-five hundred years. It's always been that direct transmission. It's not about understanding sutras, it's not about doing certain liturgies, or incantations, or so on. It's about realization, and the realization being transformative—actualized."

If Loori thinks this, I wonder how he conceives of cyberspace. I ask him.

"To me, it's just a very large network of computers. It's like the network we have here, except it includes the whole world."

"Do you consider it sacred space in any way?"

"No. Sacredness is something that's earned through time. Kyoto is sacred. Jerusalem is sacred. Rome is sacred. Stonehenge is sacred. These are sacred places because of what has been put into them. These mountains are sacred, because of the Native Americans. It was sacred to them, the way they treated them. You feel sacredness when you enter a sacred place. It speaks to you. There are places on this mountain that are sacred. Three of them. The space communicates it, and I think cyberspace in a thousand years or so might."

"What about your Web pages? Do they have a sacred aspect to them?"

"I think they are pointers to that sacredness, but in and of themselves they're not sacred."

As if on cue, a set of wind chimes begins to tinkle. Loori walks me back toward the monastery offices. Before we say good-bye he jokes about how he's toying with the idea of trying to incorporate into the CD-ROM a virtual counterpart to the stick traditionally used to strike, and thus awaken, monks nodding off during meditation. He laughs heartily at the idea, then looks me square in the eye as he shakes my hand. Walking down the slope to the monastery's gate, I ponder how impressed I am by this man, by his directness and lack of pretense, by the graciousness with which he entertained all of my questions, even the ruder ones.

Back across the gorge, reading a book while waiting for the bus back to the city, I hear voices and look up. Not ten feet away stands the owner of the inn. She's talking to what looks like a guest. I think of throwing her a nasty look, but behind her I notice the path to the monastery. I flash to my long conversation with Loori, and I realize that I don't feel like being nasty to her anymore, not at all.

The home page of Zen Mountain Monastery is located at *http://www1.mhv.net/~dharmacom/1htmlmro.htm.*

KEY SITES

The number of Buddhist sites on the Net, most of which originate in the United States, far exceeds the relative number of Buddhists in America. This is so partly because American Buddhists tend to be highly educated and affluent, and thus are more likely to be wired. It may also be so because, of all the major world religions, Buddhism supports basic beliefs that may lend themselves most easily to the Net, with its lack of a center and emphasis on interconnectedness. Unlike Judaism, Christianity, Islam, and Hinduism, Buddhism doesn't posit a

God or a Creator. The basic philosophical concept underlying Buddhism is that of emptiness, which means not nothingness but rather that all things are regarded as lacking inherent independent essence, and as existing only in relation to all else that exists—much as a Web site does not exist in and of its own accord but only as a temporary arrangement of information that at any moment is dependent for its existence upon other temporary arrangements of information—upon, for instance, the browser used to access it. Emptiness applies to the nature of the self as well, which can be experienced in cyberspace, through the adoption of various identities, as fluid rather than fixed.

Tibet in Exile (*http://www.gn.apc.org/tibetlondon*)

Like Jews, Tibetan Buddhists have suffered a scattering of the flock, theirs at the hands of Chinese invaders. In the physical universe, the Tibetan government in exile is headquartered in Dharamsala, India; in cyberspace, it is located at this Web site, which is maintained and updated by the Office of Tibet, the official agency of the Dalai Lama in London. The site's many pages serve as a constantly updated mini-encyclopedia of Tibetan Buddhism, offering information on subjects ranging from the Dalai Lama and the Panchen Lama, Tibetan medicine and astrology, and the structure of the Tibetan government in exile to "Guidelines for Future Tibet's Polity" and advice on how to work in a practical manner toward freeing Tibet from Chinese rule. The page devoted to the "Latest News on Tibetan Affairs" carries reminders, often tragic, that the Net and the world have much work left before the Liberty Bell can sound around the globe: "London—3 Feb, TIN A 13 year old girl died from exposure while trying to escape from Tibet last month, her third attempt to flee to India, and a boy of the same age died in Kathmandu as a result of injuries received during the flight across the mountains. 500 Tibetan children try each year to reach India in the hope of getting Tibetan-medium education there. . . ."

The Tricycle Hub (*http://www.tricycle.com*)

Tricycle: The Buddhist Review is America's leading Buddhist magazine in terms both of circulation and of influence. Its Web site, rich in graphics, reflects the magazine's smart, searching tone. A portion of each issue is reproduced on the site. Other offerings include a concise hypertext introduction to Buddhism ("Buddhism 101"), a directory of dharma centers around the world (emphasizing American centers), an interactive Buddhist glossary, and some well-chosen links. Though not the most complete Buddhist site on the Web, this may be the most user-friendly, and is highly recommended for beginning Buddhists and the curious. (Please note: The preceding site discussion, though accurate, is not objective, as I am a consulting editor to *Tricycle*.)

CyberSangha Home Page (*http://www.hooked.net/~csangha*)

CyberSangha is a small-circulation (thirty-five hundred to five thousand) print quarterly with a big aim: to provide, as its Web site says, "alternative perspectives" on Buddhism, particularly through exploring "alternative methods of Buddhist practice, especially electronic means such as the Internet." Published by the Tiger Team Information Network, pioneers in the field of cyber spirituality, *CyberSangha* has for several years spearheaded the discussion about Buddhism and cyberspace. Its Web site, which features a graphic of a Buddha sitting in meditation on a modem, includes the "CyberSangha Buddhist Library," billed as "the largest on-line collection of Buddhist Texts in the world," and, generously, the text of every feature article published in the five most recent issues of the magazine.

Gyuto Tantric Choir (*http://www.well.com/user/gyuto*)

The Internet is a palace, vast and mysterious. Some of its sites glitter like throne rooms; others are smaller and hidden away like servant's rooms. Then there is the attic, where old sites neither die nor fade away but are frozen in time. The Gyuto Tantric Choir site is one of these, and though it hasn't been updated since May 1995, it's still worth a visit for its audio clips of this legendary group of Tibetan Buddhist monks engaging in "multiphonic chanting, in which each monk sings a chord containing two or three notes simultaneously. This remarkable, transcendentally beautiful sound, thought to arise only from the throat of a person who has realized selfless wisdom, is like nothing else on this earth." The site carries an audio clip of one of the monks' chief boosters, former Grateful Dead drummer Mickey Hart, commentating on the monks' sound, which is a legacy of centuries of vocal training carried out at Gyuto Tantric University, established in Tibet in 1474 but, because of the Chinese occupation, now housed in Dharamsala.

The Electronic Bodhidharma
(http://www.iijnet.or.jp/iriz/irizhtml/irizhome.htm)

Sponsored by the International Research Institute for Zen Buddhism (IRIZ) at Hanazono University in Kyoto, Japan, the Electronic Bodhidharma contains the largest collection of primary Zen Buddhist documents on the Net. This site is an exemplar of sites that wrap important information in tired packaging. With its dull interface and confusing organization, these pages will tax those relatively unfamiliar with Zen or with software file transfer protocols. Dedicated scholars, however, will find the Electronic Bodhidharma to be a seriously useful Zen resource.

The Zen Garden
(http://www.nomius.com/%7Ezenyard/zenyard.htm)

Topped by a map of the site laid out as a traditional Zen garden, this gentle, austere collection of pages captures the spirit of Zen as few sites do. The Zen Garden encompasses five attractions: a passel of short Zen stories; a permanent presentation of a classic Zen tale, "Ten Bulls"; a collection of koans; a small art gallery (plus Zen links); and a bunch of sound clips including crickets, frogs, and a thunderstorm. The site is sponsored by Nomius, a Web-design firm.

The White Path Temple (*http://www.mew.com/shin*)

Shin Buddhism, although overlooked by most non-Asian American Buddhists, is the most popular form of Buddhism in Japan and among Japanese-Americans. Taking its name from its founder, Shinran (1173–1262), Shin differs radically from Zen, Tibetan, and Theravada Buddhism. Its followers are all lay. Its basic teaching is that liberation cannot be achieved through one's own efforts but only through the power of Buddha Amida. Its practice consists of chanting the name of Amida. The White Path Temple, "a virtual Shin Buddhist Temple in the Cyberspace," is an outstanding site that offers a broad yet profound overview of Shin Buddhism and Shin resources both online and off. Like the Dunya Web site detailed in chapter 3 of this book, the White Path Temple employs a virtual guide—Mida Buddy, a hippopotamus in a green suit who adds a welcome surrealistic note to this otherwise rigorously organized site, which is webmastered by Claude Huss, a Japanese Shin Buddhist.

Engaged Buddhist-Dharma (*http://www.mrtc.org/~lesslie*)

During our time together, Abbot Loori noted three evolutions in Buddhism during the past century: the influx of lay practitioners, the increase in the number of women practitioners and teachers, and the spread of "socially active" Buddhism. The latter, generally known as *engaged Buddhism,* informs this morally astute, though overpacked, site. Sponsored by "lesslie," the site presents little original material, instead providing an enormous number of links to coverage of human-rights issues around the world, from the terrors enacted against street children in Latin America to the suppression of the democracy movement in Myanmar. Links connect visitors to news agencies, to activist agencies like Amnesty International, and to government officials (one linking page lists the e-mail address of every wired member of the U.S. Congress). This is Buddhism from the heart and on the line.

talk.religion.buddhism

The "talk" can be raucous, even raunchy, on talk.religion.buddhism, but those with thick skin will find this freewheeling, heavily trafficked forum the most invigorating Buddhist-oriented newsgroup on the Net. Discussions in mid-February 1997 centered around Buddhist conceptions of hell, possible parallels between Buddhism and Judaism, the merits of vegetarianism, Chinese oppression of Tibetans, alleged religious discrimination on AOL, and a series of back-and-forth rants under the title "born to love": "I am the antibuddha. When the buddha gazes upon me, his eyes bulge in terror, he bursts into flame, and is swallowed through a crack in the Earth!" The newsgroup periodically posts an excellent introductory FAQ to Buddhism, available on the Web at *www.cis.ohio-state.edu/hyptertext/faq /usenet/buddhism-faq/top.html.*

#tibet

The most active IRC channel devoted to Buddism, this site, which focuses on Tibetan Buddhism, always seems to have two or more visitors ready to rumble, generally in a good-natured way, about any aspect of the religion. "What do you want to get out of this channel?" one asks another. "Are you here to learn, to give, or to destroy?" The response given, "I am here to learn," doesn't apply by a long shot to all participants, but the opportunity to listen to the destroyers as well as to the givers and learners makes this channel, like others on IRC, an open window on the workings of the human mind and spirit.

CHAPTER 8

Virtual
Reality

An Annotated Conversation
with Jaron Lanier, Part 2

What I'm trying to do is to save Western culture from
being destroyed by information.

—JARON LANIER

After going over the transcript of my first conversation with Lanier, I felt that certain of his thoughts deserved further elucidation. I also wanted to talk with him about some ideas we hadn't covered, including the idea of the possible arising, through networked technology, of a global brain.

Six days after our first talk, I found myself back in Lanier's loft, this time accompanied by Tracy. She and I sat on the sofa while Lanier, dressed in black jeans and a blue shirt, again nestled into his armchair. As I glanced around the loft, I noticed something I'd missed before: snakes. A green rubber snake, a black plastic snake, and a red-and-brown wooden snake lay coiled on top of items of furniture. *The Atlas of Snakes* lay on a desk.

JEFF ZALESKI: During our previous conversation, when you were talking about your idea that musical notes only came to exist with the advent of the computer, you used the word *objective* to describe the existence of those notes, within the context of how VR can allow one to perceive the workings of consciousness. I'm trying to relate that statement to what you said about Dawkins's idea of memes. You seem to lend a coherent, objective existence to the note, but not to the meme. Why is this?

JARON LANIER: I think a good way of saying something exists is that you're capable of saying what isn't it. If something is so diffuse . . . an argument about whether God exists is hopeless, for instance. Whether an apple exists is a somewhat more hopeful argument because at least you can say that some stuff isn't the apple. Regarding notes represented on a computer, rather than the recognition of the note being an interpretive activity of human behavior, which is a very, very complex phenomenon without any natural boundaries built into it, it instead becomes an a priori construction that's embedded in a computer program. And that's different for the reason that the a priori construction is limited whereas human behavior isn't necessarily limited.

I've been practicing raga a lot lately on the sitar. In raga there are notes, but they're not notes in the Western sense at all. It's inconceivable that Western notation could capture raga because it's all between the notes, it's all in the way you slide between the notes that the particular raga has its meaning and character. Here's where you have to remember the limits of the empirical process. Perhaps I'm getting too technical?

JZ: No, I want to get into empiricism.

JL: Empiricism is, on the one hand, our Western way of having objective knowledge. It's a very good way because it results in working technology. But on the other hand, it's one of these things, like physics, which, if you look at it through too fine a microscope, the edges are soft. You can never really know the universe perfectly. All you can do is create a successive series of better and better hypotheses and experiments, but you never reach the conclusion. So the possibility of making perfect musical notation doesn't exist, because the possibility of understanding people perfectly doesn't exist, because people are part of nature and you can never understand nature perfectly.

So when notes are used interpretively, as they always have been in Western music, they can pretend to control music but they never do. When you use them in an a priori way, which was done for the very first time with the advent of computers, they actually do limit what music can be, in the way that they cap those interpretations. A MIDI note cannot be anything other than a MIDI note. A MIDI note, if you're working in the world of MIDI raga, doesn't exist.

MIDI stands for *musical instrument digital interface.* Introduced in 1983, it is a communications protocol that allows electronic musical instruments such as synthesizers to communicate with one another. The information communicated passes in the form of bytes, as with a computer. MIDI defines precisely every aspect of a musical note: pitch, duration, intensity, and so forth.

JZ: If I understand what you're saying, you seem to be lending a sort of independent, inherently existing reality to musical notes in a computer. And isn't that, in a way, what Dawkins is saying—that information is something that exists of its own, that it is not necessarily interpretive?

JL: If you think about it too carefully, you can't really talk about what music is, you can't really talk about what a note is, the whole thing falls apart. But there are different strata at which these things come into focus and exist. I think that relates to the very deep process by which consciousness itself exists, and by which the objects that we recognize, the gross objects of the world that physics is indifferent to ultimately, can exist.

The only kind of physics that's been able to survive the empirical process is quantum physics. Quantum physics deals with a multitude of little particles. It doesn't deal with gross objects like apples and houses. Physics doesn't need those gross objects. They're not necessary to a complete theory. But consciousness does. And so there you have this sort of intermediate layer of unnecessary reality that comes into focus.

What I'm trying to do is to save Western culture from being destroyed by information. I think we talked a bit last time about the difference between the way Bach is played today and the way it apparently used to be played.

JZ: No, we didn't.

JL: A friend of mine in San Francisco who builds clavichords collected all the earwitness accounts he could of Bach and his sons actually playing, by people who were writing about it in a letter or something. When you read what was written in these earwitness accounts, you get the impression of a klezmer musician or some sort of almost schmaltzy musician. There's talk of clavichords imitating laughing and weeping and screaming. There's talk of rollicking rhythms and things that sounded like grooves—that sort of thing.

So you get the impression that what we know about Bach's music is not complete. And that's very reasonable because all we have is these little dots on paper. We have these little abstractions of these whole notes that undoubtedly couldn't capture the whole music. So we've ended up with this sort of neobaroque style, which is analogous to neoclassical architecture, where we have these gray columns where the originals of which they're a copy were probably painted in psychedelic colors. We have this thing that's a lesser version. The way we know Bach today is still something wonderful, but even the way we play Bach today isn't captured by the notation. Even so, there's something beyond it.

So the question is, What's the role of notation relative to music? And that's just one version of the question, What's the role of information relative to life? It's one little model of that very important question, and that question is the single most important question about computers and culture. And so the way I think it should be treated is that they are ideas between people, but it should never be confused with life itself. It should never be confused with the real thing. It would be unthinkable to listen to Bach as played by a computer, rigidly, with no information other than what's contained in the notation. If all you have is the notation, it just comes out like . . .

JZ: What does it sound like?

JL: It sounds rigid, and unfortunately it's a sound that will be entirely familiar to you because since the advent of the MIDI standard, there's been an influence on popular music. Especially when it first started to catch on in the eighties, with this kind of rigidity and plastic quality to popular music. The current music we hear, grunge and alternate music and all that, is a sort of reaction against what happened with MIDI.

When I say that notes didn't exist before, I'm dramatizing the difference. The idea is that notes shifted from being only an after-the-fact interpretation to being an important factor when they're embedded in a computer program. The other important thing to realize is that computer programs embed human ideas in a new way that they've ever been embedded before. They've been turned into a working method instead of an interpretation.

JZ: What a MIDI note represents is mathematically defined, is that correct?

JL: Yes. But the key part isn't the mathematical part, the key part is that it's defined, it's constrained. A note that's part of the MIDI standard can only be a certain kind of note. Whereas any other note in the world has this open agenda that's not constrained.

TRACY COCHRAN: Another way to put it is, The map is not the place. What's intriguing to me is that you're suggesting that our passivity is greater than it used to be.

JL: I think there are three different things that can happen. One is that you can be just wandering around on a place, another is that you can have a map. The third, and it's what happens with computers, is that you install a trolley system and you can go only where the trolley is going. That's much more analogous to what happens when you create culture using programs.

As soon as a computer program becomes your tool for creation, you can create only what was conceived of in the ideas embedded in the program. That's the nature of programs. Programs are not the same thing as nature. That's a distinction that is often confused by people like Dawkins and all, the whole batch of them—that simulation is the same thing as nature, ultimately. So what I'm saying is that notes have become a trolley system. They used to be a map, now they're a trolley system.

TC: When I hear you talk about music, what comes up for me is the difference between consciousness as it's understood in most of the conversations I've read about computers, and musical consciousness. Within my life, there are higher states of consciousness and more conventional states of consciousness. I recently read a profile of a young musical prodigy. His understanding is apparently extraordinarily subtle, but it's nonlinear. His intelligence evinces a kind of luminosity . . .

JL: Sure.

TC: . . . a dissolution of the separation that the trolley system is enforcing.

JL: Sure.

TC: Rigid notes and not the space between the notes.

JL: Absolutely. But we have to distinguish the ancient problem from the modern problem. The ancient problem that still persists has to do with maps and words and so forth. Ways that with maps and words you create these artificial distinctions. But the modern problem is the trolley-system problem, to use that metaphor. It's more severe, because words and maps don't necessarily force you into a box. They can confuse you, they can seduce you, but they don't force you, whereas the trolley system does. And there really is a difference.

TC: How can we not be passive in front of this trolley system, and still make use of it?

JL: Well, the way to use the trolley system is to get off it frequently.

TC: How do you get off the trolley system? You just take a break?

JL: The way you get off the trolley system is by directly contacting the mysteries of nature. There's nothing wrong with the trolley system as long as you get off. The problem, the nerd way of using the trolley system, to carry this metaphor on, is to stay on it all the time.

JZ: That relates to something you said the other day about the erotic quality of the Net. Which is really akin to the trolley system. You sit on the trolley, and it's almost as if you're just taken for a ride.

JL: Boy, this station was really dull, but maybe . . .

JZ: I wonder . . .

JL: What's the next one like? Yeah.

JZ: It's almost built into it. It's very hard to get off. It's definitely a moving trolley. When you're on the Web, you don't just sit there.

JL: Well, I don't want to mix metaphors too much right now because that's certainly a different thing. Let's not confuse our trolley systems.

JZ: All right. The first time I was ever on a computer and did anything, I played *Zork,* in the mid-eighties. It was magical, and I couldn't get enough of it.

Before there were graphic computer games like *Tetris* and *Doom,* before most PCs even had graphics capability, there were text adventure games. Of these, *Zork,* written in 1977–1979 at MIT, was the titan, unsurpassed in fame and influence. Set in a kingdom described only through words, filled with trolls, grues, robbers, and other horrible, seemingly unpredictable creatures, encompassing more than one hundred locations including a mysterious house, a river, a volcano, and a dungeon, *Zork* opened an imaginative world unlike any that I, and most people, had ever experienced before—because it responded to us as we searched for treasure.

"West of House," the opening screen read. "You are in an open field west of a big white house with a boarded front door. There is a small mailbox here." To this, I might type in the words "go north." To that, the game would reply, "North of House. You are facing the north side of a white house. There is no door here, and all the windows are barred." How to get into the house? Would the command "open window" get me inside? Dangers and puzzles and surprises and traps followed in quick succession. So did—much too often by my reckoning—virtual death, as I, not sly enough, took an ax in the head from a troll or was served up as fast-food dinner for a hungry grue.

In a classic episode of the original *Twilight Zone* TV series, a man flips a penny that lands on its edge, causing time to stand still. While I was an undergraduate at Wesleyan, I did the same thing. Time didn't stand still when my penny stood upright, but I sure did, stunned into an utterly alert immobility. I felt exactly the same sensation when I first entered cyberspace by playing *Zork* for the first time. I booted up the game on my Tandy 1000A, a PC that came with only 128K of RAM and no hard drive. That's a scrawny machine by today's standards, but it was powerful enough to make me feel the magic of *Zork,* of exploring and manipulating an alternate reality. The game sucked me in like a typhoon and for hours, even days, on end I spun happily in its vortex. So what if my dog needed walking? He could wait.

JL: Sure.

JZ: Can you speak a little about that?

JL: Well, the computer represents the first opportunity for people to have the outside world fluidly respond to their imaginations, without having to achieve some kind of mastery or craft first. That's why it's so important to children. It gives children an opportunity to validate the imagination by having it affect something outside of their heads, at a much younger age than they normally could. And it's a very, very important thing. It's the best thing about computers.

JZ: The only thing you have to master is the interface.

JL: But compared to becoming a sculptor, it's easy.

JZ: My daughter learned to use a mouse when she was three.

JL: Right. And that's as opposed to learning to play the violin or something. It's a much readier access to that kind of experience.

Do you want to pick up the thread about memes?

JZ: Sure. I'd like to know what you see as the difference between your conception of defined notes within computer space and—

JL: Memes?

JZ: And memes.

JL: If we're going to talk about ideas, if we're going to think of ideas as being metaphorical to genes, we'd better understand what genes are really about. And you have to understand that the method by which evolution proceeds is violence. That the reason that certain genes exist and others don't is that the ones that don't were held by creatures that were killed. And to a much lesser extent, they were held by creatures that didn't attract mates or didn't have as large litters or whatever. But the dominant issue here is violent death.

What we're talking about with this process is Kali, essentially. [Kali is the Hindu goddess who personifies the destructive forces of nature. She wears a string of human skulls around her neck.] It's the Western version of Kali. We're talking about the destruction of the weak.

JZ: Well, you're applying moral standards to a natural process.

JL: If a moral standard applies anywhere, it applies to evolution. I think the moral imperative of being human is to overcome evolution. It's the halting of evolution that characterizes the best aspects of civilization.

What happens to bad genes is that they die. Now, that happens sometimes to ideas, but are those bad ideas? When Hitler burned books, or when the library at Alexandria burned, then for just a moment ideas were turned into memes. If ideas don't really die, then they're not acting like genes, and they can't be memes. So the problem with calling ideas *memes* is that it encourages this evolutionary style of thinking. And it leads to a sort of eugenics of ideology. It's a very, very bad idea.

JZ: OK. There's another philosophical point I'd like to clarify. You said the other day that experience is a-empirical. You seem to be saying that the scientific method should not, or cannot, be applied to internal experience. Or am I wrong about that?

JL: Logic and the scientific method are two different things. Utterly. Utterly, utterly, utterly. They're related. Logic stands on its own. Logic is capable of truth, at least within its own context. The scientific method is not.

JZ: Doesn't the scientific method rely on logic?

JL: It relies on logic, but not solely. It relies on logic in the sense of the desire to not have theories contradict each other and both remain standing, although that happens.

JZ: All right, then, foregoing logic for a moment, just looking at the scientific method.

JL: The scientific method concerns the way we confront the mysterious physical world. There are several ways logic can play into that. Logic can play a role in the way we formulate theories, in the way we evaluate theories, and combined with other theories, it can relate to the way we design and interpret experiments, and evaluate whether an experiment has invalidated a theory or not. And it can be used in modeling alternate worlds in computers. Logic can be a tool, but the core of the process is not logic, the core of the process is this theory, and attempts to disprove the theory. It's this successful approximation of this mysterious real world out there.

JZ: Now, do you think that can be applied to internal phenomena?

JL: Because you include the word *phenomena*, the answer is yes. As far as any particular thing that goes on in our minds, such as a thought or a feeling, yes, I think so because there seems to be a very, very strong probability that all those things correlate to states of things that are inside the skull for the most part. They'll correspond to the neurons' states and firing patterns and all of that. Experience itself, the existence of experience itself, is, I think, a separate matter.

JZ: All right. Then can computers, which operate on logic, play a role in exploring inner phenomena?

JL: They can play a role in exploring the phenomena. But then they are no longer inner phenomena. And for that matter, if dualism turns to out to exist, they might eventually be able to explore chakras or whatever, because eventually there might be a sensor for such things. Anything that's a phenomenon ought to be subject to the empirical process at some point in the future, potentially.

JZ: A phenomenon is not experience.

JL: Right. It's the content of consciousness, but it's not consciousness itself. Except in the sense that all gross objects are brought into focus—and into being, therefore—by consciousness. A universe without consciousness wouldn't have gross objects, including ideas in the brain, or brains for that matter. You would just have a collection of particles with identical positions.

JZ: Is it because of this that you said, "What is transubstantiation if not virtual reality?" It brings the mystery down to a phenomenal level. That statement is going to haunt you.

JL: I know. I'm going to get into a mass of trouble for it.
    Did I tell you that the last time I was in Italy I was blessed by the Pope by accident and I caught his flu?

JZ: I thought the Pope didn't bless anybody by accident.

JL: I think in this case he did. What happened was, he'd been touring northern Italy. He's a little frail, he's not in the best of health. He was going out to the areas of strong papal support, which tended to be smaller, off-the-beaten-track places. So I was in one of these places and here comes the Pope's helicopter, and there weren't too many people. It was very carefully filmed so there appeared to be a much larger crowd on the evening news. Furthermore, the Pope operates with a laugh track. They had these big speakers up that created the roaring sound of a large crowd.

JZ: Are you serious?

JL: I'm absolutely serious. Whenever the Pope would say something that needed applause or that needed laughter or something, these sounds would come out of the speakers. A live laugh track. And they were sort of herding us to get blessed and there weren't that many people, so I got blessed. I actually saw myself on the evening news getting blessed by the Pope. I guess they said, "Oh, who's the guy with the dreadlocks? That's interesting."

And the Pope sneezed on me and I got a flu right after that. So I caught the papal flu.

JZ: That atones for a lot of sins.

JL: I suppose. Anyway, I think of that as being very strange.

TC: Extremely strange.

I don't consider myself a computer person, and I've always wanted to ask this question. It seems to me that there are certain kinds of knowledge that can be gained only in the body. There are certain things that I can know only because I'm incarnate. It strikes me as curious that people are investing hopes in computers the way they are. They are extraordinary tools, but what do you think we have bodies for?

I've heard Tibetan Buddhism, for instance, called an *inner technology*. There's a science to it, and it depends very much on completely embracing the body, and the emotions. And not going straight for the head. I wonder what your thinking is about that.

JL: I've always thought that virtual reality is essentially a way of bringing the body into computer culture. It's a very somatic type of experience. It's no longer a head trip. I sometimes want to cry when I see these pictures of computer classrooms where they have rows of modern computers and mice and kids sitting there staring at them. That's such an awful, wrongheaded way of thinking about kids and computers.

But on a deeper level, if you were talking to someone in that information-positivist crowd, like Marvin Minsky or Crick or Dennett or any of those people, who I think do represent the dominant voice in the computer world now, what they would say is that of course the body is vital, the body is a critical part of the way we understand things, but, just as the mind is simulatable, so is the body. That it's all information. And that you can think of the body as a different kind of specialized computer, if the mind is one. And that an artificial intelligence might someday have a simulated body.

TC: I've been most touched in my life at times when I felt like I was adopting some ancient posture, of surrender or receiving. But the technological culture seems so geared toward applying something, or adding something. When maybe what we need to do is to take something away.

JL: I think that computers are better at confusing us than previous media because they're more narcissistic. When you work with a computer, you're looking at a little miniature model of the world, a simulated universe that's built entirely of human ideas. So it's like a flattering mirror. It's a mirror in which you see the world represented and seeming to be alive.

JZ: When I was talking to Barlow, we touched upon the idea of a global consciousness, and that the global electronic network may have its own consciousness. I'm curious what you think about this prevalent theme within computer culture.

JL: This relates to what I was saying before, about how I think evolution should properly be thought of as equivalent to evil. There might very well be, and I suspect that there probably are, life-forms, potential life-forms, and there might be a particular life-form that's comprised of Arcturus plus your little finger together, or something. I mean, who knows? The fallacy is to think that any particular one is more special than the others, or will have any more special relationship to us than the others. Ultimately, it's just another distraction from one's own consciousness.

What I'm saying is that the global brain might very well exist or might come to exist, but that there isn't anything special about it. Is that going to compare to the global mind of the Amazon rain forest? It's just another thing in the universe, it's not that big a deal.

JZ: There's an attitude of worship toward it.

JL: Yes, I know, and that seems to me to be a bit silly. Once again, it is a form of narcissism: "Oh, we're building a global brain." To the degree it's true, it's also unimportant, and to the degree it's not true, it is important. Do you know what I mean by that? If it really is true that there's a global brain that's being formed, then it's just another one of those weird life-forms in the world that's ultimately inaccessible to us, separate from us, unconcerned with us. We're not connected to it. To the degree that it's really there and autonomous, it's unimportant.

JZ: How can you say we're not connected? Presumably it includes our brains as part of its wiring.

JL: No, no, if it's really true it's there, it's unconfirmable that it's there, and it's just this other thing, it's just this other way of looking at the Net.

JZ: Do you see this as an evolutionary step? You don't see any particular vector in evolution?

JL: One can. I had this argument with Jonas Salk just before he died, because he was one of the people who believed this. And what I told him was, "Evolution is the victor's word for genocide." That it potentially can continue, but it's a bad thing to promote it. It's not something we should wish to see more of. We shouldn't wish happen to us what our ancestors did to those who didn't survive.

JZ: Perhaps what's important is the religious fervor that's attached to it.

JL: Yeah, that's interesting. That's interesting sociologically. We have to distinguish what level of importance we're going to be interested in. If we're interested in it sociologically, then of course it's fascinating.

As I said before, I think a lot of this culture is really a new form of death-denial fantasy. The notion is that if computers can become conscious, then it presents an opportunity to transfer consciousness from the brain to them and avoid death. So there's a tremendous investment in all of these related fantasies because they provide a new way or hope to evade death. So in a sense, it is a new religion, very precisely, as opposed to a new spiritual path. It's like a new kind of organized religion that's based on death-denial fantasies.

JZ: That's a very interesting distinction because that's part of the crux of it: It's not a spiritual path.

JL: And as with all the religions, perhaps it already has, or will come to have within it, a sort of a mystical core.

JZ: Will you please repeat that creation myth that you told me last time? [At the conclusion of my first meeting with Lanier, he recited to me a creation myth he had devised, but I failed to capture his words on my tape recorder.]

JL: OK. This is a creation myth, a syncretic creation myth. You can fully believe this creation myth and still be a good scientist, I think.

Once upon a time, long, long ago, there were some people who had wonderful, wonderful technology. They had all the toys that we see on *Star Trek,* but they really worked. They had transporter booths, and they had time machines, and through this technology they could dart about anywhere they wanted in the universe, instantly, much faster than the speed of light. And they could be in two places at once and they could move back and forth in time.

Suddenly they had a horrible crisis, which arose because they could always see the next moment. They could always see everything around where they were, and every other place. They stopped having experience. They could no longer be surprised by the next moment. So as they become so powerful, life became very, very, very dull. They couldn't be surprised at all, and time turned into a perfect point, and stopped flowing. So they convened an emergency meeting about their lack of experience, as they knew they would. And as they knew they would, they went through a lot of options at this meeting to be able to get back the sense of experience and to have time flow again. And as they knew there would be, there was only one solution: They got all of their machines and they put them in a great bonfire and destroyed them.

They moved into caves. There, they suffered a great deal. Sometimes they died of starvation, sometimes they were eaten by giant cats. But this was OK. Because at the start of this adventure they could see it all in advance. They could see it was the only way.

Gradually, their descendants started to pick up a few little tricks. They came up with the idea of fire, the wheel, and then we descended. Now we're on our way back.

CHAPTER 9

Hinduism and Yoga

It's not good if you start becoming friends
with your computer.
—SWAMI ATMA

It's 10:30 P.M. I'm about to go online for thirty minutes to explore the digital Hindu-Yoga universe. At the same time, I hope to explore the nature of that exploration—the nature of the online experience itself. I've just turned on a tape recorder to capture my impressions. These words are my running commentary, filled in and smoothed out for publication.

I'm in the "real" world now, in my small home office. The impressions I'm receiving are rich, vivid, and meaningful. I see yellow walls that I painted myself, and a tin ceiling that someone else slathered with a thick coat of wedding-cake white. The room is crammed with bookshelves, filing cabinets, a chest of drawers, an armchair, a futon. On the wall before me hangs a map of Malta, where my mother was born; some drawings by Alexandra; and a blow-up of the postage stamp of the young Elvis (who never used a computer).

From the next room I hear the squeak of a steel wheel as our hamster makes his race to nowhere. From farther away comes the swish of tires on a snow-slick street. Out the open window to my right I can see dim stars and a sliver of moon. The air is cold and smells of wet wood.

I'm sitting at a round oak table. On it rest a desk lamp, a pad and pen, a tiny bear hand-carved from coal, and a small stone gargoyle that Alexandra thinks looks just like me. Taking up most of the table are computer peripherals—a keyboard, mouse and mousepad, modem, speakers, and a fifteen-inch computer monitor. My minitower computer stands nearby on the floor, my printer on one of the filing cabinets.

I close my eyes. Swirls of red and white blossom like nebulae against the dark of my eyelids. I hear the whir of the computer's cooling fan and the louder hum of the printer. My chest rises and falls in time with my breathing. I sense the weight of my back against the chair, the press of my slippered feet on the hardwood floor.

Opening my eyes, I consider the monitor. I know it's a three-dimensional object, but as if to presage the flat world of cyberspace it shows me only its height and width. The screen is an ebony glass rectangle framed in beige plastic. Already it is presenting me with information, for in the glass I see reflected a strip of yellow wall, a bookcase, and a shadow figure—myself. But this isn't the information I'm looking for. The monitor seems like a field of possibilities. I expect something of this machine, I realize, and in that expectation I must be granting it the sort of autonomy that Jaron Lanier warned against.

I flick on the modem, punch the buttons that turn on the monitor and computer. Words in white letters cascade against the black of the screen, from top to bottom. My computer is reporting on itself—on its processor, its memory, its cache. It's almost as if it is responding to me in some way, although not in a flexible, living way, for each time I turn it on it responds in exactly the same way.

The scrolling words disappear, replaced by a screen that reads:

MS-DOS 6.22 Startup Menu
1. Windows

2. Games
Enter a Choice.

The computer is demanding something of me and I respond habitually, as it does. I reach out and tap the "Enter" key on my keyboard, launching Windows for Workgroups 3.11, the operating system that organizes and presents as information the data that my computer computes. The screen spews further information about drives and peripherals. Then, like Dorothy's world when she stepped into Oz, my digital world shifts from black and white to color (and from alphanumerics to images) as a giant logo trumpets the arrival of Windows. Chimes ring from the tinny speakers and the logo is replaced by another drawing—of a red brick wall, my desktop "wallpaper" of choice. It occurs to me that Bill Gates's decision to model Windows after an office exemplifies the blandness that Lanier spoke of. Why not a spaceship? Or for that matter, a cathedral?

In the middle of the brick wall hovers a small hourglass. Of all the words and images presented during any Windows-mediated trip into cyberspace, this hourglass is the most common. It pops into view whenever the system is busy processing information. (The Mac counterpart is a wristwatch icon.) Over 90 percent of the world's personal computers run on Microsoft Windows. The global population of computer users, I figure, probably spends a half million hours a week all told staring at this little icon. The hourglass signifies down time. As I watch it, I remember my frustration at being stuck in John Perry Barlow's bathroom, at the interruption in the expected flow of my life. Seconds pass. The hourglass remains, and I acknowledge a choice: Do I resist the pause of the hourglass and strain toward the future, or do I relax into the present moment?

Before I can answer, Program Manager, the principal Windows interface, fills the screen. It glows in shades I've selected—pale green, navy blue, and gray. As I admire their harmony, my toe catches on a loose thread in my slipper.

Immediately my attention is drawn away from the screen—out of the screen—to my foot. As if waking from a dream, I realize that I have a body, and that my body is sitting in three-dimensional space, in my home office. My perspective widens. I sense the whole of my body, my posture, my breathing. I see the monitor, the table, the wall. There's the map of Malta, and the picture of Elvis crooning. I vaguely recollect how, when the first words appeared on the screen, my attention flowed from my body into the screen like water into a drain. My world narrowed to the screen alone. I know from past experience that again and again during the next twenty-five minutes, I will find myself waking up from the dream of cyberspace, startled to find myself back in my body, my breath shuttling in and out, the cold air passing along my bare arms and neck.

I reach out and lay my hand on the mouse. I move my wrist. On the screen, a small white arrow moves with it. Even as I lost my body before, I am extending it now through a virtual prosthesis that, like a real prosthesis, is discernible to the five external senses but cut off from the inner sense by which I know that my hand is mine, not yours.

I maneuver the arrow over the on-screen icon labeled "Netcom" and click twice on the mouse. Netcom is my Internet provider, another intermediary through which I go online. With each mediation, information is further arranged for me. What information I receive will be formatted according to the designs, and hence the intentions, of others—of the artists and technicians who created these interfaces. I hope they are men and women of good will.

Within Program Manager, a large rectangle appears—an expansion of the Netcom icon. Inside this rectangle, further icons are arrayed, including a tiny red sphere around which orbits, in yellow letters, the word *Netcruiser*. Maneuvering around two-dimensional cyberspace seems to me a game of geometrics, a kind of virtual tic-tac-toe. I center my arrow over the sphere and click.

As I tap my finger to click on the icon, I experience the movement as fluid. Yet what results from that click—the springing up
of the hourglass, the abrupt arrival of an altered screen—I experience as apart from what came before, as discrete. I see that,
behind the sleight-of-hand of the hourglass, in cyberspace rab-
bits really are pulled out of hats, made to materialize and disappear in an instant. The presentation of information through
cyberspace is largely an accretion of discrete events, though it
can be experienced as a flow, just as the discrete frames in mo-
tion-picture film blend into continuous movement.

Now a light green rectangle leaps onto the screen. Within it
lies a field in which to type in my password, which I do. Behind
and partially blocked by the rectangle is displayed a bigger, detailed version of the Netcom icon, an azure Earth bearing conti-
nents colored red. I slap the "Enter" key. My modem begins to
dial, to buzz and whistle. Messages flash across the top of the
rectangle, reporting on the progress of my online connection.
The rectangle disappears and the globe stands fully revealed. A
sense of adventure overtakes me. The digital world is mine. I
feel like Stanley, ready to cut through the brush to the heart of a
virtual Congo.

A series of icons—a spider's web, a pair of lips mouthing the
letters *IRC*, a smiling cartoon gopher—marshal like friendly na-
tives above the globe. They're cheery, as if to promise me a jolly
good time if only I'll click on them and follow them wherever
they may lead. Cyberspace is full of Pied Pipers. But floating
near them is a drawing of a ship's steering wheel, the icon for
Netscape, my Web browser. I click on the wheel and a larger
wheel appears, announcing Netscape Navigator 2.01. It is soon
replaced by a large gray screen topped by several toolbars—representations in word and image of functions such as document
saving—as well as, to their right, an icon that's cousin to the
hourglass. This is a square that depicts shooting stars sweeping
past the horizon of a dark planet. The stars will fall each time I
flip from one Web page to another. These toolbars and this icon

will shadow my every move online, framing my view of cyber-space like the mount that circles a telescope's lens. There is no peripheral vision in cyberspace.

The stars are falling, because the Netscape homepage is load-ing. I know that I won't find there the information I'm looking for, so I click on the toolbar button labeled "Stop." The stars in-deed stop falling, making me smile—I'm a Jehovah in cyber-space, I think—and the page stops loading. I decide to head for Yahoo.

Fingers flying over the keyboard, I type in the URL (uniform resource locator, or Web address) for Yahoo in the narrow green field provided by Netscape. I tap the "Enter" key, the hourglass appears, the stars recommence their fall, and, as if from no-where, Yahoo pops into existence for me, appearing as a collec-tion of hypertext links in neon blue against a gray backdrop. This collection is known as a *menu,* an appropriate word since on the Web, as in a restaurant, choices are precisely defined and limited to those presented by the chef—in this case, the webmas-ter. Free will is a multiple-choice affair in cyberspace.

On Yahoo's menu I note entries for "Arts and Humanities," "Business and Economy," "Education," "Entertainment"—so many places to go, so little time to go in. I feel a familiar urge to trash the task at hand, to surf to my heart and hand's content. I shake it off and move my arrow over various links toward the one called "Society and Culture." Each time the arrow floats over a link it turns into a little white hand. The index finger—not the middle finger—of the hand points up. Maybe cyberspace isn't quite as subversive as Senator Exon thinks.

Clicking on "Society and Culture" brings up a new Yahoo page, this one containing a menu that begins at "Affirmative Ac-tion" and ends at "Weddings." I find the link for "Religion" and click again. On the "Religion" menu, I locate "Hinduism" and click once more. A further page reveals twelve links, "Art," "Bhakti Yoga," and "Temples" among them. I find that I'm reading through these choices quickly now, scanning them really. This isn't at all the sort of contemplative reading practiced by Brother Richard and his fellow Benedictines in *lectio divina*. But I am wired now, caught in the movement. "This is media with velocity," Jaron Lanier told me, and I'm feeling that velocity now.

Beneath the Hinduism group links I find links for individual Hindu sites, including one promising an introduction to that religion. I click and find myself on a drab brown page. The brown switches to tan, its expanse etched with drawings of a sitting Buddha and overlaid with black text. I see embedded in the text scattered words highlighted in blue, further links to further sites. I begin to read the page from top to bottom ("Statistically, there are over 700 million Hindus, mainly in . . . ") but feel propelled to leap ahead. My eyes jump from one blue word to the next (*Bharat, Veda page, Minor Upanishads*). Like barkers at a carnival, each seems to asking me to ignore what lies beside it, to enter now, please, for a most magical mystery tour. I spy a catchy link, "Ganesha." Ganesha is the Hindu elephant god, and because I like elephants, having rooted for Dumbo as a youth, and for no more reason than that, I click on the neon-blue word *Ganesha* and am transported to another page filled solely with text. Too much text, I think. Right now I want some visual snap and not just words—this is the Web!—so I look for a way out by scrolling to the bottom of the page, where I find a link that reads, "Back to Yoga Page." Why not? This is fun, clicking and leaping like a virtual grasshopper to what promise to be ever-greener fields. I click and find myself at the "Spirituality, Yoga and Hinduism Page" (*http://www.geocities.com/Rodeo Drive/1415/index1.html*). This page is framed, divided into rectangular segments filled with words and images including a dazzling depiction of a red-lipped, heavy-lidded Hindu goddess laden with jewelry. Around her neck coils a speckled snake. Now, this is more like it.

I decide to continue to explore the Hindu-Yoga universe by way of AltaVista. I plug the word *yoga* into that powerful search engine, which locates 90,159 appropriate pages, presented in batches of ten. Might as well start at the beginning, I figure, so I click on the first listed link, which reads, "Power Yoga by Beryl Bender Birch. One of the two best-selling yoga books of 1995. Now in the 5th printing. Over 75,000 copies sold. A wonderful gift for . . ." I land on a pleasing page (*http://www.power-yoga.com*) that flashes words in purple and lays down a color reproduction of the book's dust jacket, but looking at that jacket reminds me of my book-writing acquaintance Rick Fields, editor in chief of *Yoga Journal,* and it occurs to me that maybe I should see if he's written anything of late that I've missed. I return to AltaVista and type in the letters "Rick+Fields," which brings up eighty-nine entries, and I begin to scan them and see links relating to *High Times* magazine and *Tricycle* magazine, one headed "News Release," another for "Universal Zendo Book Recommendations," but nothing that grabs me. I'm surfing hard now, looking for that special site, so I click to the next ten documents and find a link for "Table of Contents for The Awakened Warrior Living with Courage, Compassion and Discipline," apparently a new book edited by Rick. I click and jet to a page (*http://www.mca.com/putnam /books/awakened_warrior/toc.html*) with an image of the book's cover and, as promised, the book's table of contents, enumerating an enticing collection of pieces including ones by Rick, James Hillman, and Stewart Brand, plus an interview with "Carolos [*sic*]" Castaneda, and I scan down and at the bottom of the page I spy some linking icons including a steaming cup of coffee labeled "Cafe," which reminds me that it's late and I could use some coffee, so I click on the cup and move to a page (*http://www.mca.com/putnam/cafe.html*) touting a few authors and books including William Gibson and his new novel, *Idoru,* and since Gibson's always worth a look I click on the word *Idoru* and land on a black screen (*http://www.mca.com/putnam /idoru*) that reads "Enter," first in red letters, then in white, that slowly appear only to fade like a school of digital fish swimming past, replaced by the words *It's here,* and I have to find out what's here so I click again and come to a new page (*http://www.putnam.com/putnam/idoru/launch.html*) that offers me the chance to download a sound clip of Gibson reading from *Idoru* or to read an excerpt from a recent Gibson essay, "The Net Is a Waste of Time, and That's Exactly What's Right About It."

A Waste of Time? With a shock, I remember myself and my task, and sense my attention surging back into my body. I find myself hunched over the keyboard, my upper body arched toward the monitor like a speed swimmer about to take a dive. I breathe deeply but it's only a token breath, because I know where I want to go and nothing's going to stop me now, and before I can take a second breath I dive back into the screen.

KEY SITES

Sivananda Yoga "Om" Page (*http://www.sivananda.org*)

This is the homepage of the most sophisticated Yoga site on the Net. From the spinning "Om" symbol on the homepage to the "Spiritual Utilities" page that includes, among other downloadables, an audio clip that replaces the customary Windows opening chimes or chord with a trio of Sanskrit mantras recited by Swami Vishnu-devananda (1927–1993), the founder of the International Sivananda Yoga Vedanta Centers, this site is a delight.

The Sivananda Yoga Web site promotes the teachings of Sri Swami Sivananda (1887–1963), whose Sivananda Yoga, or yoga of synthesis, combines elements of the four traditional paths of Yoga: jnana yoga, or the yoga of wisdom; bhakti yoga, or the yoga of devotion; karma yoga, or the yoga of the path of selfless service; and raja yoga, the yoga of the mind. (Hatha yoga, the yoga of physical postures and breathing, is generally considered a branch of raja yoga.) The site details Sivananda's teachings, includes information on the activities of the Sivananda Yoga

Vedanta Centers, and offers free subscriptions to an electronic newsletter with the delightful moniker *Gurugram.*

Featuring 117 interlinked pages, 173 graphics (full-color, duotone, gray-scale, and line-art), two audio clips, and six animated illustrations, the Sivananda Yoga Web site has won multiple online awards. Its vivacious mix of image and text has been nurtured with care by the site's creator and webmaster, Swami Atma, a thirty-five-year-old Frenchman who doubles as the director of the Los Angeles branch of Sivananda. Swami Atma, as I learned when I interviewed him by phone, speaks English in a quiet voice made silky by a strong French accent.

> JEFF ZALESKI: Will you please tell me a bit about your background and how you came to be the webmaster of Sivananda?

> SWAMI ATMA: In February '95, I was in the ashram in the Bahamas. [An ashram is the Hindu equivalent to a monastery, a place apart from the world where devotees gather around their guru or their guru's teachings.] When I came back, one of our students was involved with the Internet, so he introduced me to it, to the World Wide Web and so on. I got a simple connection with Netcom and started to browse the Web, and I thought it would be a good tool for us to promote our organization.

> So what I did for a few months was, I learned about the concepts, and then started to prepare some pages to do a presentation to our board of directors. Two months later, I had prepared thirty-five pages or so, with some of the pages we have about the teachings, some centers, and our teachers. The board liked it very much and told me to go ahead. So pretty much on my own, I found a commercial server, and then I keep on updating, a little bit every day.

> JZ: What is the purpose of your Web pages?

SA: The purpose is basically separated into three in my mind. One is to put the teachings out and to spread them so that they reach as many people as possible. The second is to give people a chance to come to our centers and ashrams; so it's to give information about our different locations, about the organization itself. The third is to have an online bookstore that will directly sponsor the Web site.

JZ: Your pages present a mix of graphics and text, and then you have the downloadable audio clips. What kind of impression are you trying to give when you create these pages?

SA: I tried to do something that's not too plain, because of course some people recommend you put almost no graphics, so that it can be easily downloaded. However, I wanted to go a bit beyond this, to use some of the more advanced features of the Web. I wanted the general appearance to be quite pleasing, but also to be useful right away. I presented most of the links in the form of text, and included the links in the text so that somebody can feel that already at the first page they can learn something, and move on. There is a lot of text because this is what I think downloads the best. You feel that you are learning already.

Now, on each page I try to go to one or two or three or sometimes a bit more graphics, so that it's more fun to watch. But I try to keep in mind always not to make it too heavy graphically, so that it's quite easy to download.

It takes many more bytes to digitize any picture than any word, so images, particularly photorepresentational ones, take longer to download, braking the online experience. But because the Web involves multimedia, most people moving through it expect and even crave images, as I did during my thirty-minute sojourn. Finding the right balance between text and images isn't an easy task, but as Swami Atma understands, it is an important one for webmasters eager to attract visitors to their sites.

JZ: How successful is the site? Do you know how many people have accessed it?

SA: There are about eight hundred people per week. Of course compared to very successful sites, that's very small. But last week we had twenty-three thousand hits. Some people visit and see quite a few pages, and, you know, every graphic, every text file is a hit. We get about twenty-five hits a person, regularly.

Like every webmaster I spoke to for this book, Swami Atma measures his site's popularity in terms of hits. Another measure is page view. One page view equals one download of any Web page, irrespective of subsequent downloads of files embedded in the page. The big commercial Web sites earn a huge number of page views daily. CNN Interactive (*http://www.cnn.com*), for instance, receives between 1.5 and 2 million page views a day.

JZ: What would you like to put up on your pages in the future that isn't there now?

SA: We will definitely expand a lot in terms of the teachings. You know, there is so much to explain, regarding the four paths of Yoga, the different philosophies, even some of the techniques that people can do every day. So I think the site is going to grow to become very large.

JZ: It's already large. You have, what, over 150 pages at this point?

SA: I would like people who are, let's say, interested in Yoga, if they are living far away from a center or an ashram, to be able to get really exhaustive information.

JZ: That raises an interesting question. I can read plenty of books about Yoga, and I can even watch videotapes, which of course you could put on your Web pages, although the download time might be prohibitive. But all this wouldn't be the same as my studying with a Yoga teacher in the flesh. Or would it?

SA: That's right. It will never replace that. Many people who have a computer phobia, their first reflex is to say, "People are going to access all this and then they will never come to the ashram." But I believe that's not going to be the case. That's like saying because of all the books on Yoga, less people are practicing or are going to see a teacher. No, it's a springboard to encourage people to get more involved. Of course, they can try a few things from the book or from the videotape by themselves, but most likely it's just going to encourage them to try to find a teacher, and to learn from a teacher.

JZ: Why do you think it's important that people do that, and not just stop at whatever they can get from the computer or the book?

SA: It's in the nature of this teaching. With Yoga practice and spiritual practices, there is something more subtle that has to be transmitted. Of course, we could think about it in terms of the technical details, such as "If they do a posture, there must be some external eye to see any fault" and so on, but it's more subtle than that. There's a certain energy and something that's passed over in a living relationship with a teacher that cannot be replaced by any other medium.

JZ: You don't feel that can be transmitted through cyberspace?

SA: No, it will never replace having an actual Yoga teacher. When I started Yoga, the first two years I started with books, so I can really talk about this. It was quite different. When I started to take actual Yoga classes with a teacher, then I started to make much more progress and discovered what it was really about. I already benefited a lot from doing Yoga from the books, but there was a different dimension when I met a teacher.

JZ: On one of your pages, there is a definition of the word *Yoga* that says that Yoga includes "a union between one's individual consciousness and the universal consciousness." You may be familiar with a school of thought that holds that the Web is leading toward a global mind, and is going to bring humanity together. What do you think of that?

SA: The way I look at it is as a tool, basically. Like a book is a tool. It's just a more powerful tool of communication, and the tool can be used either for the good or for the bad. So on the one hand, it can help people get better education and information. I think the Web and the Internet already have brought people together quite a bit. But it also has some negative aspects. Our viewpoint here is, we know this tool is available, so we might as well use it to promote the traditional teachings of Yoga, which are very beneficial for humanity. So we try to make the best out of it. But it's not the ultimate solution. I don't put all my hopes in it. It has its limitations.

JZ: Regarding the potential negative aspects of the Web, one thing I've noticed from my own experience is that I get absorbed in it very quickly. There's always a propulsion to find out what's on the next site, and the next site, and the next site.

SA: Like TV a little bit.

JZ: Do you find that's the case? I'm curious as to what advice you'd give to people to use when they're actually sitting in front of their computer, to help them to be more aware of themselves, especially of their bodies. My own experience is that using a computer promotes one's going straight up into the head. And staying in the head.

SA: One thing I think, and even though it's also specific to the Web, it's true for computers in general: The type of energy or vibration that's around a computer is not very good for you. If you sit for two or three hours in front of the screen, you can already feel that it's affecting you, not for the best. So what many people recommend is to take some breaks and do something more physical—some of the yogic practices, easy exercises or breathing techniques, or walk around the block even, something like this. To help bring all this into balance, because it's not affecting our nervous system and our minds very well.

JZ: Can you get more specific about how you feel it's affecting the mind and the nervous system?

SA: Well, I have read quite a few things about the EMFs, electromagnetic fields. I believe the computer is emitting quite a bit of them. You know, our body and mind, our being, is already influenced by the psychic atmosphere around us and a lot of subtle things around us. So, our *pranic* system, or our energy system, is basically of an electrical nature. When it's in a natural environment, then it's functioning more or less in harmony. When we are in an artificial environment, such as most people in front of a computer in an office or even at home, where there are many electrical devices, this EMF—there are probably other reasons as well—can contribute to disturb the harmony of the psychic system and physically of the nervous system and so on. I cannot explain it in medical terms, I'm not a doctor, but I feel myself that this is happening.

Numerous medical studies have linked, albeit inconclusively, increased exposure to electromagnetic fields, which are generated by high-power lines, cellular phones, and many household appliances, to various types of cancer, particularly brain and breast cancer, as well as to miscarriages. If EMFs are implicated in cancer and miscarriage, their effect must be on whatever in the body responds to electromagnetic influence—including, as Swami Atma says, the nervous system.

Computers generate only a weak EMF. A much stronger EMF is generated by the typical desktop computer monitor, which is a CRT, or cathode-ray tube (but not by the liquid crystal displays [LCDs] used in some laptop computers). Some anecdotal evidence points to CRTs affecting the nervous system in ways that LCDs do not. In issue 21 of the mailing list NETFUTURE (discussed in detail in chapter 10 of this book), Bill Meachem writes, "After a day of working on a computer equipped with a CRT, I am frazzled. I feel 'thin'—that is, I am in touch only with the surface, intellectual part of my mind and not with deeper emotions, subtle feelings or my body. . . . In contrast, working with a flat-panel display is not at all frazzling. I am calm, in touch with myself, able to access deeper feelings, and not glued to the screen." EMF levels run much higher at the back than at the front of a monitor. Many monitor manufacturers take the medical studies, or at least customers' concerns about them, seriously enough to build EMF shielding within their monitors. A comprehensive discussion of the potential medical hazards of EMF syndrome (EMFS) can be found through the EMF-Link homepage on the Web, at *http://infoventures.microserve.com /emf.*

JZ: Your advice is basically that people from time to time walk away from the computer. But what if they have to be at the computer for long periods of time? What can they do when they're sitting at their computer?

SA: The most simple thing is, you just stop for one minute or two and you do some deep breathing. You sit up, you try to relax as much as you can—you can learn to relax the different parts of the body even while sitting—and you take ten or fifteen breaths. That can end up recharging you nicely.

In terms of the Web, I think the main problem for most people is that they use it a little bit like TV, as just a pure waste of time. So this we have to watch, not to go for the pure sake of browsing or to watch little icons, but to try to enhance our minds, not to just be there for no reason, to gaze at the thing for no reason.

JZ: My wife went to the Sivananda Yoga ranch in the Catskills this past summer. She came back with the impression that in Sivananda there is very much an emphasis on devotion. I wonder if people who rely on computers in their work and play are beginning to focus devotional energies toward them. Do you find this to be the case?

Do people worship computers? Very few if any—yet. There is, however, a pervasive devotional attitude toward the projected global mind of which computers will be a part. And if few of us worship computers, probably nearly all of us anthropomorphize them on occasion. I have cursed out my computer many times. In the future, when, through AI, computers appear more intelligent than us (and in time they will outscore humans in IQ tests), and capable of reshaping reality to our desires, it's almost certain that they will become objects of ritual worship. Those who can't wait, meanwhile, can participate in the humorously but perhaps presciently named newsgroup alt.religion .computers.

SA: I don't think it's a major issue. What happens is everybody needs to express some emotion and love, and of course a lot of people don't get enough of this from people, so they divert it toward the machine. But according to Yoga, what Yoga is about really is using all our different instincts, and tendencies of the mind, natural aspects of the mind, and transforming them, transcending them, into the higher level. The devotion is basically channeling all the emotions into a higher emotion toward God.

So obviously, it's not good if you start becoming friends with your computer. To attach emotionally to your computer is really a low type of emotion. But this is why, if we can promote these spiritual teachings through the Web, it's going to help reverse this type of process.

JZ: Do you think that God manifests on the Web or in cyber-space?

SA: Yes. We look at God as being unmanifested, meaning pure raw consciousness, you understand? Which is loving nature and bliss. But also manifest in everything. What this tradition says is, there is nowhere—there is no time and space in this whole creation—where God is not. So it's in the good and it's in the bad.

I think the content is quite important. So when there is divine content, then God is there. But when there is more negative content in the Web page, then more forces are present. I look at it as a very neutral thing, the Web and the Internet.

Hare Krishna-ISKCON International-Hare Krishna (*http://www.algonet.se/~krishna*)

"Hare Krisha, Hare Krisha, Krishna Krishna, Hare Hare." But of course the Hare Krishnas, the most missionary of all Hindu groups, are online. This is the homepage for the International Society for Krishna Consciousness (ISKCON), founded in 1966 by His Divine Grace A. C. Bhaktivedanta Swami Prabhupada (1896–1977), who in 1965, at the age of sixty-nine, came nearly penniless from India to New York City to spread Vedic (from the Vedas) philosophy and practice. Today ISKCON sponsors hundreds of communities, temples, schools, restaurants, farming projects, and businesses, including a publishing outlet, Bhaktivedanta Book Trust International, which produces, among myriad publications, *Back to Godhead Online,* the cyber version of the official magazine of the Hare Krishnas. The reach and deep pockets of ISKCON are manifest in this awesome site, a phantasmagoria of visuals and text, including a complete translation of the Bhagavad Gita, the holiest book of Hinduism, into English, along with extensive commentary on the text by Swami Prabhupada. As ever more religious Web sites will do, this site has tackled the problem of "counterfeit" sites head-on. The second page on the site, stating "It is not all gold that glitters," presents an official logo—a stamp of approval—that can be found on all Web sites approved by ISKCON. With its rigorously clear layout, encapsulated in a "Navigation Center" page, this is the best-organized site in the Hindu online universe.

The Transcendental Mediation Home Page
(http://www.mum.edu/TM_public/TM_Home.html)

The fame of His Holiness Maharishi Mahesh Yogi may have peaked when the Beatles embraced him on bended knee in the late 1960s, but thirty-eight years after he unveiled the technique of transcendental meditation (TM), he and his teachings remain a powerful force in the field of consciousness research. The text-rich pages here offer information on the maharishi, TM, and the Maharishi University of Management (MUM), located in Fairfield, Iowa. They also offer a small description of the practice of Yogic Flying, accompanied by a photo that depicts what looks to be three young males hovering in the lotus position over a hill of grass on the MUM campus. Someone should tell NASA about this.

SPIRITUAL TEACHERS

The institution of the guru—the spiritual teacher or guide—is integral to Hinduism. Over the millennia, many gurus have achieved great fame through direct contact and word of mouth and, in recent centuries, through their writings or through writings about them. Electronic media have intensified the celebrity of some gurus—for example, of the Maharishi Mahesh Yogi.

The Net is bound to heat this process further, particularly as the subcontinent of India, the main geographic bastion of Hinduism, wires up.

At the same time, the Net may undermine the tradition of the guru, which historically has pivoted upon the direct transmission of subtle energies between guru and student. (With its lack of any central governing authority, however, Hinduism as a whole will probably flourish on the Net.) It's probable that, in millennia to come, virtual gurus will arise and gain disciples, but, assuming that virtual life lacks *prana,* it seems these virtual gurus won't transmit the *something* that Swami Atma mentioned. When disciples are able to jack in directly to the computers that generate virtual gurus, however, these gurus may be able to transmit other, albeit coarser, energies to their willing—and, in a worse-case scenario, unwilling—disciples.

Not all gurus are famous. No doubt many, shunning publicity, continue to spread their light in obscurity, but others, living and dead, are represented on devotional pages on the Web. Some of these pages are charming, some are eloquent, but nowhere on the Net is the lack of *prana,* the absence of the living presence of the human being—in these cases, the presence of the gurus themselves—more keenly felt. Not all gurus are to be trusted, either, but here are homepages about three whose message shines with the sacred, as well as a homepage about a fourth who stands apart from all other spiritual teachers and teachings.

Sri Sathya Sai Baba (*http://www.sathyasai.org*)

"I have come to light the lamp of Love in your hearts, to see that it shines day by day with added luster." So declares the Sathya Sai Organization's official homepage, a pink-backdropped, text-filled place dedicated to the life and work of Sathya Sai Baba (b.1926), whom millions, particularly in his native India, consider an avatar, a direct incarnation of God. One can argue easily about Sai Baba's divinity, but only with difficulty about his good works, which number, in addition to his spiritual teachings, the establishment of free schools, a hospital, and a pure-water project in his native land. Sai Baba has influenced a number of celebrities, especially in the rock-music world. A portrait of him—his appearance is most remarkable for his gigantic halo of curly black hair—appears on the site's homepage, as well as on the walls of the Hard Rock Café in Manhattan. The claymation children's film *Gumby: The Movie* (1995) is dedicated to him.

Meher Baba (*http://davey.sunyerie.edu/mb/html/mb.html*)

"Don't worry. Be happy." These four words of Meher Baba (1894–1969) achieved wide circulation in the 1960s, in part because Peter Townshend of the Who proclaimed himself a devotee of this Indian-born spiritual master. Like Sai Baba, Meher Baba established free schools and hospitals and came to be known as an avatar. Ironically, he became best known for his vow of silence, which he swore on July 10, 1925, and held until his death forty-five years later. This extensive site, maintained by Mark Hodges and Joe Stewart, speaks for him through pictures and extracts from his writings, as well as through writings about him and an abundance of links.

Mother Meera
(*http://www.midcoast.com/~jim/Meera/MMpg7.html*)

Of all the gurus alive today, Mother Meera is at once the most surprising and, perhaps, the most consequential. Still young, in her thirties, she has for the past ten years been considered by an increasing number of followers as an incarnation of the Divine Mother. Through her *darshans,* or blessings by the laying-on of hands, conducted at her house in Thalheim, Germany, she has, according to testimony, transformed the lives of thousands, including several high-profile authors—Andrew Harvey and

Mark Matousek among them. Maintained by an anonymous devotee, this site presents not only many pictures of Mother Meera smiling sweetly, but also detailed directions to her house and pointers on how to behave during *darshan*.

Krishnamurti (*http://www.rain.org/~kfa/gfxindex.html*)

In 1982, two years before his death at age ninety-one, Krishnamurti spoke to an audience of perhaps twenty-five hundred, one of whom was me, at Manhattan's Felt Forum. He looked tiny and frail, sitting on his plain wooden chair on the bare stage, but when he spoke his voice rolled through the auditorium like thunder. He proclaimed, as always, absolute self-reliance—the rejection of all religions, teachings, and creeds as impediments to the complete inner freedom that, he said, was available now, in this very moment, if one would only seize it. Krishnamurti, who rejected Hinduism but who came out of the Indian tradition, was the most radical spiritual guide of the century, perhaps of all time. On this elegant site, the Krishnamurti Foundation of America presents, through word and picture, a thoughtful introduction to his life and his teachings.

MORE KEY SITES

Yoga Journal's YogaNet (*http://www.yogajournal.com*)

Yoga Journal is the West's most influential Yoga magazine in part because, in addition to providing substantive monthly coverage of all aspects of Yoga, it explores the broader spiritual, social, and health contexts within which Yoga teachings function, particularly in the West. The magazine will thus run side by side, as it did in its April 1996 issue, a discussion by Donna Farhi, a New Zealand Yoga teacher, of yogic breathing methods, and an extensive article by myself about Yoga online—an early formulation of some of the issues examined in this book. The magazine's tidy Web site features the same provocative range of coverage. It highlights the current issue of the magazine, including the cover article (in the January/February 1997 issue, "Dream Yoga," by Peter Ochiogrosso) and selected other pieces; a small archive of articles from past issues is provided as well. In addition, the site offers a "Monthly Pose" with graphics and detailed instructions for beginners and continuing students; "selfcare pages" that "provide the latest research on a variety of alternative health care topics"; a "Yoga Watch," which currently presents dispatches from the magazine's senior editor about her travels in India; an online marketplace of audios, videos, and literature; and an online users' forum.

#meditation

If you want to meditate with others on the Net, #meditation is the place to go. This IRC channel is scarcely ever empty, but it is always silent. No one types messages on this site. Its de facto purpose is to function as an electronic meditation hall. The last time I entered it, I joined six others—a man logging on from NASA, a clergyman with an e-mail address at the Pentagon, someone from the University of Washington, someone from MIT, and two visitors whose e-mail addresses I didn't recognize (any IRC participant's e-mail address may be obtained through a simple browser function). For twenty minutes we all just sat there, and I, for one, felt calmer for the experience.

Global Hindu Electronic Networks: The Hindu Universe (*http://www.hindunet.org*)

The Global Hindu Electronic Networks, or GHEN, is the richest Hindu site on the Internet. Sponsored by the Hindu Students Council, it contains hundreds of pages or links flush with images and texts, scriptures and commentaries, dedicated to Hinduism, Jainism, Sikhism, Buddhism, Yoga, vegetarianism, Ayruveda, festivals, anti-Hindu activities, Indian news—anything that derives from, or touches upon, the world of Hinduism.

soc.religion.hindu
alt.hindu

Like GHEN, these two newsgroups, the leading debate forums about Hinduism on the Net, are sponsored by the Hindu Students Council. All three are masterminded by one man, Ajay Shah, an Indian immigrant to the United States who in 1990, while working toward his doctorate in chemistry at the University of Mississippi, cofounded the council. Shah is one of the true unsung pioneers of cyberspace. Even so, and despite his current position with a software company that develops chemistry-related programs, he has never formally studied computer science. To learn more about his activities, I telephoned Shah at his home in San Diego. He proved to be a wonderful interview—refreshing for his lack of pretense, inspiring for his passion for the Net, which he conveyed through a torrent of words spiced by a thick Indian accent, and revelatory for his rare insights into Usenet and its newsgroups.

JZ: How did it happen that GHEN created the Hindu Universe Web site?

AS: Well, we were a new organization and we didn't have too many other means of contacting people, because Hindus are dispersed all over the U.S. In India, everyone around you is a Hindu, so if you start an organization, you just call out and a lot of people with similar interests will join you. But here we have to find some other means of gathering people, of communicating with them. That's how we ended up using electronic mail, because it was virtually free for all the people who went to universities. It was a quick and easy way of communication, so we started all our electronic activities in late '89, beginning of 1990. We started with several projects. One is an Indian mailing list, which now has over thirty thousand subscribers.

There was a time when it was anonymously edited, and I used to be the editor of that list. That got me into the moderation of a mailing list. Because of the other things I was doing, I decided to quit as the editor in '92.

So the electronic activities of Hindu Students Council grew, because Internet also grew. There was no really Hindu Usenet newsgroup when I started looking into newsgroups in 1990. There used to be soc.religion.eastern, and that's a good newsgroup, but still the name *Hindu* was missing. So I started out by creating a newsgroup called alt.hindu. It still exists, but now it has been superseded by a group that I also moderate. I created the other group last year in October. We moved to a soc. hierarchy, and created soc.religion.hindu.

When we started the Web activities, it was almost at the beginning of Web. We were one of the first sites to be created.

JZ: What year was that?

AS: Gosh. It was created maybe two and a half years ago.

JZ: That's ancient history as far as the Web is concerned.

AS: Well, one of the things that helped us is that I was keeping all the archives of alt.hindu. So I had almost two thousand documents at that stage just to start with. People had asked all kinds of questions, and other people had answered all kinds of questions. So we had almost an instant set of documents that we could start with. All I had to do was to convert them into HTML form.

JZ: What is the main purpose of the Web site?

AS: Just today, I got two messages from two different teachers from two different school systems. One of them wants to learn more about a Hindu festival, and the other wants a list of Hindu festivals to put in the interfaith calendar they're putting together. So we are a repository of information about Hindu dharma, where anyone can come and find all kinds of information.

We also have started some activities that include a lot more community involvement. For example, sometimes some of the newspapers write things about Hindus that are not true, or that are somewhat derogatory. If some really bad remarks are made about Hindus, then we can put out a call for action. So we have a Hindu antidefamation page.

Another purpose is to provide the Hindu community with resources. For example, we have a list of Hindu temples in America. If, for example, someone just moves to Los Angeles, and they want to look up where the Hindu temples are, we have that information available.

Also, a lot of us have come from India, and we would like to propagate some information about India. We have a page on Indian history, and we have some pages on the current events that are going on in India.

Another aspect is to bring the Hindu community from around the world together on one platform. So, for example, in Fiji, if the Hindus are treated badly, people from Fiji can write to us and we would at least pass the information along to other people. We cannot really do much from here, but at least we can provide the information to everyone.

JZ: Have you been successful in that? Are you reaching out to people around the world that way?

AS: I think we've been very successful. We get letters from places in the world that we never thought we would get letters from. We have people reading the Hindu documents from Eastern European countries, from Russia, or in South Africa, where people write to us and say, "Now I feel like I'm not alone."

Also, we get hits from countries like Kuwait, and from Bahrain and places like that—some of those Middle Eastern countries where even carrying the Bhagavad Gita is illegal. You can't even take those books there, but people from Saudi Arabia can access the Web pages and read it. Just as I would enjoy reading about different parts of the world. We are not really trying to convert anyone, because there's no such concept in Hindu, of converting people.

JZ: Well, there's a difference between converting and making something available to people, yes?

AS: Exactly.

JZ: Do you think that the Web pages are beginning to supersede the Usenet groups, or do they serve different purposes?

AS: I think it will happen one day, but that day is not yet here. To some extent, they're serving a different audience. If I want to find some information, say, about a particular ritual, if I go to a Web site, I might or might not find the information. But if I post it on the newsgroup, I would get the information. But as Web sites have more and more information, people will find that material there. There's another aspect that a lot of people enjoy, and that's discussing and debating with other people. If you go to soc.religion.hindu or soc.religion.christianity, soc. religion.islam, or whatever, you can debate with several people on several topics in one place.

The real problem with the Usenet groups is that more and more people will spam the newsgroups. [*Spamming* is the practice, universally condemned by Usenet aficionados, of posting the same message in a multitude of newsgroups. It is employed primarily by commercial outfits posting advertisements.] And if we don't come up with a better way of countering the spamming, if we don't keep out the people who are there just to bring down the newsgroups, then the Usenet future is not very good. When the newsgroups were fewer, and the readership was smaller, they were much more easy to manage. Now some of the newsgroups—for example, soc.culture.indian—have a readership of a few hundred thousand. That one is unmoderated, and people can post virtually anything, and they do.

JZ: On the two newsgroups that you moderate, soc.religion
.hindu and alt.hindu, what sort of criteria do you use to decide what's allowed to be posted and what's not?

AS: Well, each newsgroup has its own criteria. I've been
working on a sort of liberal criteria in the sense that as long
as the post is relevant to the Hindu way of life, Hindu philosophy, Hindu politics—anything—it's acceptable. I don't
accept posts that exist just to malign Hindus, and I don't accept posts that use four-letter words. And I don't allow personal attacks.

JZ: What if I came on and wanted to post something explain-
ing why I thought Christianity was superior to Hinduism?
Would you allow that?

AS: Yes, that would definitely be allowed. I think those kinds
of ideas are definitely worth discussing. That doesn't mean
that everyone would agree with them or disagree with them,
but the Usenet forum is there to give people the opportunity
to express their opinion, and I would definitely allow a post
like that.

JZ: You've spoken about the general purposes of the Web
pages and the Usenet groups. What do they serve for you
personally? Why are you doing this? This must take an enormous amount of time.

AS: Oh, it does. I've been here in the U.S. for about fourteen
and a half years now, but even when I was back in India, I
did things that did not necessarily give me any monetary returns. This doesn't give me any monetary returns. Most of
the time I end up spending a lot of my own money. I can always say that I'm doing it as a community service, and most
of the people who are doing some kind of Web site or this
kind of work would always say that, but I also would say
that it's a need of the hour, and somebody has to do it.

I think my name appears only once on the Web site, on one page. So I create this for the community, but not necessarily to say to everyone, "Well, okay, I'm the one who is doing everything." We have been trained in such a way, back in India, that you do it with the spirit of community, but also you do it in such a way that you're not really out there to take credit for yourself, or looking for something in return, even fame.

JZ: Is there a spiritual purpose for you in doing this?

AS: No. I'm not a very spiritual person to begin with, although I moderate the religious newsgroups and I create religious sources. I'm more action oriented than I'm spiritually oriented. According to Hindu philosophy, *spiritually* is defined in multiple ways, and one of the ways you can be spiritual is by doing actions. I'm not someone who sits and studies or meditates or things like that. I just do action.

JZ: I recall reading on some of GHEN pages the idea that we may be moving toward some sort of global transformation. As I'm sure you know, that idea isn't uncommon within computer circles. What are your thoughts along these lines?

AS: It's amazing to see how the world has come together on one platform. I know when I say, "The world has come together," it's limited. The Web started only two years ago and we see there are 22 million people in the U.S. who are on the Net. I think I read yesterday that by 1998, 100 million people around the world will be on the Net. So as the technology becomes cheaper and as the connections worldwide are faster, and people have equipment, there will be a time when people will be able to communicate with each other much more effectively. There are a lot of universal ideas that hold that we should respect each other's beliefs, and that we should seek world peace and prosperity. These ideas will have a better chance of propagating from one country to the other, one person to the other.

I'm not naive, and I do believe that, just as many good ideas are going to propagate, bad ideas are going to propagate. But being an optimist, my belief is that not only will the good ideas be propagated around the world, but issues such as human rights will also propagate much more effectively. China is a great example of this. They used fax machines and the Net and e-mail so effectively during Tiananmen Square.

JZ: But it didn't do them a lot of good there, did it? It's true that we found out about it, but still the forces of oppression won.

AS: That's true.

JZ: But perhaps slowly it will change.

AS: Perhaps it will slowly change.

And perhaps not so slowly. In Bill Clinton's second inaugural address, he claimed that "for the first time in all of history, more people on this planet live under democracy than dictatorship." The day after the speech (January 21, 1997), the *New York Times* ran a piece by David W. Chen that found Clinton's claim to be "correct," citing a 1996 survey that estimated that, currently, about 3.1 billion people live in democracies, while 2.66 billion do not. As the Internet is known to have hastened the downfall of the USSR and its Communist empire, particularly in drumming up international support for Boris Yeltsin during the dramatic days of August 1991, it is accurate to say that the Internet has played a direct role in the global movement toward democracy. As Internet penetration of nondemocratic nations intensifies, we can hope that this movement will, like the Net, gain in velocity.

JZ: You spend a lot of time in front of a computer screen. You say you're not spiritual, but I'm sure you're aware of the way your mind works in front of that screen. Do you find that you lose your sense of yourself and kind of flow into the screen?

AS: I don't necessarily flow into the screen, but I flow into the issue which is on the screen. That political issue takes me over at that given moment.

JZ: In that way, it's no different than a book.

AS: Sometimes I feel it's much more absorbing than a book. Because you've gotten into this mentality of thirty-second commercials, and so you easily flip from one page to the other much more quickly.

I know so many people who are actually addicted to newsgroups. They never write, never write, they just read them.

JZ: What do you think that's about?

AS: To some extent there's a show-biz aspect to it. It's so much entertainment value. To have two people or three people or several groups of people fighting with each other, it's so absorbing, it's like looking at a World Wrestling Federation fight.

CHAPTER 10

Sacred Cyberspace

Be aware of every breath.
—ANONYMOUS (SUFI)

Twenty years ago, the first time I tried to meditate, I placed a pillow on the floor, sat on it with crossed legs, and shut my eyes. I didn't know what to expect. Visions maybe? A whisper of enlightenment? What happened knocked me right off the pillow. I found that I simply couldn't bear it, trying to sit still, to do nothing but watch my thoughts. My body rebelled and so did my head. Before a minute had passed I jumped up as if stung by a bee. I paced the room, snapped on the TV, snapped it off, paced some more. I felt as scattered as a set of billiard balls after the break.

The next day the same thing happened, and the next, and the next. By the end of a week, I was able to sit for a full minute. By the end of a month, five minutes. Now I sit for up to a half hour each morning, trying to wake from my dreams long enough to count my breaths, observe my thoughts, sense the energies coursing through my body. That's nothing compared with what some do. Abbot Loori and his students engage in periods of intensive sitting meditation that run seventeen hours a day, seven days a week.

The first time I logged on to the Web, I couldn't get enough. I happily clicked from one site to the next, slaloming along the slopes of the digital world, letting my mind and my fingers take me wherever. When I thought to check the time, I saw that I'd been online for close to two hours. Navigating the Web had engaged my attention wholly, but when I was done I didn't feel refreshed and open to the world as I do after meditation. I've been surfing the Web on and off for two years now, and the experience remains the same. Invariably, the screen catches and squeezes my attention.

I don't avoid snow because it's cold, and I don't plan to unplug my computer any more than I plan to give up building snowmen with Alexandra. A low-level entrancement seems to be my lot in life anyway, except during rare moments. It's not as if my computer is a Darth Vader come to vaporize my spiritual hopes. But it's good to know the lay of any land you cross, and if cyberspace presents a particular challenge to the attention, as my experience shows me it does, I want to know as much about that challenge as possible.

Attention, the focusing of mind, is key to excellence in all fields. I can't learn if I don't mind my lessons. In the spiritual life, attention allows us to begin to see—and to begin to see past—the veil of illusion, the constructs of self that screen us from ourselves as we really are, the world as it really is. And as we begin to see, we begin to accept, for seeing is an act of acceptance, of inviting the world into our field of awareness.

Paradoxically, the finer our attention, the greater the mystery unveiled. Every morning I drink coffee out of a blue glass mug. I scarcely notice the mug—it's just my usual coffee cup, that's all. But if I attend to the mug with eyes wide open, if I allow it to fully enter my consciousness, it elaborates itself into an object of unexpected complexity. I note the curve of its rim and the angle of its handle, the slight ripples embedded in its glass, the play of light and dark along its surface, not just *blue* at all but a flow of shadings from violet to royal purple to indigo to black, shifting as the sunlight shifts through the window. The more closely I look, the more is revealed, and the cup seems to take on a presence, to *be* in a way that I can't begin to fathom. For a moment, I sense the mystery of matter, and the mystery of myself sensing this mystery—and then I lift the cup and sip some coffee, because it's just my usual coffee cup after all, and I need to get to work.

The attention I can bring to the mug is a free, focused attention, an attention not compelled by what it surveys. I can allow this attention to pass on to the hand holding the mug, to my breath, to my thoughts—or to open up to the impression of the computer screen glowing before me.

The religious traditions say, and observation confirms, that most of the time our attention is not so free. We are caught in daydream, distraction, illusion, conception, judgment—in a state known variously as sleep, attachment, or identification, the realm of samsara and sin. This is difficult to know as true, just as it is difficult, when we are asleep in bed, to know that we are asleep. Twenty years ago, I was given a simple challenge to drive home the truth of my usual state, and it's one that I take up from time to time as a reminder of that truth: During the course of one day, I try to be aware, each time I step through a doorway, that I am stepping through a doorway. It sounds easy to do.

In the Garden of Gethsemane, as Jesus prepared to meet his fate, he told three of his disciples, "My soul is exceedingly sorrowful, even to death. Stay here and watch with me." But after he went away and prayed, he "came to the disciples and found them sleeping, and said to Peter, 'What, could you not watch with me one hour?'"

The *watching* of which Jesus spoke is the free, focused attention held sacred by every great religion as a path to inner freedom. This attention is a natural faculty, but it is covered over as we mature and accommodate to the world. What covers it over are our habits of mind, which separate the heart from the head and the head from the body. What's needed to allow this attention to flourish is to get out of its way. A simple step, really, but one not easy to master, as the disciples learned on that fateful night, and as I saw during my thirty minutes in the Hindu-Yoga online universe.

Within the traditions, meditation—the direct observation and training of the mind—is considered the gateway to the path of this attention. Christians may practice meditation through the Centering Prayer or the Prayer of the Heart. Buddhists may practice it through mindfulness. Muslims, through *zikr;* Hindus, through yoga; Jews, through *kavvana.*

There's a traditional Sufi saying that conveys the intensity of attention necessary to achieve spiritual awakening: "Be aware of every breath." This is an extreme advisory. On most days we go from morning to night without giving our breath a third thought, or more than a few moments' attention. Even when trying, it's difficult to remain aware of the breath for more than a minute. Thoughts, feelings, physical sensations derail the attention.

Practice shows that it's far easier to sustain awareness of the breath while sitting in a quiet room than while sitting in the stands at a football game or rushing to catch a train in Grand Central Station. Meditation and other sacred endeavors— prayer, contemplation, ritual—that rely upon free, focused attention thrive most readily within a supportive environment. This is one reason why monasteries exist. Most of us don't care to be monks, so spiritual traditions have devised other means to support the attention and to direct it toward the holy. The most prevalent is sacred architecture—the building of churches, temples, and mosques that instill through their proportions and design a sense of the sacred. Gothic cathedrals were constructed according to mathematical formulas derived from the assumed proportions of the Universal Man, whom Christ was said to incarnate. Bound by arches that surged upward in a mirror image of the many hands below templed in prayer, these cathedrals inspire worshipers to focus their attention, metaphorically and literally, toward the higher. Other spiritual seekers—Pagans, animists, practitioners of the African religions and their offshoots—sometimes turn to nature for their inspiration, conducting rituals outdoors.

The daily prayer cycles of Muslims; the keeping of kosher by Jews; the crosses that so many of my Italian Catholic neighbors dangle next to their hearts; the *tilak,* or dot, worn on the foreheads of Hindus in honor of Lord Vishnu; the altars that grace

Buddhist homes—all are reminders of the sacred that invests this world of matter. In the virtual world, however, similar reminders, and explicitly sacred design, are comparatively rare. This isn't surprising, since cyberspace is a secular creation, molded in large part by programmers who have too rarely recognized the limits of empiricism. (In a cover profile on Bill Gates in the January 13, 1997, issue of *Time*, the Microsoft mogul is quoted as saying, "Just in terms of allocation of time resources, religion is not very efficient.") The paucity of explicit sacred symbol and design in cyberspace wouldn't be such a problem if online activity were only neutral toward the cultivation of free, focused attention. But most computer-human interaction is, in fact, subversive to this attention.

Any excursion into digital reality is a heady experience. At the start of his influential essay about virtual reality, "Being in Nothingness" (available on his Web site), John Perry Barlow announced, "Suddenly I don't have a body anymore." This isn't literally true, since it was Barlow's body that wore the hardware that allowed him to enter virtual reality in the first place. Still, the sweep of the VR experience is so powerful that, in VR, it seems as if one has lost one's body. This tug on the mind away from the body exists as well in the everyday experience of looking at a computer monitor.

Meditative practice is grounded in the body, for the body is steadier than the mind. Through sensation, the meditator can return to the body as a touchstone of what is real, again and again and again. It is impossible to sustain free, focused awareness without grounding that awareness in the body. The body is also the medium through which we experience sacred energies. It is a laboratory of the Divine. Meditators often adopt special—sacred—postures during their practice, ranging from the erect-spine lotus of Theravadan Buddhists to the pretzeled positions of Yogins to the submissive prostrations of Muslims. These postures enhance the flow of subtle energies through the body and catalyze the emotions toward the sacred. Any medium that diminishes our sense of body, of our incarnate nature, puts our consciousness, our attention, and our spiritual possibilities at risk.

The break with the body in cyberspace is most apparent when meeting other people through live, text-mediated chat, as in IRC or the chat rooms of AOL. The *prana,* the subtle energies, are lost. The incarnate being, the human being, behind the words can only be imagined, just as the reader of these words can only imagine the writer. What fills the space left by the absent *prana* is self-projection. In online encounters, words are clues to a puzzle of infinite complexity: another human being. They misdirect as often as they hint. Some chat forums now employ online "avatars," pictorial representations that allow forum participants to disguise, or to reveal, themselves by adopting any digitized image—of a cartoon cat, of Marilyn Monroe, of Jesus, or perhaps, as a nod to the future, of a supercomputer. But these virtual embodiments are amputations, golems of the mind—toys, really—and using them, while fun, bears the same relationship to a face-to-face meeting as standing in a basement and directing a remote-controlled car from Radio Shack has to speeding along in a Corvette convertible on a warm spring day. This is not to say that communication isn't possible in cyberspace, because it is—even heart-to-heart communication. But it has its limits.

Recently, a number of commentators have claimed that the experience of surfing the Web induces *flow,* the term used by the psychologist Mihaly Csikszentmihalyi in his classic book *Flow* to describe what he calls "the psychology of optimal experience." Flow, as Csikszentmihalyi explained in the September 1996 issue of *Wired* magazine, means being

completely involved in an activity for its own sake. The ego falls away. Time flies. Every action, movement, and thought follows inevitably from the previous one, like playing jazz. Your whole being is involved, and you're using your skills to the utmost.

Many of the times I've surfed the Web or engaged in live chat in IRC or on AOL, I've felt totally involved in the experience, and time flew. I don't know that my ego fell away, though, and I'm certain that my whole being wasn't involved—certainly not my body, at least not the attuned body, quickened in perception, that I sense during meditation. I doubt whether these experiences, or any online experiences, actually correspond to what Csikszent-mihalyi means by flow, for they lack the balance of body and mind that he emphasizes in his book. Call it *flow* or not, the experience computers offer, albeit pleasurable, seems to bear little relationship to genuine spiritual work, which always incorporates the truth of the suffering that comes with having a body.

The Net has the power to pull me, and millions more, back online again and again, perhaps more than we might like. Is the online experience addictive? When I asked John Perry Barlow that question during my first interview with him, he had this to say:

"The way I look at addiction is that addiction is something that arises as a result of a system that almost works. If you've got something that provides intermittent, unpredictable, positive feedback, it has a high addictive potential, because then you try to engineer the system so that it will be predictable and non-intermittent. And of course it's not in the nature of the system to be engineered in that fashion. The harder you try the worse it gets, and the next thing you know you've got yourself a Jones.

"I've applied that theory to a lot of different kinds of addiction, and it seems to work pretty well. It certainly works very well with the online thing, because what is broken there is the *prana*. So you can try to horse it into some kind of configuration that is really going to give you a sense of satisfaction, and you can feel that you're nanometers away from it, but there is this missing element—and that is going to prevent you from feeling whole."

Barlow added that he didn't see much evidence that people stay there, an observation I've heard expressed by others, and one that I share. The year I bought my first modem, I spent perhaps fifteen hundred hours in cyberspace. That's a lot of time, more than was healthy for me, and I knew it. I knew that I was hooked—by the thrill of meeting new people, exploring new vistas, adopting new identities, and, above all, of abandoning my body and succumbing to the "flow" for hours on end. It all felt a bit godlike, and is there any feeling more intoxicating than hubris? I knew that in going online I was looking for the control—the predictable outcome that Barlow spoke of—that eluded me in my offline life. I even understood that in seeking this control I was sabotaging my spiritual work, by substituting a more malleable virtual world for this recalcitrant real one, by refusing to accept this world as it is. I was neglecting my family as well. But when you're hooked, you're hooked.

Psychology professionals are starting to recognize and to attempt to treat Net addiction, which they sometimes refer to as Internet Addiction Disorder. Twelve-Step groups, however, which abound on the Net (and are discussed in detail in chapter 11 of this book), and which more readily recognize the spiritual aspects of addiction, have generally shied away from dealing with Net addiction, especially on the Net itself, likely for the same reason that A.A. doesn't hold meetings in bars. The sort of abstinence recommended by Twelve-Step programs seems an impractical solution for Net addiction anyway, because, for a variety of reasons, many of us have to go online. (A group called Netaholics Anonymous does exist. Their homepage can be found at *http://www.safari.net/~pam/netanon/index.html*.)

Fortunately, though the pull of the online world is great, the pull of the organic world is greater still, for it's embedded in every cell of our bodies. Eventually, my own online Jones, to use Barlow's phrase, wore off—not all at once, but steadily, a little bit at a time. The real world reasserted itself, and slowly I welcomed it back.

Used intelligently, time spent in cyberspace can be therapeutic. Cyberspace has been likened by more than one sage (including

Partenia's Jacques Gaillot) to dream space. It is a realm where the laws of time and space grow hinky, where nothing ages and there's no gravity to keep us from flying, in this VR or that, high above the earth. Though the illusory power bestowed on the cybernaut can be addictive, it can be liberating too. A taste of godhood does wonders for self-esteem. In cyberspace, moreover, we can heal psychic wounds in a relatively safe way by reexperiencing, through role-playing, the trauma that opened them. And online, by experiencing the fluidity of the self, we can experiment and explore every side of ourselves, including the shadow side. We can play.

Still, this can be a dangerous game, and the "flow" that's built into the Web is only one of the potential pitfalls in cyberspace. In the absence of sacred design, secular design rules. As Jaron Lanier explicates so eloquently in his online essay "Karma Vertigo; or, Considering the Excessive Responsibilities Placed on Us by the Dawn of the Information Structure" (available on his Web site), the network architecture—the technical way a computer network is constructed—that we put in place today will influence our human culture, including its spirituality, for generations to come. As examples, Lanier cites the discreteness of much computer interaction (a phenomenon touched upon in chapter 9 of this book) and the existence of "files (instead of a big connected sea of information)." Other examples, some relating to software design, come to mind: the modeling of the Windows interface as an office; the cut-and-paste function of word processors, which leaches words of their gravity; hypertext, which though beneficial in its challenge to linear thinking can also inspire conceptual clutter; the anthropomorphizing of computers and software (which reached a nadir in the unpopular Microsoft interface *Bob*).

One of the clearest voices cautioning against the seducements of cyberspace belongs to, of all people, an editor at a leading publishing house of technical books about computers. He is Stephen L. Talbott, an editor at O'Reilly & Associates, the author of *The Future Does Not Compute: Transcending the Machines in Our Midst,* and the founder and editor of the electronic newsletter NETFUTURE (available through e-mail subscription, or on the Web at *http://www.ora.com/staff/stevet /netfuture*). I've interviewed Talbott twice by phone from his home in upstate New York. The first time we spoke, in 1995, he made the point that cyberspace "gives us a world of indirect interaction . . . an abstracted world [that] seems to run counter to a certain basic requirement of spirituality, which has to do with encountering reality in the most intense and profound way, and thereby penetrating to what lies behind it—the forces, energies, potentials from which the visible is taken to have descended. It's hard to imagine that kind of profound penetration of reality occurring more easily in a context where you scarcely have access to the reality to begin with."

During our second conversation, conducted a year later, Talbott reemphasized the peril of replacing direct, real-world experience with abstraction, and of substituting human creative response with what he calls *automatisms*. (His preferred example of the latter is the practice by which banks officers, who used to make loan decisions partly by assessing an applicant's character, now rely solely on software that leaves the human out of the equation.) During that second talk, Talbott said something most unexpected. "I think," he told me, "that we confront such grave, sometimes almost overwhelming challenges in the world precisely because we have a need to develop the capacities that enable us to overcome those challenges. I think we're facing the challenge of technology in modern life simply because it's time for us to wake up in a way that we have not yet waked up, and this is a requirement for our waking up."

The intelligent response to online enchantment seems to be not to turn off the screen but to take up the challenge, as Talbott recommends. To do that entails a willingness to foster awareness of the body and the sacred energies that flow through it even while the screen is on. Making use, like a resourceful explorer, of the terrain itself can help—for instance, taking the pauses in flow symbolized by the hourglass not as unwanted intrusions but as reminders to bring the attention back to the body. Another way to take up the challenge is through the sacralizing of cyberspace.

A historic step toward the creation of sacred cyberspace was taken by a Tibetan Buddhist monk in 1989–1990. During that time, working with graduate students and faculty at Cornell's Program of Computer Graphics, Pema Losang Chogyen developed a digitized three-dimensional representation of the thirteen-deity Vajrabhairava mandala. In Tibetan Buddhism, a mandala is a mind palace that is home to a deity, an interlocking system of sacred symbols that is visualized during meditation. Mandalas can be extraordinarily complex. The Vajrabhairava mandala is as ornate as Ali Baba's cave, encompassing a room and antechambers built of intricately inlaid walls, ceilings, and pillars, festooned with silk banners. To visualize such a mandala in all its detail taxes the abilities of even the most advanced meditators. For the untrained, to attempt this sort of visualization is like trying to climb Mount Everest in a pair of Keds.

"In a visualization, you are supposed to visualize every detail," Chogyen told me when I visited him in his threadbare, book-filled apartment in a run-down building on Manhattan's Upper West Side. (As with so many Tibetans, Chogyen's spiritual gifts outpace his material riches. He himself is frail and thin, though possessed of a heartwarming smile). "Obviously," he added, "it is difficult for beginners. Visualize something like a ball at the navel, a ball the size of a mustard seed. Within that ball, you visualize the entire mandala with the deity. Within the deity's navel, you again have the mustard seed—so you are going into infinity. So you train your mind. Usually we don't really train our mind, we let our mind go."

To learn to visualize any particular mandala, beginning meditators often must rely on a two-dimensional representation of that mandala, often in the form of a sand painting. This,

Chogyen explains, serves as "a blueprint, a layout of the visualized three-dimensional mandala." It takes practice to read a two-dimensional mandala properly. To aid this effort and to demonstrate how three-dimensional mandalas are built up in layers of detail within the mind, Chogyen and his colleagues at Cornell created the computer program *Encountering the Mandala*.

This program isn't available to the public on diskette or on the Net, although a page about Chogyen's project, including images captured from the program, is located on the Web at *http://www.graphics.cornell.edu/~wbt/mandala*. The visual images produced by the program have been transferred to a videotape, however: *Exploring the Mandala*, which runs ten minutes, depicts the unfolding from a sand painting of the three-dimensional mind palace. To the bass chanting of Tibetan Buddhist monks from the Gyuto Tantric Choir, brightly colored geometric forms blossom from the sand painting like a fantastic plant, seemingly in three dimensions, until the fully constructed palace begins to spin like a top, finally descending into the head (shown through live footage) of Chogyen, meditating on a field of grass. To watch the video is to be awestruck by the deep powers of the human mind.

There is another digitized Tibetan Buddhist mandala in motion that can be purchased on disk. This is the Kalachakra, or Wheel of Time, mandala, available as a screensaver. I have it on my computer, and it's a wonder to behold. Like many screensavers, the *Peace Mandala Screen Saver* accretes from a black screen. From the center of the screen out, pixel by pixel, a multicolored, two-dimensional image of the Kalachakra sand mandala, the most complex of all Tibetan mandalas, appears. The process takes five minutes.

The *Peace Mandala Screen Saver* springs from the resourceful mind of Barry Bryant, the founder and director of the Samaya Foundation, a nonprofit organization begun in 1973 to promote Tibetan Buddhist teachings in the West. The foundation and Bryant are headquartered in a rambling loft/apartment complex located in the heart of Manhattan's Soho. Within rooms decorated equally with Tibetan *thangkas*—sacred scroll paintings framed in silk—and batteries of computer and video equipment, Bryant, a middle-aged fellow who makes a natty appearance in spectacles, a trim beard, and pastel clothes, spoke to me about the screensaver, its purpose and genesis.

Bryant first dealt with computers in the early 1960s, when, as the budget director of a small company, he supervised a transfer of records from handwritten logs to computer entries. (Back then, he recalls, computers were "these giant things" that worked with punch cards.) At the same time, he pursued a second career as a painter, later branching into video and film. In 1973, in Copenhagen, where he was working for Danish television, he filmed the Dalai Lama, who was then on his first European tour.

"I asked him," Bryant said, looking at me intently, "if he felt as though the mass media and spiritual media were ultimately one. He paused for a moment and asked what I meant by *mass media*. He asked, 'Do you mean physical media?' I said yes. He answered, 'Yes, ultimately they're one.' And that it's important for us to realize that nonseparation, that oneness. In that instant, the Samaya Foundation was born."

Much of Samaya's early work involved the videotaping of Tibetan lamas, representatives of a culture devastated by the Chinese invasion of Tibet in 1959. Bryant kept up with his more personal art projects as well, and in 1984 generated what he believes to be the first digitized Buddhist icon, *Atari Buddha,* in which a Buddha is drawn in white lines on an orange backdrop on an Atari, one of the earliest makes of PCs. Some years later, a San Francisco TV station invited Bryant to transmit an electronic image of a Buddha in place of the test patterns that used to be broadcast in the wee hours of the morning. Shortly after that, in 1991, Bryant broadcast an electronic, psychedelic-colored image of Tara, the Tibetan Buddhist female deity of compassion, on the Sony Jumobtron in Times Square, a sight that must have made the local hustlers and hookers blink. About the same time, Bryant came up with the idea of doing a Buddhist screensaver, first of Tara. He soon discarded that image in favor of the Kalachakra mandala, which he produced after a couple of years of work with his nephew, Warner Bryant Scheyer, who was then in his midteens.

"For me," Bryant said as he handed me a cup of herbal tea, "the whole world of high technology is content shy. It's content needy, in need of inspired content. I have unshakable faith in Kalachakra in terms of what it can do for the world, and I feel that we should use all the various media available to us to express that, and to make this available to the world."

The Kalachakra mandala is part of the Kalachakra tantra, or system, ascribed to the Buddha. It is, according to information given on the "Help" menu of the *Peace Mandala Screen Saver*, "a road map of the universe. It explores the interrelationship of the heavenly bodies, the human body, and the workings of the mind." Traditionally, the mandala is created as a sand painting during the Kalachakra empowerment, a ritual that runs twelve days, as monks painstakingly release sand in tiny trickles from elongated funnels to fashion the mandala. As it appears on the computer screen, the mandala seems a universe in itself, a stupendously intricate, otherworldly maze, drawn to precisely prescribed measure, filled with gods and humans and animals and signs, all together representing the five-story palace of the deity Kalachakra.

Like any sacred symbol, however, the Kalachakra mandala can lose some of its resonance through familiarity. Employing a sacred symbol as a screensaver seems especially problematic, since screensavers are themselves like habits, running through the same routine over and over again. Familiarity with them breeds not contempt, but invisibility. Stopping the construction of the Kalachakra mandala each time I need to return to work on my computer, moreover, strikes me at times as vaguely blasphemous, like cutting off a crucifix at the knees. Still, when seen afresh and allowed to run its course, the *Peace Mandala Screen Saver* is an astonishment.

"I think it can be an awakening for our practice," said Bryant. "I would love to see sacred symbols filling up all of our computers from all of the traditions of the world."

Many of the key sites discussed in this book offer sacred words, images, or audio clips that can be downloaded into home computers. One unusual software program that speaks of the sacred and that is available for downloading as shareware resides at *http://ourworld.compuserve.com/homepages/empower tools*. This is the *I Ching Empower Tool*, a digital version of the I Ching. Taoists and Confucians alike have for eons considered the I Ching a sacred text. Ostensibly a book of divination, the I Ching serves more profoundly as a guide to spiritual growth. *The I Ching Empower Tool*, created largely by Roger Norton of Roger Norton Consulting, is consulted just like a real-world I Ching, through the tossing of three coins six times to generate a hexagram that corresponds to a specified reading. In the software version, the coins are virtual and it's a click of the mouse that sets them spinning.

In an e-mail interview, Norton explained that "the coin toss in the *Empower Tool* uses a random-number-generating procedure." Traditionally, the tossing of coins (or, in a more elaborate procedure, the throwing of yarrow sticks) is done by hand, a method that seems to allow the questioner to play a more direct role in the outcome than clicking on a mouse to generate a random number. I asked Norton about this, and to my surprise, he agreed. "There is no way to randomize the physical act of coin striking coin," he wrote. "There was no way to differentiate the user's shake of the coins or flick of the wrist. There was no way to duplicate the bounce of the coins on a variety of surface materials. For all those reasons, we feared the program would be inaccurate or totally useless.

"But judge for yourself," he continued. "There is another factor involved here that somehow makes it work. When all is said and done, I honestly don't know what it is. . . . Perhaps the seed of all sixty-four situations [the sixty-four hexagrams] lies within every problem we bring to the I Ching, so any answer is relevant. . . . That's a rational explanation. Or maybe our unconscious minds affect the physics involved in a computer's operation in ways we can't imagine. That's pure speculation. Maybe the true answer is much more spiritual than we realize. I think I like that answer best."

In most religions, not just sacred texts but the books that present them are treated with respect. Few Christians would choose to use their Bible as a coaster or a doorstop. Perhaps we should treat a digital version of the I Ching, or an FTP file containing the text of Genesis, with the same reverence. The evanescence of cyberspace, the way we can make it appear or disappear at will, makes this a difficult task, but it may be that, in the end, cyberspace will be only as sacred as the care—and the attention—that we bring to it.

Exploring the Mandala is available from Snow Lion Publications (Box 6483, Ithaca, NY 14851–6483 [*http://www.well .com/user/snowlion*]) for $19.95.

The *Peace Mandala Screen Saver* is available from Samaya Press (75 Leonard Street, New York, NY 10013) for $39.95.

CHAPTER 11

Community

The only reason to get online is to find other people.
— STACY HORN

The idea of the virtual community has gained common coin.
Virtual communities do exist. Cyberspace connects people
to one another. This doesn't ensure community, as the connec-
tivity made possible by cyberspace is too often a one-way,
broadcast flow of information, but where there is interactivity
online, a mutual exchange, there, in a broad sense, community
exists. Sometimes the community is as evanescent as a lightning
flash, as when a group of strangers meet by chance and for one
time only in a chat room on America Online. Sometimes it's
longer lasting, as on Echo, or East Coast Hang Out, a virtual
community discussed later in this chapter. How do virtual communities compare with real-life communities in nurturing spiritual work?

No movement that speaks of the sacred depends more on
community than the Twelve-Step movement. Though the fundamental principle of the Twelve Steps (formulated by Bill Wilson,
cofounder of Alcoholics Anonymous) involves surrender to a
"higher power," this surrender manifests through work with
others. The Fifth Step of A.A. reads, "Admitted to God, to ourselves, and to another human being the exact nature of our
wrongs"; the Twelfth, "Having had a spiritual awakening as a
result of these steps, we tried to carry this message to alcoholics
and to practice these principles in all our affairs." To follow

these imperatives, many individuals in recovery, as well as recovery-oriented groups, have reached out to others through the Net (A.A.'s own homepage is located at *http://www.alcoholics-anonymous.org*). One of the first to do so was a fifty-year-old from San Diego who, in accordance with the Twelve-Step tradition of anonymity, goes by the name of Bob Y. He hosts a charming site on the Web called "Recovery Is Good for You" (*http://www.users.cts.com/crash/e/elmo/recovr.htm*). In a phone conversation, Bob described for me how he came to A.A. and the Web:

"I was on a twenty-four-year career of drinking and drugging. For a long time it was fun, fun—and trouble. It was a lot of fun but, gee, I lost a marriage here, lost a house there. But I was still having fun. Then I reached the point where it was all trouble. The last four or five years were like that. I pretty much lost everything except my job. I became suicidal. I was brought into the program in the middle of a suicide attempt. That was about seven and a half years ago. August 21, 1989."

It apparently doesn't take a sober head to use a computer, since Bob had been using them on his job since the early 1980s, when he got his hands on an IBM 8086, with "640K of memory, no hard drive, a fourteen-inch CGA monitor." After several years in recovery, that experience stood him in good stead. "I got interested in the Internet," Bob told me, "and somebody said that homepages weren't that difficult to program, so I thought I could learn how to do it, just for myself. The Alcoholics Anonymous international convention was about to begin in San Diego. So I thought, 'Well, why don't I create a page about the convention?'"

The "Recovery Is Good for You" site grew from that page. It is, Bob admitted, "real vanilla, nothing real fancy in HTML code or anything." The vanilla is flecked rich with information, though. It includes a schedule of recovery-oriented conventions and gatherings around the country, a collection of personal stories of recovery that people have e-mailed to Bob, numerous

links, and, in Bob's groundbreaking contribution to online spirituality, information about his "On-Line Internet Sponsorship." In
Twelve-Step programs, sponsors are program members who have
been drug and alcohol free for at least one year and who act as
guides to those with less time sober. As Bob put it, they are people
"willing to share experience, strength, and hope via e-mail."

The idea for an online sponsorship itself came to Bob via
e-mail, from a visitor to his site. To enact it, Bob explained, "I
asked for volunteers from a mailing list, and I posted on a few
of the newsgroups. I now have eighty volunteers from Alcoholics Anonymous, Narcotics Anonymous, Overeaters Anonymous, Cocaine Anonymous, Al-Anon, a few others. When
somebody asks me for the list of sponsors, I send it to them. I
currently receive one to three requests for that list every day."

Bob insisted that online sponsorship shouldn't replace face-
to-face sponsorship except when absolutely necessary. He called
online sponsorship "an additional tool for our journey." He
pointed out, however, that "there are some people who have access to the Internet who live in very remote areas, and you know
they can't get to meetings. They can't have a live sponsor who
they can see regularly. There also are disabled people who are
homebound, who spend lots of time on their computer but can't
go out of the house. And for them, the list is working."

"But why isn't online sponsorship enough?" I asked. "Why
do people need a 'live' sponsor?"

"I don't think you can replace the sense of intimacy that is
possible in a live situation. And I believe that a sense of intimacy
and complete trust are required for successful sponsorship. You
can't get a hug via e-mail, you can't get taken out for a cup of
coffee. As a sponsor, you can't say, 'I can tell by the look in your
eyes that something is wrong. Why don't you tell me what it is?'

"But I think there are some real good things on both sides,"
Bob hastened to add. "I've gotten responses from people saying, 'You know, even with my sponsor, there was something I
couldn't tell him. But the anonymity of e-mail made it so that I

could tell this guy that real deep, dark secret I never wanted to tell.' And getting rid of those deepest darkest secrets is critical to our success in this program."

That you can't get a hug via e-mail is driven home to me when I attend an online A.A.-style meeting on the IRC channel #AA. (A schedule of this meeting and others like it is posted regularly on the Usenet group alt.recovery.) Although not officially sponsored by A.A., these meetings usually draw a crowd of active A.A. members. The give-and-take is friendly but, due to IRC architecture, scattered, as the following sample (with screen names masked) indicates:

> POSTER 1: bottom line is we cant ever drink again . . . so we have to go to HOW EVER MANY meetings such action requires

> POSTER 2: hahaha we LIVE now Poster1, there isn't enough hours in the day for all there is out there now :) at least not in my life now

> POSTER 1: I guess of course I have a rocking home group..we sponsor all kinds of cool sober stuff..so that is why I go everyday . . . Well I go everyday..but I never got to the point of drinking everyday..but I go everyday in order to never get there..and to be able to practice all the principles..:)

> POSTER 3: well, that's your program Poster 1

> POSTER 4: That's great for you Poster1 :)

> POSTER 1: In order for me to keep my primary purpose..which is to stay sober and help another drunk

> POSTER 5: Today I dont have the need to go to meetings on a daily basis . . . doesnt mean tomorrow I wont have that need

> POSTER 6: AMEN

> POSTER 4: hey anyone live in San Diego??

POSTER 4: there is a great speakers meeting in about 1 hour

It's telling that so much of the talk in this online ersatz A.A. meeting revolves around the necessity (or not) of attending real-world meetings. Also notable is the following entry, posted shortly after the entries above:

>>>[name deleted] strolls thru the room huggin
\{{{{{{{{{{{{{{{{{{{{{{{{{{(everyone)}}}}}}}}}}}}}}}}}}}}] and the ladies twice ;-)

That is an online hug, and it's a ghostly thing. Similarly, indigenous online religions pale next to real-world faiths. Many are intentional jokes, such as the popular Church of the Mighty Gerbil ("Go forth upon this Earth and spread the holy words of the Sacred Gerbil on Earth. Go Forth and Prosper!"), which is located at *http://www.gerbilism.sanpedro.com* and proclaims itself to be engaged in "the first Holy War to take place on the web," against the equally popular Church of the Bunny. On its own site (*http://ourworld.compuserve.com/homepages/bunny church*), the Church of the Bunny responds to the threat, declaring alliances with the Church of the Mighty Shrew and the Orthodox Church of the Hamster. Silly stuff, but these churches, particularly the Church of the Bunny, claim a number of followers as well as distinct theologies. The Church of the Bunny is linked to a somewhat more serious church, the Universal Life Church (*http://ulc.org/ulc/index.html*), which has only two tenets: "the absolute right of freedom of religion and to do that which is right." This church offers instant ordination; prospective ministers need only enter their name and address into the church's database. ("This is to certify that the bearer hereof, Reverend Jeff Zaleski, has been ordained this Second day of March, 1997," reads my own ordination certificate.)

Then there are wholly serious cyber religions, nearly all of which proclaim the gospel of reason and of technological progress. The Church of Virus, for instance, located at *http://www.lucifer.com/virus/lb_index.html*, "provides a conceptual framework for leading a truly meaningful life and attaining

immortality without resorting to mystical delusions." Whether
they're serious or not, it's difficult to take these religions seriously, but neither are they to be ignored. Their existence indicates a dissatisfaction with established religions, and may hint
at more vigorous, and darker, cyber religions to come. The mass
suicide of the 39 members of the Heaven's Gate cult in March
1997 highlights the Internet's ability to harbor and foster spiritual communities of every kind, including the most dangerous.
The Heaven's Gate cult, which arose in 1975, didn't spring from
the Net, but it did broadcast its message to thousands through
its now-defunct Web site and postings to various newsgroups.
At least one of the suicides, 39-year-old Yvonne McCurdy-Hill
of Cincinnati, a post office employee and mother of five, initially
encountered the cult in cyberspace and decided to join in response to its online message. Cults like Heaven's Gate find cyberspace a welcome medium. Those most vulnerable to a cult's
message—the lonely, the shy, misfits, outcasts—are often attracted to the Net, relishing its power to allow communion with
others while maintaining anonymity. While the Net offers an
unprecedented menu of choice, it also allows budding fanatics
to focus on just one choice—to tune into the same Web site, the
same newsgroup, again and again, for hours on end, shut off
from all other stimuli—and to isolate themselves from conflict-
ing beliefs. Above all, the headiness of cyberspace, its divorce
from the body and the body's incarnate wisdom, gives easy rise
to fantasy, paranoia, delusions of grandeur. It wasn't a great surprise to learn that the members of Heaven's Gate were described
by residents of Rancho Santa Fe, California, where the cult was
headquartered, as being "unnaturally pale," or that they em-
phasized nonsexuality even to the extent of castratation and
hoped to "shed" their bodily "containers" in order to pass on to
the "Level Above Human."

In his seminal book *The Virtual Community: Homesteading
on the Electronic Frontier,* Howard Rheingold defines virtual
communities as "social aggregations that emerge from the Net

when enough people carry on . . . public discussions long enough, with sufficient human feeling, to form webs of personal relationships in cyberspace." But do most virtual communities really "emerge from the Net"? The Well, the West Coast–based virtual community that Rheingold focuses his book on, didn't. It began in 1985 as, in Rheingold's words, a "cultural experiment," designed by Stewart Brand, Larry Brilliant, Matthew McClure, and other alumni of cultural experiments of the Sixties, including Ken Kesey's bus (Brand) and the Hog Farm (Brilliant). These men, and probably other charter Well members, knew one another before they launched the Well. They already shared a web of personal relationships. Most virtual communities, especially the successful ones, spiritual or secular, do not spring from the Net fully formed like Athena from the head of Zeus. They begin, and generally remain after some fashion, extensions of or counterparts to real-world communities. Observation shows as well that people who meet online often want to meet offline. This is just human nature, which exhibits an irrepressible curiosity about the body.

"For me, the online connection isn't complete until you meet someone offline," says Stacy Horn, founder and president of the virtual community Echo. This seems a startling admission from someone who makes her living in the digital arena, but Stacy, to whom I was married years ago, before she or I ever went online, has always had a knack for voicing bottom-line truths.

Echo bills itself as "the virtual salon of New York City." *Salon* seems too genteel a word to convey the passion felt by many of Echo's thirty-five hundred members, or Echoids, for this virtual community launched a virtual eon ago, in March 1990, as a deliberate East Coast counterpart to the Well. As one member exclaimed recently on the ever-changing tag line on Echo's homepage (*http://www.echonyc.com*), "I joined Echo to get laid but now I do it for love."

Echo is an online service where words matter. The smart, savvy tone of the conversations it hosts, conducted through serial postings in more than sixty "conferences" ranging from "Parenting" to "Twelvestep" to "Into the Mystic," have attracted a panoply of New York intellectuals and artists, as well as such organizations as the Whitney Museum of American Art, *Ms.* magazine, and the *Village Voice,* all of which have their own discussion forums on Echo. This virtual community has received extensive media coverage in *Newsweek, USA Today, Wired,* and elsewhere, in part because of its unusually high complement—40 percent—of women users. The subtle key to its success, though, may be that it exists in the real world with nearly as much vigor as it does in the digital realm. Echo members don't meet only online. They get together regularly in "f2fs," or face-to-faces—at discussion dinners, readings, bar parties, softball games, and group excursions.

"The only reason to get online is to find other people," Stacy tells me when I visit her at the Echo offices, located in Tribeca, within shouting distance of Jaron Lanier's loft. She should know. Over more than a decade, the number of hours she has logged online are Olympian (or, as she puts it, "ridiculous, just ridiculous"). After some friendly small talk within earshot of Echo's handful of employees, we've moved for privacy into the smaller of Echo's two office rooms. Against a brick wall rises an enormous set of shelves holding dozens of modems. In a glass case next to it stands Echo's server. Otherwise the room is nearly bare, its space punctuated by a wide-screen TV and the red metal folding chairs we're sitting on, face-to-face. Stacy is small enough to sit cross-legged on her chair. In blue jeans and a black sleeveless shirt, she looks as gamine as ever.

"What are people looking for on Echo?" I ask.

"The same thing they're looking for in their lives."

"But why do they turn to Echo?"

"It's not that they turn to Echo or anyplace else. Echo is just another place to inhabit. They'll try Echo out, and if they find people that they feel comfortable with they stay, or they go on to someplace else." Stacy mentions diversity as one advantage

Echo offers over the real world. "On Echo," she says, "there's a slightly greater probability that I will have a conversation or a relationship that I wouldn't have had otherwise. And that allows for a slight stretching of the tolerance muscles."

Stacy's description of Echo as a *place* intrigues me. "Do you picture a place, like a room, when you're on Echo?"

"No. There is no picture. I've asked other people on Echo, 'Where do you feel that you're going when you go to Echo?' They say they don't feel like they're in their room anymore, and they don't feel like they're in their computer, and they don't feel like they're in my computer. But there's definitely a feeling that some people are over here, some are over there. The Central Conference is here, the Culture Conference is there. There's a sense of movement from place to place. It's how you would feel if you moved around the room with your eyes closed."

No sight, no picture—and no bodies, I point out. What does she think about the lack of the body in cyberspace? Her answer paves an unexpected middle road.

"It's like cybersex," Stacy says. "When people have cybersex they're describing what they're thinking and feeling. You don't have that when you're having physical sex, saying, 'I'm thinking this, I'm feeling that.' Cybersex is not quite enough, and I'd love to say that physical sex is, but it isn't either, because it's kind of neat having those thoughts that you don't normally have. You misunderstand when you separate the two. When you get online and talk to someone, you're not getting the whole picture, and you misunderstand what people are saying. When you're in person you misunderstand all the time, based on what someone looks like, on their physical presence. You need both for the big picture."

Sex, including cybersex, implies intimacy. "Do you feel that you've had genuine heart-to-heart communication with people online?" I ask.

"Only with people that I've also met in person. I need both. It doesn't quite complete the picture until I meet someone."

"Here we are," I say. "We're sitting here and talking, and there's subtle communication going on. I don't mean just visual cues. There's always some sort of psychic energy exchange going on between people. Do you think that exists in online communication?"

"It does happen," she says with a nod of her head. "The same 'No, we're not communicating, now it's getting better, yes!' Those same things are happening. It's not as if you can get online and not feel, or not communicate. I've found that people are exactly the same online as they are in person. There's a little bit of playing around at the beginning, but eventually they settle down and they're themselves. They absolutely cannot help it."

I bring up the absence of the subtle energies in cyberspace—the absence of *prana*.

Stacy looks at me skeptically. "I totally disagree that there's no *prana* in cyberspace. That's like saying you have to lose your humanity because you're using a different form of communication. That you lose the breath of your life, or anyone else's, just because you happen to be using a different medium to communicate with them. Here is Echo. It has created this interview, it has these people in these rooms, it has people who are married, who have kids, who get together constantly. We get together all the time in person, we talk online, we talk on the phone. It has created a world. Where is the *prana* not?"

I tell Stacy about how some of the other people I've spoken to believe that sacred energies can't manifest in cyberspace. "They believe that there's something in life, in real life, that can't be manifested or duplicated in digital reality."

As before, her answer is a rug-puller. "I don't think that there's such a thing as digital reality. That's the best way that I can put it. I don't think that you can separate life from life. Let's say that someone gets online, meets a priest, and their faith is sparked as a result of something the priest says online, and then they get together with that priest in person, and eventually they take Communion. Where is the digital reality? Where is the digital reality in the picture? If somehow that experience online led to Communion, where is the *prana* not?

"To think that you can separate any element of me from me," Stacy concludes, "and to say that here I don't have *prana*, here I do have *prana* . . . " She shrugs her shoulders and smiles. "I have *prana* wherever I am."

Stacy's insight that virtual reality and physical reality inform one another is, I think, essential. I disagree with her about *prana*. I believe that it does break in cyberspace, limiting the medium's potential for spiritual work in communities as well as on the individual level. But *limit* does not mean *negate,* and spiritual work, which calls upon us to accept others, to love them as ourselves, does take place in virtual communities—for instance, through the "stretching of the tolerance muscles" that Stacy mentioned. Virtual and physical reality exert a gravitational pull on one another. At present, virtuality is the moon to the real world, bound by its greater mass, but just as the moon influences the tides, spiritual work in virtual communities is influencing and will continue to influence that work in real-world communities.

CHAPTER 12

Omega

An Annotated Conversation
with Mark Pesce

*I am pretty sure that the World Wide Web is the physical
manifestation, the activation, of Ajna
chakra. The Third Eye.*
—MARK PESCE

Here comes Mark Pesce, striding along Avenue A. He's shifting worlds as easily as a race-car driver shifts gears, now focusing down on the screen of his handheld USRobotics Pilot
minicomputer, now glancing up to avoid colliding with a bunch
of kids on the sidewalk of this main drag of Manhattan's East
Village. He's tall and big-framed, kind of gawky, but he's got
style, with his lime checked shirt and his cool silver glasses and
his shaved head that makes him look like a monk.

Pesce is no monk, though. Now in his mid-thirties, he's a
world-class scientist, the cocreator of VRML, virtual reality
modeling language, the protocol that is turning the Web from
Flatland into the 3-D universe of our dreams. He is also, and
not at all incidentally, a practicing witch—a "known homosex-
ual" witch who is "known to harbor revolutionary/anarchist
tendencies," as he puts it on his Web site.

How did a self-described "bright boy" from a middle-class family in North Kingston, Rhode Island, turn out like this? A Roman Catholic upbringing had something to do with it, instilling in Pesce a yearning for the sacred but also a need to rebel when he admitted to himself and to others, as a student at MIT, that he was gay. Rebels who long for the light often turn to drugs, and so did Pesce, who spent his first year at MIT, 1980–1981, majoring in psychedelics and pot, with a self-directed minor in philosophy (and writing; he won the school's Freshman Fiction Award). This course of study was what got him kicked out of MIT during his sophomore year, but not before he'd connected with digital trailblazers like Nicholas Negroponte, founder of the school's Media Lab, and Danny Hillis, a major figure in the development of parallel computing.

The next decade saw Pesce working as a software engineer and experimenting with spiritual teachings from Pentecostal Christianity to the Gurdjieff Work. Then came in rapid succession three events he calls epiphanies. On Christmas Day 1990, Pesce read Gibson's *Neuromancer* and learned of the "consensual hallucination" known as cyberspace. Three months later he experienced what he calls a "vision" of a "unification of communication," which he soon related to the mythic image of Indra's Net, an infinitely large net held by the Vedic lord of thunder; in each eye of the net glistens a jewel whose facets reflect the infinitude of other jewels. The third epiphany erupted courtesy of Jaron Lanier, who in an interview read by Pesce spoke of virtual reality as the telephone, not the television, of the future. The interactivity promised by Lanier galvanized Pesce, who in 1991 moved from Boston to San Francisco, where the best and the brightest programmers worked, to set up a company to develop a low-cost HMD (head-mounted display) for VR navigation.

"We were going to rule the world," Pesce tells me as he reaches for another slice of the spicy Indian bread known as *pappadum*. "Crush Nintendo and all that shit." We're talking over lunch at an Indian restaurant a couple of blocks away from where I first spotted Pesce hiking toward his meeting with me.

Pesce is being unduly modest here, for his intention was not just to rule the world but to save it. After his three epiphanies, he says, "I thought about this, and thought about it, and thought about it." All the thinking made him realize that the problem with cyberspace was that "when you're in cyberspace, you don't know what's around you," and so you don't know where you are. Hence his quest for the low-cost HMD that would allow users to know exactly where they were in cyberspace—and that would allow something of much greater import as well.

"In order to modify your behavior," Pesce tells me through a mouthful of vegetable *pakoras*, "you have to become conscious of it, okay? It became apparent to me that although cyberspace was a separate universe, it existed in order to augment our understanding of this one. And that in fact we can build something to be able to see the planet better. If we can see the planet, we won't fuck it up. Because, let's face it, the planetary ecology is pretty fucked right now. So what I was interested in doing was creating something that could manifest the wholeness of the planet. I know that this was why I was doing it—that, in fact, getting rich didn't have very much to do with it.

"We'll call this my *delusions of grandeur* period," Pesce says, shaking his head. "I developed a low-cost sourceless orientation sensor for virtual reality, for which I now have a patent. As far as we know, I'm the first Pesce to be granted a patent, which made my father tickled purple. But I found that at the end of this year and a half of really intensive work, I was absolutely dry inside—empty, burned out, and unfulfilled. And then my partner fired me."

The company fell apart soon after that. "It was an incredible liberation for me," Pesce says, leaning forward. "I learned that, in fact, cyberspace tends away from any attempt to dominate it. There's something about it, its *it-ness,* that tends away from any attempt to dominate it."

That comment strikes me as much more interesting than my lamb vindaloo. I put my fork down. "Let's put on the brakes here for a moment," I say. "Cyberspace has sentient qualities?"

"That's the thing," Pesce chirps. I notice that although his hold on his body seems less than masterful—he twitches at times—Pesce uses his voice with authority, playing it like a violin. "I took this up with one of my first spiritual friends. He said, 'Well, Mark, we're all at the ends of the terminals, so cyberspace has sentient qualities that are equally us.' I went, 'Oh, that's an interesting way of looking at it.'"

Indeed. Can Pesce please elaborate?

"In order to control," Pesce says , "you must rigidify, right? I mean, that's essential Taoism. And yet what you're dealing with here is quintessentially mutable, and therefore with any attempt to control it, you lose your ability to dominate. All right? And this is one reason why the dance between Microsoft and Netscape is so very interesting."

Pesce leans farther forward, pinning me with his gaze. "I know the next step in both players' courts. Most people don't. And I can't tell you, otherwise I'd have to kill myself or something. Most people don't understand that the Web you see now is not the Web. It's as much Web as we can deal with now."

He's practically flat over his plate now. He drops his voice to a stage whisper. "But it's not the Web. The Web is so much broader than what we are capable of conceiving. It's now 30 million documents, whatever that means. That word—*documents*—is going to go away. The Web is not a document space. I think by the millennium it'll be close to a billion—*things*.

"*Things?*"

"*Things*. Entities. Avatars. Whatever."

That the Web will be filled with *things* rather than documents results from Pesce's work on VRML. Pesce first beheld the Web in October 1993, when he downloaded the first graphic Web browser, Mosaic (designed by Netscape founder Marc Andreessen), into his workstation. The vision transported him;

if not Indra's Net, it was awfully close. But the Web lacked something, he realized: the sensual three-dimensionality of VR, which corresponds to that of the real world. Was there a way to infuse the Web with this quality?

There was, and it didn't take long to come up with it. Within weeks of setting to work with fellow engineer Tony Parisi, Pesce and his new partner had come up with the first prototype for VRML, which they dubbed *Labyrinth*. They then made a decision that would set the course of Pesce's life to date (and back up his statement that "getting rich didn't have very much to do with it"). Rather than patent and market the prototype, they decided to turn it over to the world by presenting it at the First International Conference on the World Wide Web in Geneva. There, the new 3-D protocol gained its present name, VRML (pronounced *VER-mel*). A VRML mailing list set up shortly afterward with the help of *Wired* magazine attracted two thousand people, and Pesce's dream of world domination had transmuted fully into one of world salvation.

VRML isn't VR. The three dimensions it offers don't track with movements of your head, at least not as presented on a flat computer monitor. It does grant 360-degree presentation and navigation of *things*—say, a building—represented through the monitor. VRML hasn't yet taken the Web by storm, but it will. Proliferation was slowed by the need for processing power to catch up to the demands of the protocol—VRML is a crawl on a 486 or on weaker Pentiums—and by the sluggish integration of VRML browsers into Web browsers, particularly into Netscape, which now supports VRML on its Navigator 3.0. VRML applications are arising daily on the Web. (An excellent index to many exists at the VRML Repository, at *http://rosebud.sdsc.edu /vrml/repository.html*.) They range from biomedical atlases to corporate presentations; from molecular models to mathematical representations; from a three-dimensional street scene of Edo-era Japan to—in what will certainly be the most popular VRML application—"virtual worlds" such as the entertainment complex Virtual Vegas (a "virtual gambling environment" located at *http://rosebud.sdsc.edu/vrml/repository.html*) and Terra Vista (a "grass roots effort to create a virtual community on the Web," located at *http://www.terravista.org*).

It seems impossible to separate the spiritual from the material in Pesce's life story. At about the same time that he was being fired from the company he'd founded, he experienced what he calls an "opening of the floodgate" in his spiritual life. As is so often the case in spiritual transformation, it was the proximity of death that blew the gate open. On the July 4, 1992, Pesce's close friend and roommate fell gravely ill with what, Pesce says, was essentially a temporary form of multiple sclerosis that kept him from manufacturing antibodies. Distraught and compelled to do something, anything, Pesce invited another friend to his house, where the two descended to the basement and "toned."

"We put a lot of energy into the boy," Pesce tells me, "and he made, as the doctors termed it, 'a miraculous recovery.'"

The gate opened, and with it a new vista for Pesce. "I remember thinking persistently that I needed to pick up my spiritual practice again. But not only that: I looked around, and all of my friends, all of my close friends in San Francisco, were witches. Some of them used that term, some didn't. The names vary, the soul is the same. I looked around and I said, 'I'd better stop fighting it.'"

Pesce began a formal study of witchcraft, under the tutelage of "some really effective witches." The witchcraft he now practices isn't the broomstick and black cat variety. It seems to belong to the tradition whose teaching is as often referred to as "magick," which claims roots dating back to the Hermetic books attributed to the Egyptian god of wisdom, Thoth (whose name was translated into Greek as Hermes Trismegistus), and is celebrated for the formulation "As above, so below." This stream of the teachings grouped under the general rubric of "Paganism" gained notoriety early in this century for the antics of its leading modern interpreter, Aleister Crowley, best known for his own formulation, "'Do what thou wilt' shall be the whole of the law." Crowley is a poor choice of role model—he died a penniless heroin addict; Gurdjieff pronounced him "filthy inside"—but Pesce quotes the man known as "the Beast" often. At the same time, Pesce puts a likable spin on his own witchcraft that one can't imagine coming from the mouth of the pompous, exploitative Crowley. "People always ask," he tells me, "'Are you a good witch or a bad witch?' And I say, 'I'm a silly witch. It guarantees I'm good.'"

Being a good witch, Pesce explains, "means that you have both a gift of attunement, and a responsibility to that attunement." He is proud of being a good witch at such a relatively young age. As for younger witches, they are rare, he says, "because generally you're so chaotic in your twenties that you can't focus your will."

Will. I wonder exactly what Pesce means by that word. I ask him to relate his understanding of will to the phrase taught by Jesus, "Thy will be done."

"There is no God but man," he retorts. "Clearly. But that's not to diminish the higher power either, which is to say, 'As above, so below.'"

"Then what do you mean by will? Is there a difference between will and desire?"

"Yes. Whether desire is there or not has nothing to do with what your will is. In my own understanding, the essence of witchcraft is timing. The secret lies in knowing when to do what to do. Because then it takes a minimum of effort and, generally, it's in balance with what should be going on. Will is an attunement to your timing, such that you know, and then can do, whatever's called for whenever it's called for."

"Do you use your computer to express your will?"

"Absolutely. That's the vector of my own work, I guess."

Pesce's will found a particularly resonant expression through computers in a ritual he calls the CyberSamhain, which he identifies as "a definitive, pure act of will." A few days before

Halloween 1995—on the very day, Pesce tells me, that was the twenty-fifth anniversary of the birth of the Internet—he directed, at Joe's Digital Diner in San Francisco, where a crowd of about seventy had gathered, his own version of the ancient Celtic festival of Samhain. The ceremony served as Pesce's test for his First Degree (one of several rankings in traditional magick). Its primary purpose, however, was far grander.

Samhain, Pesce explains, marks the time of the year when "the veils between the worlds is thinnest. It has been my own supposition from my own magical training that any distinction we make between the shadow realm and cyberspace is largely a category error. So I said, 'Okay, let's do a ritual that's reflective of that. Let's welcome the god into cyberspace. Let's create a place for sacred being in cyberspace.'"

To create this place, Pesce designed a variation on traditional Pagan ritual, which squares a magic circle with four "Watchtowers" situated around the circle, one in each of the four cardinal directions. On the night of the CyberSamhain, he substituted the candles commonly used to symbolize the Watchtowers with four PCs, their monitors facing one another. A naked priestess traced a circle on the ground between the PCs while each PC ran a VRML edition of the circle that had been posted on the Web. As Pesce chanted and called forth various gods, a handful of people at other locations duplicated the ritual while using VRML browsers to view the magic circle on the Web. Others at other locations participated by viewing an HTML version of the circle.

"What we did was an 'Above, so below,'" Pesce tells me. "We did this doubling between real space and cyberspace, all right? We achieved, as much as we could, a resonance between the form in cyberspace and the form in RL [Real Life]. That was my goal—to have this absolute resonance between the two forms. The idea was, inasmuch as possible, to sanctify cyberspace. If we don't bless our creations, they dehumanize us."

Did the ritual work? Pesce insists that it did. But how does he know?

"Everyone involved with that ritual has had very good computer juju ever since," he says. "VRML really started to take off after that. Draw of that what you will. It was also one of the first pieces that stated that there needed to be a dialogue between the sacred part of ourselves and cyberspace. And that dialogue is now ongoing and is taking up an increasingly interesting portion of some people's minds."

My own included, I think. We've finished lunch now, but Pesce and I have more to talk about—specifically, about his "operating theory," which he promises to elaborate for me over coffee elsewhere. We walk up the block and around the corner to the Yaffa Café, a popular local watering hole. In Yaffa's back garden, over straight American coffee for me and decaf cappuccino for Pesce ("If I have any more caffeine today it'll be bloody," he tells the waitress), I learn of his ultimate vision.

MARK PESCE: Okay. Here's my operating theory. It's a theory and I'm doing my best to put it to the test. The Yogis talk about the chakras. My own theory is that the planet has chakras, as well as human beings, and that the planetary body is actualizing those chakras. I am pretty sure that the World Wide Web is the physical manifestation, the activation, of Ajna chakra. The Third Eye. [As elaborated in Kundalini Yoga, the seven chakras in the human body, ascending from the genital area to the top of the head, are spiritual nerve centers that correspond roughly to biological nerve centers.]

VRML is one aspect of the manifestation of that perception. It was time for it. It was time. It could have been something else, if something else had been there at that time. I had my finger in the breeze. We did it.

Where does that leave us? It leaves us with one other chakra unactualized.

JEFF ZALESKI: And that chakra is?

MP: The next one is Crown chakra. Crown chakra represents connection with the Divine, connection with the universe. It's interesting because the Mayans indicate that this is what they call "the end of the galactic activation cycle." And what I see now is that there are three events that have happened in the past three months that allow me to provide circumstantial evidence for that. I'll give them in order.

The Crown chakra is beginning to activate. The first thing that the Yogi would say is that you are experiencing the endarkenment of that chakra, which is its shadow nature. You've seen *Independence Day?*

JZ: No.

MP: You haven't? That's a shame. It's a very interesting movie. Ships appear from outer space as giant rings, and immediately locate themselves over the exoteric centers of power. With a little central ring in the middle.

JZ: And that means?

MP: They crown these places. They crown the White House, they crown the Empire State Building. They crown them. And when these machines activate, a beam of fire shoots down and all of reality is burned away. That's the shadow nature of the activation of the Crown chakra. Because as soon as you've activated the Crown, you've activated your cosmic connection. And it's the shadow nature, and everybody gets really scared and says, "Oh my God, the ships are from outer space, the aliens are evil, they're coming to get us." The film was in some ways a very weak film, but at the same time it was extremely resonant with what was going on in people's heads. So that's factoid number one.

Factoid number two: If you were going to present the opening to the galaxy in the most benign, most simple, most acceptable possible way to human reason, which is very good at filtering out things that are just unacceptable to it, how would you do it? You'd find a very simple relic, of a very simple life-form, on a very near planet.

JZ: I know what you're referring to. [Pesce is referring to the discovery, announced days before this late September 1996 talk, of possible fossils of Martian life in a meteorite.]

MP: Yes, absolutely. It is in all ways acceptable to our reason. Which is significant, because if a spaceship suddenly landed from Sirius and little men walked out, it wouldn't be acceptable to our reason. You've read *Childhood's End?* If you remember, the Overlords refuse to show themselves for fifty years, because if they had originally they would have been mistaken as devils. So they had to acclimate human beings to their presence before they could come forth as they were without causing a panic.

The third factoid: Scientists announce there's a third basic class of life on the planet. The Archaea. Who are so dramatically different from us. They share only 20 percent of the DNA with any other phyla, and they're capable of living in environments where we could not possibly consider life occurring: Venus, Mars, Jupiter. And so now, all of a sudden, the universe, which was utterly dead, is looking like it's teeming with life. There's the beginning of an opening, and that opening says all of a sudden that life is not local. It's distributed and universal.

Now, I draw my own conclusion from this from Sheldrake's work—that in fact the reason that life developed on earth the way it did is because DNA happens to be morphically resonant, because there's a lot of it around in the universe. So those reactions were the ones that had the clearest pathways open for them because they are common throughout the universe. I'm sure that when we finally get a good sample of the Martian bacteria, we'll find out that its structure is relatively similar to that. That's how we were able to recognize it at all—because it's somehow morphically resonant with what we think life should be like. The reason for that is because there's a lot of it around.

Rupert Sheldrake is the biologist who, in his 1981 book *A New Science of Life,* introduced the concept of *morphic resonance.* This concept posits that there is a collective memory in nature and in the behaviors of nature (including us) that creates a morphic field, a field of habit, that grows ever stronger over time. A snowflake that will fall next winter will look like those that have fallen for hundreds of millions of years because of its resonance with the morphic field generated by these past snowflakes. According to Sheldrake, morphic fields organize all self-organizing systems—molecules, ecosystems, trees, dogs, languages—by modifying the probabilities of random events. For this reason, the concept of morphic resonance does not apply to computers, which act utterly predictably and thus allow for no modification of their behavior (other than through deliberate reprogramming or through malfunction).

The principle of morphic resonance would at first glance indicate that the forms that religious behaviors—and particularly religious rituals, which are a kind of sacred habit—take in the virtual world will follow those of the real world. But Sheldrake leaves room in his theory for the arising of entirely new forms, which, when established, generate their own morphic fields. It may be that the break between the real and virtual worlds, and the breaking of *prana,* will prove sufficiently severe to shock into being entirely new forms of religious behavior.

> JZ: I don't quite understand how the discovery of, let's say, the Martian fossil life relates to the opening of the chakra. Is there a force engineering this?

MP: Or is it morphic resonance? I don't know. I don't want to invoke causality. I simply want to observe. Unfortunately, it's a characteristic habit of human beings to try to fit things into systems by which they make sense. But if I were a higher power, and if I were going to introduce humanity into knowing that there's life out there in the universe, that is undoubtedly the most benign way to do it. It's a planet that's sort of closest to ours in terms of climate, in terms of overall structure—sure, life could have happened there. It's a really interesting thought! And it's not outside the realm.

At the same time, the most amazing thing is how—although this is probably the most important discovery of the twentieth century—essentially nonplussed everyone is. I was out all night with friends, partying it up, smoking dope, whatever. I came back to the hotel room, turned on the TV at 3 A.M., and all of a sudden CNN is talking about life on Mars, and I'm like, "I didn't dose, this must really be happening!" And yet the next day the front-page story on *USA Today* was on AOL, not on life on Mars! People took it in stride because it was just so mellow.

JZ: It was mellow, and most people already believe that there's life in outer space.

MP: Yeah. But believing is way different from direct experience. It will shatter worldview.

So this is how I interpret those three factoids: They fit into an eschatology in which I see the next sixteen and a third years as being an opening of that last chakra. What I am positing in relation to this theory is that the next sixteen years will see an increasing broadening of our awareness of how alive the solar system is. Sheldrake says that he thinks the sun thinks. Because it's got all these weird electric fields and there appears to be no rhyme or reason that we can understand. I don't know if the sun is a big brain directing evolution on all the planets, but that's Sheldrake's thesis now. And he's a very bright man.

So my functioning thesis is that there is a *telos,* that there is in fact a directioning, there.

JZ: How unscientific of you.

What I should have said was, "How unscientific of you, in terms of the beliefs of the scientific mainstream." Contrary to the popular belief that evolution progresses from simplicity toward complexity, orthodox science recognizes no direction to evolution, no end toward which evolution is moving, and no purpose to its movements. Today's best-known evolutionist, Stephen Jay Gould, argues forcefully in his most recent book, *Full House: The Spread of Excellence from Plato to Darwin,* that evolution is a matter of variation of individuals within populations, and evinces no evidence of favoring increasing complexity. As an example, Gould points to bacteria, which he declares to be the most successful adaptation in the history of life. Future species are, according to Gould, as likely to be simple, like bacteria, as they are to be complex, like us. If Gould and the many scientists who agree with him are right, then the ideas of Teilhard de Chardin (discussed later in this chapter), which have inspired much of the more speculative thinking about cyberspace and its effect on humanity's spiritual future, are wrong.

MP: Planets have a direction. I don't know if it's unscientific. What I'm trying to do is to produce elements that are testable, like Sheldrake. Okay? What I'm saying is that, if this theory's true, there should be a broadening consciousness that the universe is in fact universally alive. And that in fact any boundaries we draw between the biota and the non-biota are category errors.

Destroy duality as you would destroy falsity. I think that's partly what the activation of that last chakra is about.

All right. So my own work: The interesting thing about any simulation is that the longer you interact with it, the more tightly you become coupled to it. That's what a good interface is. Interface is seduction, at least a good interface is. Bad interface is domination. What I expect an emergent property of this intense modeling of the world will be is a collapse of boundary between singular ego and Gaian ego. Or I should perhaps say between singular *ontos* and Gaian *ontos*. That's probably a better way of looking at it, because I don't really know anything about Gaian ego, but we all know something about Gaian *ontos*.

By *Gaian ontos,* or Gaian being, Pesce is referring to one aspect of the Gaian Hypothesis, formulated in the 1970s by the British biochemist James Lovelock while he was working with NASA to detect life on Mars. According to this hypothesis, the earth, or Gaia, is a giant living, self-regulating organism. As humans are one element of the many that make up the earth, and as we think, according to the Gaian Hypothesis it may be said that the earth itself thinks, through us.

JZ: This will happen in the case of the individual?

MP: Well, let me put it this way. Before electric media, we were circumscribed by the distance we could travel and directly experience. And now all of a sudden, "What hath God wrought?" God hath wrought the unification of the human noosphere wherein electrical cables connect us to each and everyone else. And all of a sudden there are parts of us that aren't parts of us. But they are parts of us. Where do I end? Where does CNN begin, or MTV? Or Jeff Zaleski? We live in a different ontosphere than my great-great-grandfather did. Very different. We don't know that because we're in the milieu, we're structurally coupled to the milieu, so really the only thing we can intuit is our own structural coupling to the milieu. My thesis is that producing an effective evocation of the planet, which is not one evocation but many, many different ones, will bind us more closely to its ontological nature, to its beingness. Until in fact the simulation of the planet, and our apprehension of the planet, are similar. Or similar enough.

Noosphere is the word Teilhard de Chardin used in his extraordinary book *The Phenomenon of Man* to describe the "thinking layer" that evolution has spread "over and above the world of plants and animals." By Teilhard's reckoning, the evolution of the noosphere depends upon two factors: "the roundness of the earth and the cosmic convergence of the mind." To Teilhard, humanity is key to the noosphere, for with the arising of humanity, "for the first time in a living creature instinct perceived itself in its own mirror" and "the whole world took a pace forward." The phrase *a pace forward* implies, in a distinctly non–Stephen Jay Gouldian fashion, that the world, through evolution, is marching in a particular direction. Toward what? Toward "Omega," which is, in Teilhard's language, "*a distinct Centre radiating at the core of a system of centres;* a grouping in which personalisation of the All and personalisations of the elements reach their maximum, simultaneously and without merging, under the influence of a supremely autonomous focus of union."

Teilhard's influence on thinking about cyberspace is incalculable. Nearly every formulation about the arising of a global brain—the global network of computers with human beings at the terminals—finds its roots in interpretations of his thought, as does the ancillary idea that this arising will lead to some sort of transformation of humanity, and hence of Gaia. As John Perry Barlow wrote in his widely distributed essay "The Great Work" (available on his Web site), "Whether or not it represents Teilhard's vision, it seems clear we are about some Great Work here . . . the physical wiring of collective human consciousness." But Teilhard's specific formulation is Christian, indeed Roman

Catholic, as he was a Jesuit (although he was forbidden by his religious superiors in the Church to publish his major works; *The Phenomenon of Man*, written in 1938, first appeared in print only in 1955, the year Teilhard died). By "*a distinct Centre*" Teilhard means precisely the "personal God" of Christianity. Furthermore, Teilhard acknowledges the presence of evil: "Evil may go on growing alongside good, and it too may attain its paroxysm at the end in some specifically new form." These fundamental characteristics of Teilhard's work are often glossed over by cyber philosophers (though not by Barlow), who seize upon Teilhard's vision of a converging global consciousness and wrench it to conform to supremely hopeful thinking. For some, Teilhard's words have become a magic mirror in which they see whatever they want. One commentator claimed in *Wired* that Teilhard's idea of "tangential energy" is equivalent to virtual life, when in fact Teilhard defined this energy as that "which links the element with all others of the same order." This same writer went on to state that "according to Teilhard, this invisible virtual life has been with us since the beginning." But, again, Teilhard was a Christian, and the Omega he describes is—although nonmaterial ("detaching the mind, fulfilled at last, from its material matrix")—not digital but mystical.

JZ: Similar enough for what?

MP: Well, we'll probably behave differently as a result.

JZ: Can you give me an everyday example of how behavior will be changed?

MP: Well, yeah. If it's very clear to people, say, that driving polluting cars in Los Angeles is causing an ozone hole to open in Los Angeles, which is causing skin cancers to go up, and cataracts to increase, that may be a powerful determinant of behavior in Los Angeles. It may in fact be something that causes a sense of social constraint in people participating in behaviors that are considered to be antithetical to that ecology. That's what we realized about the ozone hole, because before we saw the ozone hole, with computer imaging of the planet via satellite, we didn't decide to stop dumping chlorofluorocarbons into the atmosphere. So that's a concrete example.

JZ: It sounds as if what you're talking about is merely a very radical extension of what's already here. At home in Brooklyn, I don't throw my newspapers out into the garbage anymore. I set them aside to be recycled. And I do that because I'm aware of global deforestation. So, yes, this sort of awareness changes my actions in that sense. And I suppose on a very subtle level it changes my sense of self, because I feel more connected with the globe. But I don't think that it has changed my basic perception of myself. I'm still caught in the ego.

MP: But ego is a manifestation of physicality, right? It's an emergent aspect of physicality. Although the funny thing about ego is that when you go looking for it, you can never find it. And it's never there when you need it.

JZ: Do you think that what's going to come is going to affect people's sense of themselves in the world, either in the same way, or to the same degree, that long periods of meditation do? In meditation you observe the self, and you can see the play of the self, and you can encounter what lies behind the self.

Let's use a Buddhist word, *mindfulness*. A traditional Buddhist might say that it's only through mindfulness that you can achieve liberation. The sort of changes you're talking about, will they increase mindfulness?

MP: Do they increase mindfulness of whom? See, what I'm shifting is *whom*. I'm saying that if the Gaian biota is also a whom, then yes, they will increase mindfulness of that. Will they increase mindfulness of the personal whom? Certainly I don't know if what I'm doing will necessarily do that.

JZ: I'm looking around this garden and I see a lot of people. Most of the time, they're just vaguely people to me, animate moving objects. I don't realize their humanity. But if I'm mindful, that does increase my perception of their humanity.

MP: You see the buddha-nature in them, right? Ideally.

JZ: Hopefully. But my question then is, How do I realize through a model that this is the same as me? When I really see another human being, I recognize him or her as the same as me. And that somehow I'm intimately connected to them. I don't see how that can happen through digital modeling, except maybe through art. Certainly, art can quicken the moral sense. But most of the technology I've experienced falls short. I do remember, in 1970, watching the funeral of Nasser, the Egyptian leader, on TV, the hysterical crowds reaching for his coffin, and being struck by the power of the media to bear witness.

MP: We have to remember that models are always models, that the menu is not the meal. You have to keep that in mind, always. You have to keep that in mind when working symbolically in the universe in general. But I don't think there's anything fundamentally different in it from the way we understand our own perception. Because we're almost always in playback mode. At least that's what the cognitive psychologists tell us—that we're almost always in memory rather than actually in the moment.

I don't think that this should seek to replace the experience of the natural. It seeks to augment the experience of the natural. I want to be very clear on that. Because the natural is immediate and, insofar as communication, unmediated. This is why I'm going to the Catskills next week to write— because I'm going to be writing about facilities to manage the planet. And I want to be in a natural surrounding when I do that.

This is a different kind of meditation. With a different self that we didn't recognize before, but which is as present. Buddhists practice right livelihood, which is, I think, their own recognition of their own essential is-ness, being-ness, with the planet. My own life has been more or less voluntary simplicity. I did not buy, and I do not buy, into the Silicon Valley, get-rich-quick-right-now myth. I see it, in fact, as a bit of a mania that distorts one's own ends.

Let's get back to teleology. I have a poser for you. I don't know if it's a koan or not. What's the difference between good VR and bad nanotech?

JZ: I have no idea.

MP: They are both ontologically equivalent. This has been noted not just by me but by others. At the end of nanotech, and at the end of virtual reality, the world truly does conform to your will, all the time. Then there's no differentiation between your will and your reality. I think that's the convergence point in 2012.

The convergence point will come at 6:00 A.M. on December 21, 2012, according to the metaphysician and ethnonaturalist Terence McKenna, whose conclusion Pesce is citing. The date arises from McKenna's elaboration of a mathematical function that he calls Timewave Zero and that was influenced in its conception by the I Ching as well as by McKenna's experiments with psilocybin mushrooms and ayahuasca, a psychedelic derived from the bark of the Amazonian banisteriopsis vine and containing a potent dose of DMT.

McKenna, whose interests are summed up in the title of his book *The Archaic Revival: Speculations on Psychedelic Mushrooms, the Amazon, Virtual Reality, UFOs, Evolution, Shamanism, the Rebirth of the Goddess, and the End of History*, is a major figure on the technopagan-Pagan scene, in which Pesce is also a principal player. Technopaganism is an expansive movement that includes techno-"witches" like Pesce, techno-Wiccans, techno–goddess worshipers, techno-Druids, techno-shamans, and ravers. Technopagans tend to hang out in MUDs like Divination Web (*telnet: bill.math.uconn.edu.9393*) or in Usenet groups like alt.pagan and alt.magick. An outstanding Web guide to Pagan resources exists at Arachne's Web, located at *http://www.cascade.net/arachne.html*. Not all Pagans are technopagans, of course, but what unites all technopagans is a consideration of cyberspace as magical space, as dream space, wherein reality corresponds to imagination and to will. The use of alternate realities, including dream space and psychedelic space, is an ancient and honorable way of knowledge. Whether the alternate reality that is cyberspace presents equal access to the knowledge available in dream space and psychedelic space is questionable, however, as both of these arise within the body and seem to depend upon the body's subtle energies.

JZ: By 2012 this is going to happen?

MP: Absolutely. I used to think, "No, there's not enough time." Now, every day that passes I see it, because the Web has amplified human intelligence enormously. It's a giant intelligence amplifier. The Internet first, and now the Web as the emergent property. The propagation of the Web so quickly means it's probably morphically resonant with forms that occur elsewhere. If not this elsewhere, then other elsewheres. And we've only just started to use that intelligence amplifier. We're still not quite aware of its ability, but once we become conscious of its ability, the amplifier really starts to feed back. And things happen more quickly. The interesting thing about the noosphere is that innovations propagate across its entire breadth instantaneously. Thirty million copies of Netscape downloaded in a week. That speed is not slowing down, and intelligence amplification is not slowing down, and—hopefully—wisdom is not slowing down. That is my own personal experience. There appears to be a lot of wisdom mind around now, capable of being picked up and used. And in fact we, as inhabitants of the late twentieth century, have had access to most of the mysteries of most of the mystery schools for at least the last three or four thousand years. Which is an incredible body of wisdom.

JZ: Most, but not all.

This small interjection refers to a big development in traditional spirituality occasioned by media, particularly electronic media. One reason that mystery schools are called *mystery* schools is that much of their teaching is secret, never written down, passed on orally from teacher to student. Every major world religion contains its own versions of mystery schools, an esoteric core of spiritual teaching reserved for initiates. Pesce told me that, in the very public CyberSamhain, "there were certain things I couldn't do, because I was sworn to protect the secrets of the tradition." Similarly, Abbot John Daido Loori mentioned to me that the vast majority of what goes on during the last two years of Zen training is not written down, because it is only for the ears of "a student who can hear." The primary rationale given by most teachers for this secrecy is that esoteric teachings laid open to the world will be distorted or misinterpreted, often to the detriment of those who try to employ them before they are ready. Students of Kundalini Yoga, for instance, which deals with powerful, potentially destructive energy flows in the body, are nearly always enjoined to practice the yoga under the tutelage of a teacher who will show the pupil how to channel the energies step by step.

There is a popular saying in cyber circles: "Information wants to be free." This saying invests information with an autonomy that seems inappropriate, but it is true that many people want information to be free—and as widely distributed as possible. Sometimes these people are the spiritual teachers themselves; and so the Dalai Lama, for instance, has urged the distribution through media, including Barry Bryant's screensaver, of the Kalachakra initiation and mandala, which for thirty-five hundred years were protected as secret teachings. More often, it is people disaffected with a particular religion who are broadcasting its secrets, as in the recent publicized instance of secrets of the Church of Scientology being posted on the Net. Some secrets can't be expressed in digital form, because they relate to direct energy transmissions between teacher and student. I suspect, however, that in years to come the secrets that can be expressed on the Net will be. This development will have its beneficial side, as too often esoteric secrets are hoarded by spiritual seekers in order to support what the Tibetan Buddhist teacher Chogyam Trungpa called "spiritual materialism . . . the ego's constant desire for a higher, more spiritual, more transcendental version of knowledge."

MP: It makes sense now to serve and instruct. Remember I said that being a witch means being aware, and having a responsibility to that awareness—that when you're aware of something, it's for a reason. And that you have a responsibility to be mindful of what you're aware of, or what your attention is drawn to, and then to face it squarely, and do what needs to be done. The CyberSamhain needed to be done. I intuited that, and I acted.

When the astronauts went into orbit and beheld the body of the planet, they had mystical experiences. Howard Rheingold told me that there was some outer-space fair, and there were both Russian and United States astronauts at the fair. And at one point a Russian astronaut and an American astronaut got into a capsule together. They closed it, so no one could hear them, and the Russian turned to the American and said, "So did you see God up there too?"

JZ: I know Edgar Mitchell did.

MP: Yeah. They all did. Most of them don't talk about it, because they don't want to be classified as loonies. But apparently they all did. I don't really see how you couldn't.

So the lines of history are converging. McKenna goes with this funny fractal that he calls the Time Wave, which he and his brother Dennis channeled in 1973 when they spent ten days high on mushrooms or whatever. And of course Dennis McKenna is now a very respected ethnopharmacologist, and he's figured out that there's some quantum resonance that takes place with respect to molecules. So what does that mean? Well, McKenna says that it means that the Gaian biota is speaking to us. That this is the channel of communication that it uses.

So he draws this line and he says, "This is where I place the endpoint." What I see there is a convergence point between *technos* and *ontos,* between doing and being. And that at the point of that convergence, the entire meaning of being and doing is transformed. You could call it the end of the world if you wanted to, although I'm not sure I want to. What I do want to say is that it's the point when we understand the relationship between ontology and the noosphere. December 21, 2012. It's the winter solstice.

I know it sounds ludicrous. It sounds ridiculous. But you know, every bit of information that you absorb, no matter where it comes from, changes you. You are a field, not a thing. My own feeling is we really don't know how much things have changed, because we would be shocked into some other state, which would probably not be healthy for us, if we really could comprehend, if we really could grasp, the total nature of the total change that's under way now.

Mark Pesce's homepage is located at *http://www.hyperreal.com/~mpesce/.*

The Soul of Cyberspace

May all beings never be separated from happiness.
— SIDDHARTHA GAUTAMA, THE BUDDHA

In late February 1997, a team of Scottish scientists announced that they had cloned an adult sheep. Fierce debate over the ethics of cloning, particularly of cloning humans, ensued. The Pope inveighed against "dangerous experiments." President Clinton froze for ninety days all federal funding of research that could lead to human cloning. Ian Wilmut, head of the team that created the sheep, announced, "Cloning people should be in the realm of science fiction. All those involved in this research would find it unethical."

But the cloning of sheep was science fiction until Wilmut made it science fact. Dolly, the ewe created by Wilmut, looks like any other sheep, but her placid eyes carry a chilling lesson: If someone wants to do it, and if it can be done, it will be done.

The variables are *want* and *can*. The *can*—actualized through technology—is out of control. Today, cloning; tomorrow, fully immersive artificial worlds teeming with artificial life. Only global catastrophe or an act of God will block this future. Neither seems likely. Faced by what we can do, some religions will thrive, others will mutate, still others will be torn apart. It may be that cyberspace will sweep us toward the sort of global spiritual transformation envisioned by Teilhard de Chardin.

What Teilhard told was a story, however, and stories have a way of not coming true. Still, who can say for sure? And so while some of the questions raised at the beginning of this book have been answered, others must remain open. For now, a new question arises: What do we want?

At 10 A.M. on February 8, 1996, three Tibetan Buddhist monks of the Namgyal Monastery in Ithaca, New York, walked into the monastery's prayer room. They sat down on dark mats, two of them side by side, the third facing the others. This third monk flipped open a laptop computer and brought up an image of the Kalachakra mandala. In the light of the glowing screen, the three monks proceeded to pray for half an hour, conducting a formal blessing of cyberspace.

"Cyberspace is a field that has been created where there is an absence of obstructions," explained Thomas E. Miller to me by phone from his home in Ithaca. Miller is a Namgyal Monastery official and the man who conceived of the blessing. "That's the way cyberspace was designed. Which creates the potential for something to arise. And the nature of what will arise there is dependent upon the motivations of the people that use it."

That the nature of something may depend upon the motivations of those who use it can be illustrated with the example of a hammer. If the user intends to use the hammer to build a house, it is a constructive tool; if the user intends to use it to hit another person on the head, the hammer is a weapon.

The person who gave Miller permission to go ahead with the blessing was Pema Losang Chogyen, the same Tibetan monk who pioneered sacred cyberspace with his creation of the digitized Vajrabhairava mandala. Chogyen is the director of the Namgyal Monastery. When I visited him at his Manhattan apartment to talk about the Vajrabhairava mandala, I asked him why he endorsed a blessing of cyberspace.

"Blessing means a transformation for the better," he told me. "In the Tibetan, it's literally translated as 'transformation into a higher status.'

"We know," he continued," that cyberspace is limitless, infinite, and out of control. All that we can do is to create some kind of awareness among cyberspace users. I think that is a blessing—to send a message of very positive feelings."

Our souls become what we make of them. So will the soul of cyberspace, for cyberspace mirrors us in our entirety, including our souls. Our soul is its soul. Increasingly, we will live among wonders and terrors. If, in the strange days to come, we attend to the sacred, then the soul of cyberspace, though beset by human frailty, will be a sacred one, reflecting the wishes voiced by the monks in their blessing:

> May all beings have happiness and its causes.
> May all beings be separated from suffering and its
> causes.
> May all beings never be separated from
> happiness.

The Namgyal Monastery's page devoted to the blessing of cyberspace is located at *http://www.namgyal.org/blessing.html.*

Bibliography

Crick, Francis. *The Astonishing Hypothesis: The Scientific Search for the Soul.* New York: Scribner, 1994.

Csikszentmihalyi, Mihaly. *Flow: The Psychology of Optimal Experience.* New York: Harper & Row, 1990.

Davies, Paul. *The Mind of God.* New York: Touchstone, 1993.

Dennett, Daniel. *Consciousness Explained.* Boston: Little, Brown, 1991.

Gibson, William. *Neuromancer.* New York: Ace, 1994.

Gould, Stephen Jay. *Full House: The Spread of Excellence from Plato to Darwin.* New York: Harmony Books, 1996.

Hayward, Jeremy and Francisco Varela. *Gentle Bridges: Conversations with the Dalai Lama on the Sciences of Mind.* Boston: Shambhala, 1992.

Lucky, Robert W. *Silicon Dreams: Information, Man, and Machine.* New York: St. Martin's Press, 1989.

Ludwig, Mark. "Virtual Catastrophe: Will Self-Reproducing Software Rule the World?" In *Clicking In: Hot Links to a Digital Culture,* edited by Lynn Hershman Leeson. Seattle: Bay Press, 1996.

McKenna, Terence. *The Archaic Revival: Speculations on Psychedelic Mushrooms, the Amazon, Virtual Reality, UFOs, Evolution, Shamanism, the Rebirth of the Goddess, and the End of History.* San Francisco: HarperSanFranciso, 1992.

Moravec, Hans. *Mind Children: The Future of Human and Robot Intelligence.* Cambridge: Harvard Univ. Press, 1988.

Panati, Charles. *Sacred Origins of Profound Things.* New York: Penguin Books, 1996.

Rheingold, Howard. *The Virtual Community: Homesteading on the Electronic Frontier.* Reading, MA: Addison-Wesley, 1993.

Sheldrake, Rupert. *A New Science of Life: The Hypothesis of Formative Causation.* Los Angeles: J. P. Tarcher, 1981.

Steinsaltz, Adin. *The Thirteen Petalled Rose.* Translated by Yehuda Hanegbi. Northvale, NJ: Jason Aronson, 1980.

Talbott, Stephen L. *The Future Does Not Compute: Transcending the Machines in Our Midst.* Sebastopol, CA: O'Reilly & Associates, 1995.

Teilhard de Chardin, Pierre. *The Phenomenon of Man*. New York: Harper & Row, 1965.

Tipler, Frank. *The Physics of Immortality: Modern Cosmology, God and the Resurrection of the Dead*. New York: Doubleday, 1994.

Williams, John Alden. *Islam*. New York: Braziller, 1961.